JESUS

— and His —

ENEMIES

JESUS

and His

ENEMIES

PAUL YEULETT

P&R PUBLISHING
P.O. BOX 817 • PHILLIPSBURG • NEW JERSEY 08865-0817

ISBN: 978-1-59638-832-1 (pbk)
ISBN: 978-1-59638-833-8 (ePub)
ISBN: 978-1-59638-834-5 (Mobi)

Printed in the United States of America

Library of Congress Cataloging-in-Publication Data

Yeulett, Paul, 1969-
 Jesus and his enemies / Paul Yeulett. -- 1st [edition].
    pages cm
 Includes bibliographical references.
 ISBN 978-1-59638-832-1 (pbk.)
 1. Jesus Christ--Adversaries--Biblical teaching. 2. Jesus Christ--Conflicts--Biblical teaching. 3. Enemies--Religious aspects--Christianity. I. Title.
 BT361.Y48 2013
 232.9'5--dc23
                          2013031116

Contents

FOREWORD

AS CHRISTIANS, we have the best news imaginable: the news of God's saving love, revealed in the sending of his Son on a mission to rescue a perishing world through atonement, victory and forgiveness. The message of the Bible is called "gospel" for that reason—it is good news for lost men and women.

So why don't more people respond to it? Why is the message of the Bible ridiculed, ignored, and rejected? Why are Christians often regarded and portrayed as irrational fundamentalists who mistakenly place their trust in a book that science and culture have long since discredited (or so we are told)?

Is there something about our twenty-first century culture that makes our present generation so hostile to the claims and promises of Jesus? Was it easier to communicate the message of salvation in the past?

The reality is that it was not; indeed, it never was easy to proclaim that message. No one communicated it better or more plainly than Jesus himself, the subject and object of salvation. Yet, as Paul Yeulett reminds us throughout this book, Jesus had enemies, people who were implacably opposed to him and all that he represented, from the moment he was born into the world until the moment he left it.

The opposition he experienced and endured he promised to be the lot of his followers too. That is the thrust of his teaching in John 15:18–25:

> If the world hates you, know that it has hated me before it hated you. If you were of the world, the world would love you

as its own; but because you are not of the world, but I chose you out of the world, therefore the world hates you. Remember the word that I said to you: "A servant is not greater than his master." If they persecuted me, they will also persecute you. If they kept my word, they will also keep yours. But all these things they will do to you on account of my name, because they do not know him who sent me. If I had not come and spoken to them, they would not have been guilty of sin, but now they have no excuse for their sin. Whoever hates me hates my Father also. If I had not done among them the works that no one else did, they would not be guilty of sin, but now they have seen and hated both me and my Father. But the word that is written in their Law must be fulfilled: "They hated me without a cause."

The message is clear: people will hate Christians *because* they follow Christ, and they will hate them *as* they hated Christ. If we are to maintain a constant and faithful witness to Jesus in the face of such opposition, we will do well to reflect on the enemies Jesus faced—the various manifestations of the darkness that opposed the light that had come into the world.

That is what Paul Yeulett does in this book. He examines the various streams of opposition that Jesus encountered—the demonic, political, religious, emotional, physical, and spiritual powers that combined against his person and against his gospel. In this book, Paul Yeulett helps us to understand these better, and in doing so reminds us that there is nothing new under the sun; God had predicted such opposition in Psalm 2, and it will go on until the end of time.

But alongside the experience of darkness is the marvelous illustration in the life of Christ himself that the darkness does not overcome the light. Christ has the victory. The Son of God triumphs. That, at last, is the reason why we can continue to proclaim the good news of God's salvation: because although he promises that "In the world you will have tribulation," he also says, "But take heart; I have overcome the world" (John 16:33).

As we read through this book we will gain a greater understanding of the original context in which Jesus lived and ministered, the light coming into the darkness of the world. We will have a deeper appreciation of why people reject the gospel. But we will also be given the encouragement to continue going into all the world to preach the good news to everyone.

This is a great resource: a study by one of Jesus' friends of Jesus' enemies. Use it well, and you may yet have the joy of seeing many of Jesus' enemies in your own context become his friends!

Rev. Dr. Iain D. Campbell
Free Church of Scotland, Isle of Lewis
Moderator, General Assembly of
the Free Church of Scotland, May 2012

PREFACE

IN APRIL 2010 I was kindly invited by Iain Murray to give two addresses at the Banner of Truth Youth Conference, which takes place annually in Leicester, England, and which immediately precedes the Ministers' Conference. Both of these conferences have been greatly blessed by the Lord over a number of years. It was a rare privilege to be present, most of all because of the encouragement in seeing nearly one hundred and fifty young people listening so attentively to God's Word and responding with prayer and praise that warmed the hearts of everyone there.

I took the theme "Christian Living in a Dark World" for my talks and delivered a message from the text of John 3:19: "And this is the judgment: the light has come into the world, and people loved the darkness rather than the light because their works were evil." It was this address that eventually developed into the chapter beginning this work.

Soon after I returned from Leicester it became clear that this theme could be extended a good deal further. It occurred to me that the Gospels contain records of a certain number of enemies with whom Jesus had to contend during his life and ministry, and especially as his death approached. In most cases Jesus was involved in a specific conflict with these opponents, each of which would constitute a single study. Many of these individuals and groups are obvious at the first reading of the Gospels, for example Judas Iscariot, Pontius Pilate, the Pharisees, and the Sadducees.

The aim of this book, in short, is to draw theological and pastoral lessons from these various encounters. In order to do that I have found it necessary to include a certain amount of theological and historical background in each case. Good pastoral work must always be rooted in good theology, and Christian theology is founded upon the historical fact of redemption. "When the fullness of time had come," the Son of God stepped into this world of time and space to save a people for himself (Gal. 4:4). At the same time, the Bible teaches us timeless truths, and this is the case with Jesus' confrontations with his enemies as much as any other biblical subject. Every reader of this book is personally implicated: we are all by nature enemies of God and of Christ because of our sin, but the Savior has come into the world to deliver us from that enmity. Therefore, an examination of the words, deeds, and motivation of Jesus' various adversaries should seek to address the reader's conscience.

To whom is this book addressed? Although the majority of these chapters are not transcripts of sermons, nor even adaptations of sermons previously preached, I have tried to keep the faces of my own congregation before my mind's eye as I have written. I have not assumed any in-depth knowledge of the culture and traditions of first-century Israel. Such information is briefly introduced where it seems appropriate.

The subjects of each chapter tend to follow in chronological order, insofar as a chronology can be ascertained from the Gospels. In a few instances chronology is circumvented in order to achieve a more logical sense of progress. For example, the conversation between Jesus and the Sadducees about the resurrection is analyzed before we come to consider the high priest Caiaphas, even though Caiaphas' words in John 11:50 were uttered quite some time before the challenge of the Sadducees, which took place during the final week of Jesus' life.

The first two chapters are introductory, setting the scene. Chapter 1 examines the basic causes for the enmity between Jesus and his opponents, and chapter 2 is an overview of the cosmic conflict that underlies the hostility faced by the Savior. After this the chapters deal with episodes recorded in the life of Jesus, and not surprisingly most of them are concentrated into the final days of his life and ministry. Chapters 14 to 16 are located at the cross of Calvary itself. My original intention had been to conclude the work at this point, but in order to show how the risen Lord Jesus drew one-time enemies to himself, I decided to include two more chapters, culminating in the apostle Paul, once Saul of Tarsus, who received mercy so that "as the foremost, Jesus Christ might display his perfect patience as an example to those who were to believe in him for eternal life" (1 Tim. 1:16).

The ultimate desire in this work is that men, women, and even children who pick up this book might have their hearts warmed with the love of Jesus Christ himself, the love "that surpasses knowledge, that you may be filled with all the fullness of God" (Eph.3:19).

I would like to express my gratitude to a number of people who have helped in making this project possible, even if in some cases they have not realized what a help they have been! First of all I must thank the staff at P&R Publishing for their professional assistance and very friendly advice. I would especially mention Amanda Martin, Ian Thompson, Kim McKeever, and Aaron Gottier. I am indebted to the kind and wise counsel of Brian Norton, Geoff Thomas, Eryl Davies, Iain D. Campbell, Ian Hamilton, Iain Murray, and Jonathan Watson, all of whom have spurred me on at different times. Particular thanks go to Keron Fletcher, who read through the first proof of this work and offered several thoughtful observations and suggestions, and to Brian Watt, whose painstaking patience and eagle eyes picked up many typographical errors. Additional thanks go to Will Alcock, who freely assisted me in cataloging the books in my study a few summers ago and more recently helped in producing the promotional video.

I want to put on record my high esteem and warm appreciation for all the members of Shrewsbury Evangelical Church, faithful and prayerful brothers and sisters in our common Lord and Savior Jesus Christ. Above all, none of this work could have been attempted without the love and support of my dear wife Ruth, who has not only encouraged me but also sought to apply some necessary brakes (and breaks) from time to time. It is a faithful saying that "he who finds a wife finds a good thing and obtains favor from the LORD" (Prov. 18:22). I thank the Lord for her and also for our children, Rebecca, Matthew, and Daniel, whose questions and observations about the Bible, and life in general, continue to keep us on our toes!

Why Did Jesus Have Enemies?

And this is the judgment: the light has come into the world, and people loved the darkness rather than the light because their works were evil. For everyone who does wicked things hates the light and does not come to the light, lest his works should be exposed. (John 3:19–20)

JESUS OF NAZARETH, the Son of God, the Prince of Peace, and the friend of sinners, had many enemies. Pick up and read any of the Gospels and you will quickly see the theme of conflict emerging and stamping itself upon the scene.

Begin with Matthew's gospel and very soon you will read of the scheming of a bloodthirsty tyrant, Herod the Great, who seeks to snuff out the life of the infant Jesus. Mark tells us early in his record that "the Pharisees went out and immediately held counsel with the Herodians against him, how to destroy him" (Mark 3:6). Even the cozily familiar birth narratives of Luke contain Simeon's prophecy that the child Jesus was "appointed for the fall and rising of many in Israel, and for a sign that is opposed" (Luke 2:34). In John's gospel the theme of enmity is so prevalent that the author stops and dwells on it in his prologue:

He was in the world, and the world was made through him, yet the world did not know him. He came to his own, and his own people did not receive him. (John 1:10–11)

Moreover, the conversations between Jesus and his Jewish contemporaries, which dominate the central chapters of John's gospel, invariably culminated in the sharpest of disputes. Above all, see how all four Gospels devote such copious space to the sufferings and death of Jesus. His life ended in abominable cruelty, which the gospel writers recorded in considerable detail.

Before we begin to look at the opponents who confronted Jesus throughout the course of his life and ministry, we need to ask a most important question: why did Jesus have enemies? What caused this hostility and hatred? We need to answer this question correctly from the outset of our investigation.

CONFLICT RESOLUTION

Our three young children enjoy watching cartoons. However, they invariably become quite agitated whenever there is an onscreen argument between two characters. "Who's right?" they will ask. They need to know who is in the right and who is in the wrong. They feel it necessary to engage in a childish form of "conflict resolution." Today conflict resolution is big business across the world. In a variety of professional and commercial fields, considerable resources are expended in achieving agreement between disputing parties, aiming ideally for a "win-win" solution that will be to everyone's satisfaction. In the United Kingdom, for example, the Advisory, Conciliation and Arbitration Service (Acas) seeks to resolve disputes between employers and trade unions. Although methods of conflict resolution vary across different cultures, the concept itself is a widespread one.

Now imagine that a team of specialists in conflict resolution were to be hired. Their brief: examine the evidence presented by the New Testament and seek to answer the question, "Why did Jesus have enemies?" They would quickly discover that a wide range of groups were gathered together in common cause against Jesus. The apostles of the early church listed some of these parties: "both Herod and Pontius Pilate, along with the Gentiles and the peoples of Israel" (Acts 4:27). We have already seen that the Pharisees and the Herodians, two contrasting sects in Israel, held counsel against Jesus. What conclusions could be drawn from the observation that so many contrasting groups were opposed to this one man, Jesus of Nazareth? Surely the problem lay fairly and squarely with him. He had a habit of alienating people and often seemed to be in a minority of one. Might he not have been well-advised to address this issue as a matter of urgent importance? The way things look from a distance, a "win-win" solution would seem out of the question.

However, the argument presented in this chapter, and throughout this book, is that we have no need to call in today's conflict resolution specialists because Jesus himself explains why these conflicts exist. He himself is the specialist. In John 3:19–20, towards the end of his conversation with Nicodemus, Jesus issues the pronouncement that is quoted at the beginning of this chapter.

> And this is the judgment: the light has come into the world, and people loved the darkness rather than the light because their works were evil. For everyone who does wicked things hates the light and does not come to the light, lest his works should be exposed.

With these words, Jesus delivers the divine verdict upon the state of the whole human race. It is a verdict of resounding guilt, a conclusion of comprehensive condemnation. In verse 19, the word *judgment* means the divine ruling, God's pronouncement. It could equally, and more pungently, be translated "this is the condemnation." The reason for this enmity between Jesus and his opponents is then concisely summarized—people "loved the darkness rather than the light because their works were evil."

LIGHT AND DARKNESS

When Jesus talks about light and darkness—and in John's writings these are very recurrent themes—he is speaking in a way that is wholly consistent with the rest of the Scripture, both the Old and the New Testaments. The Bible has a knack of confronting us with a stark set of contrasts that is very much at odds with our contemporary view of morality. The categories of right and wrong, of good and evil, are nonnegotiable as far as the Bible is concerned. While today there are some actions that almost everyone in our society rightly regards as wicked—for example, cruelty to young children, institutional racism, and drug dealing—for the most part people are reluctant to speak in such absolute terms. Moreover, different generations have differing views as to what ought to be condemned and what ought to be condoned.

The Bible is the authoritative disclosure of the mind of God, and therefore it never shrinks from making clear pronouncements. Right at the beginning of human history Adam and Eve were faced with the exclusive choice between good and evil. They could obey God, which would lead to life, or they could disobey him, which would result in death. There was no middle ground, and there were no other considerations to bear in mind. It was either obedience or disobedience. In Deuteronomy 28 we read the long list of God's blessings for obedience and his curses for disobedience. There is nothing that falls between these two categories. In the books of the kings of Israel and Judah we see that there were a number of kings who did "what was right in the eyes of the Lord" whereas others did "what was evil in the sight of the Lord."

This is the general pattern of Scripture: there is light and there is darkness, there is life and there is death, there is heaven and there is hell. Therefore this passage in John 3 is wholly in keeping with this biblical pattern of dealing in contrasts. See how clear and exclusive the division is made in verses 20 and 21: on the one hand there are those who come to the light, and on the other there are those who do *not* come to the light. There is nothing in between, no middle ground, no sitting on the fence.

Light and darkness are surely among the most obvious contrasts known to all of us, unless we have never been able to see. Light and darkness are opposites of which we are all deeply conscious from an early age. Moreover, they quickly take on added associations and suggestions; they become considerably more than the mere physical responses of our retinas. Children who are often afraid of the dark ask their parents to leave their bedroom door ajar so that some light will be admitted. As they grow up, light and darkness take on different, more mature associations, but the pattern continues. Light increasingly becomes linked with joy, gladness, all that is pleasant and lovely. Darkness signifies depression, gloom, sorrow, and despair. It is well known that Seasonal Affective Disorder (SAD) afflicts many people in countries like the United Kingdom, where the winters are long and dark. It is possible to purchase devices that create the appearance of sunlight in the dark mornings of early January; there is a market for such gadgets because so many people find the darkness oppressive. Further, light speaks of knowledge and understanding; darkness of ignorance and superstition.[1] Our conversations abound with colloquial expressions that illustrate these wider associations of the themes of light and darkness. "Her face lit up," we say, or "A dark mood came over him."

In Scripture the associations of light and darkness are amplified considerably more, so that there are the clearest moral and spiritual meanings attached to them. What is suggested by the human psyche is grounded in the revelation of divine character. For light is a major theme of the Bible. It is the first creation of God and the subject of God's first recorded words (Gen. 1:3). We see that the presence of God with his people in the wilderness was symbolized by the burning light (Lev. 24:2). A great light was prophesied by Isaiah to a people who dwelt in darkness (Isa. 9:2), a passage often read at Christmas.

Ultimately light symbolizes the presence of God himself and darkness symbolizes his absence. The apostle John brings this subject to a head in his first letter: "God is light, and in him is no darkness at all" (1 John 1:5). For this reason, light in the Bible is always very closely related to truth. Where there is light, there is the capacity to see what is real and true. The nineteenth-century Scottish Bible commentator, John Brown of Edinburgh, wrote that light is "truth, calculated to make men wise, and good, and happy."[2] But darkness is the very opposite of these things: it prefers "ignorance to knowledge, error to truth, and sin to holiness."[3]

LIGHT AND DARKNESS IN CONFLICT

There is a further, consequent aspect of light and darkness that we need to consider. They are not only opposites; they are opponents. The conflict between darkness and light is strong, violent, and bitter. The apostle Paul asked the Corinthians, "what fellowship has light with darkness?" (2 Cor. 6:14) Darkness seeks to overcome light. The late New Testament scholar Leon Morris wrote that "the strife between good and evil is no tepid affair, but one that elicits the bitter hatred of the forces of evil."[4]

As we have seen, light and darkness are recurring and powerful features of John's gospel, and so is the conflict between them. The light that is being spoken of in our passage is Jesus Christ himself. John has already said as much in the prologue to his gospel. "The true light, which enlightens everyone, was coming into the world" (John 1:9). Yet no sooner has John told us about this true light than he goes on to tell us about how this light has been rejected.

> He was in the world, and the world was made through him,
> yet the world did not know him. He came to his own, and his
> own people did not receive him. (1:10–11)

John is describing people who are walking around in darkness when the light is already shining all around them. Later in the same gospel, in 8:12 and in 9:5, Jesus refers to himself as "the light of the world." Both these passages are located within contexts of bitter opposition, even hatred, from his countrymen.

This then is the point: Jesus Christ is in the midst of his people, showing himself by all his words and actions to be the true light, but the darkness of the people's hearts means that they will not and cannot receive him as such. Jesus Christ is the very embodiment of light, of truth, knowledge, and love, but the vast majority of the people with whom he has come into contact have rejected him. They still do so today; and today, as two thousand years ago, this results in bitter conflict.

Actors, Not Spectators

This is not mythology; this is not fiction. Jesus' words about the conflict between light and darkness are a present-day commentary on the natural state of the human soul. The Word of God always and directly addresses the conscience of those who are reading or hearing it. We are not in some kind of spectators' gallery looking on at an evil world. We are all implicated; it is the evil in *us* that contributes to the evil of the world.

The trouble is that we are used to living in a spectator society. Many of the great dramas that intrigue us take place among people we have never met and are never likely to meet, or even among people who never existed. We may be fascinated by a television soap opera, or we may be caught up in real-life events going on in the public arenas of sport or politics, but the effects are the same. We sit in the closeted safety of our own living rooms and state our opinions at a safe distance. But if we bring this mind-set with us to the Word of God, then we are guilty of a fatal error. We are participators, not spectators, in the unfolding events of this present world. We can't press the pause button or eject the DVD from its player. Neither can the DVD have its contents deleted. The DVD is about every one of us.

This is the terribly solemn fact—men and women are by nature on the dark side of the plot. They have taken up rebellious arms against the Sovereign Ruler of the universe. Jesus tells us plainly that men's deeds are evil. Our deeds are evil because they spring from evil natures.

The Westminster Shorter Catechism, put together by the leading British churchmen of the mid-seventeenth century, asks in Question 18, "Wherein consists the sinfulness of that estate whereinto man fell?" The answer given is that "the sinfulness of that estate whereinto man fell, consists in the guilt of Adam's first sin, the want of original righteousness, *and the corruption of his whole nature*, which is commonly called Original Sin; together with all actual transgressions which proceed from it" (italics mine).

This is the cause of the judgment, the condemnation, of which Jesus is speaking: original sin, which includes the corruption of the whole human nature. Troubled Job posed the question "Who can bring a clean thing out of an unclean?" and answered it, "There is not one" (Job 14:4). Man's whole nature is corrupted. He is unclean through and through; every aspect of his nature is both guilty and polluted. Why is all humanity affected in this way? It is because our very first ancestors chose disobedience rather than obedience. Adam, by his deliberate actions in disobeying God, introduced the poison of rebellion into the human race, and every one of us inherits this original sin. Like a polluting chemical introduced into a stream in the high Andes, the vast Amazonian basin of the whole human race is utterly contaminated. Not one of us is exempted. A toddler throws tantrums and acts out of pure selfishness not only because of his immaturity, but primarily because of his sin.

LIGHT SHOWS UP EVIL FOR WHAT IT IS

Jesus speaks of the way people love darkness "because their works are evil." A sinful, corrupted nature will give rise to evil deeds. Then in John 3:20 Jesus goes on to show that people hate the light because it shows up their evil deeds for what they are. The New Testament commentator William Hendriksen likens this behavior to that of "loathsome insects that hide themselves beneath logs and stones, always preferring the darkness, and terribly frightened whenever they are exposed to the light."[5] Perhaps you have lifted up stones in your own garden and seen this for yourself. Bugs and grubs of all kinds start scurrying and burrowing away for the comfort of darkness. The light blinds and terrifies them, but under the cover of thick darkness they are secure and can go on being "loathsome insects."

This is stark and accurate biblical psychology. By nature people hate and fear God's holiness, the brightness and purity of his moral law. Every encounter with God's holiness makes sinful man want to shrink away in fear, shame, and terror. A life that is characterized by sin, whether that sin is open or secret, will by its very nature want to run away and hide from God.

Even at a merely human level it is a most fearful thing not only to know that I *am* guilty, but to discover that someone in legitimate and powerful authority *knows* that I am guilty. Perhaps you are familiar with that flushed sensation of desperate shame—like hot pins and needles in your head—that comes when you know that your wrong actions have been found out. Fallen human instinct dictates that we flee and hide from such a situation. We are most reluctant to expose our misdemeanors to people in authority because we hate that sense of shame.

If this is true in human relationships, how much more solemn this must be in the sight of God! This is just what motivated

Adam once he had sinned and knew that God was present in the Garden. He fled from God, he tried to hide from him, he covered up his nakedness. Nothing like this had ever happened before. Hitherto, Adam and Eve had enjoyed God's presence. They were created for joyful fellowship with God and had no idea what shame was. But as soon as they sinned, their entire relationship with God—and with one another—was upset, distorted, and characterized by shame and fear.

This history of Adam and Eve and its consequences for the entire human race set the scene for the ministry of Jesus in Israel two thousand years ago. Jesus spoke about light and darkness on a number of other occasions. The following passage has a strong relationship to the verses in John 3 that we have been considering:

> No one after lighting a lamp puts it in a cellar or under a basket, but on a stand, so that those who enter may see the light. Your eye is the lamp of your body. When your eye is healthy, your whole body is full of light, but when it is bad, your body is full of darkness. Therefore be careful lest the light in you be darkness. (Luke 11:33–35)

Jesus uses the familiar picture of a lamp to demonstrate the meaning of his own presence in the world. What is a lamp for? It is for enabling the occupants of the house to see what is in the house or room where the lamp is situated. The lamp should be located where the people are found. This imagery stands the test of time, of long centuries and millennia; it really makes no difference whether we are talking about a candle or an electric lightbulb. If you were to put the light in the basement while there was no one there, or under a basket or bucket, you would be wasting the light, acting both illogically and foolishly.

Imagine a family living in an average-sized house, paying a substantial amount each month for electricity. And then imagine that the lights they switched on in the living room and kitchen were always covered with bowls and buckets so that they could not be seen. The scenario would be absolutely absurd. People would be bumping around blindly, unable to see all the good and useful things in the house, endangering life and limb, health and safety, while they could simply uncover these lights so that all this inconvenience and danger could be avoided. Now we can see the point of this parable that Jesus told. The people he was contending with were extinguishing the light that they had been given. The light was among them; it was right in front of them; it had never shone so brightly—but they were covering it up, obscuring it. "The true light, which enlightens everyone" (John 1:9) was in the world, "and people loved the darkness rather than the light" (John 3:19).

Spiritual Blindness

Then Jesus develops the figure of speech somewhat in Luke 11:34. In case we failed to understand it the first time around he brings it closer to home and applies it more personally to the people. He moves from a lamp to the human eye, "your eye." What is the eye? It is the bodily organ that admits light. The eye performs the function of a lamp as far as our bodies are concerned, and therefore the eye guides the rest of the body in everything that it does. Now imagine a slightly different situation. You are in a room that is dark and dim, and you find it hard to make out its contents. What might the problem be? There are various explanations. Maybe the light is not working properly; the bulb has gone, the fuse has blown, or the power is cut. Or maybe there never was any artificial light in the room at all. Or perhaps it is the middle of the night, or possibly daytime but for some reason it is dark outside—there could be a heavy thunderstorm, or even a total solar eclipse.

But then suppose that you have carefully eliminated all these possibilities one by one. There can be only one explanation remaining. Your sight is failing you. Think how disabling it would be for any of us if our sight were rapidly taken away! The control, the freedom, the mastery we usually exercise over our surroundings would be removed. Although blind and partially sighted people may, in time and by various helpful means, be enabled to adjust very well to their disability, the fact remains that our capacity to function effectively in this world depends to a great extent on our sight. What if those of us who need glasses or contact lenses suddenly lost these accessories, or they became unavailable? Driving and many other activities that require excellent vision would be impossible.

We need to ask these important questions again: Why did the majority of people in Jesus' day resist and oppose him, ultimately plotting and carrying out his death? Why do men and women today shut their hearts and minds to the gospel of Jesus Christ and say they are not interested? The answers to these two questions are one and the same. People love darkness rather than light because their deeds are evil, and therefore they willfully shut out the light.

Although they will come up with all sorts of excuses why they do not want to be Christians, in the end it is only the Lord himself who gives the correct verdict. Why do people not want to follow Jesus Christ? Is it simply that they have not heard the gospel, and that if they did hear about Jesus they would immediately love him and follow him with all their hearts? Experience proves that they will not. They will say that they do not believe in Jesus or the gospel; certainly they will not submit to Jesus as their exclusive Lord and Savior.

Some will say that we simply lack proof. This, essentially, was the plea of the famous English atheist philosopher Bertrand Russell (1872–1970). There is insufficient evidence. God has not made himself clear enough. He should try to do a better job of convincing us. In a world with such a number of different religions there are simply far too many rival claims, and we cannot know what to believe or whom to believe. We could add to this the great question of human origins which, for many, appears to cast doubt on the opening chapters of the Bible. The authority of the God of the Bible seems to be undermined as soon as we turn to its opening pages. And everyone surely knows that it is religion of various kinds that causes strife, war, and persecution—look at history, look at modern conflicts in the Middle East and, until recently, in Northern Ireland. On and on we could go; if there were a good God, he would not allow all the suffering that goes on. Therefore people refuse to believe in him.

Many of us are used to hearing protests of this kind. What they all have in common is that they say there is something defective in Christianity itself, that the claims of the Christian faith are weak, inadequate, contradictory, or untenable; or that Christians are ignorant, naive, perhaps bigoted and harsh; or even that God—if he exists—is unfair or unkind. All this can leave Christians with a sense of defeat and deflation. They run out of arguments, they feel squashed and wonder how they will ever persuade unbelievers of the truth. The unbelieving world says, "You Christians haven't done a good enough job of convincing us—come up with some better arguments."

But we need to say it yet again: the Lord Jesus Christ completely reverses the situation. The boot is on the other foot; the fault lies not with Jesus or with his message, but with the people themselves. That is why he speaks as he does in these verses. The problem is not with Jesus or the gospel but with the human heart. Why do so many people, then as now, reject Jesus and refuse to believe in him? Because of something lacking in him or in his message? No—because of their own dark and sinful hearts. That is the verdict.

CONCLUSION

We began with the question "Why did Jesus have enemies?" and we have reached the conclusion that we are all, by reason of belonging to Adam's fallen race, Jesus' enemies. We need to see the universal extent of this condemnation. The whole world is the arena in which this light shines, and it is the whole of fallen humanity that is implicated in this charge of rejecting the light.

So this book is about Jesus' enemies, but it is written so that readers, who may be discovering for the first time that they *are* enemies, might learn how Jesus summons us to become his friends.

Invisible Enemies
in High Places

And the dragon stood before the woman who was about to give birth, so that when she bore her child he might devour it. She gave birth to a male child, one who is to rule all the nations with a rod of iron, but her child was caught up to God and to his throne, and the woman fled into the wilderness, where she has a place prepared by God, in which she is to be nourished for 1,260 days. Now war arose in heaven. (Rev. 12:4–7)

THE AIM OF THIS BOOK, as has been stated, is to investigate the major confrontations in which Jesus of Nazareth was engaged during his earthly life, from the cunning and murderous threats of Herod the Great to the mocking voices of those who reviled him at the cross of Calvary. We are doing so not out of mere historical interest, but because each of these confrontations illustrates vital lessons about the sinless Savior's encounter with this world of sin, with real sinners like ourselves.

The majority of these chapters will focus on individuals and groups of people Jesus encountered, as featured in the four gospels. But there is a further dimension to this theme that could not possibly be overlooked, and which needs to be given due prominence before the rest of this study unfolds. It is the great cosmic conflict taking place between the righteous Son of God, the man from heaven, and the forces of wickedness. This is none other than the great war "against the rulers, against the authorities, against the cosmic powers over this present darkness, against the spiritual forces of evil in the heavenly places" (Eph. 6:12). The apostle Paul, in this mighty passage in Ephesians, draws our attention to the battle that the individual believer and the church fight against these evil forces. For every believer and for every congregation, this conflict is a local manifestation of the universal holy war that the triune God wages against all his enemies—a war in which he will ultimately prevail.

THE UNFOLDING COSMIC CONFLICT

There is a clear progression in Scripture as this theme unfolds and develops. Throughout much of the Old Testament, the war between the forces of good and evil is witnessed in the arena of earthly history. We see murder, war, conquest, slavery, plague, famine, royal edicts, and much else in the history of every nation. What we might call the invisible war, the one that enlists various unseen combatants, does not for the most part appear in the pages of the Old Testament. It is true that in the first two chapters of Job the veil is drawn aside for a time and we are permitted to gaze upon the angelic realm, in which Satan along with the "sons of God" presents himself before the Lord. We also have open references to Satan in 1 Chronicles 21:1 and in Zechariah 3:1–2.

But what is largely concealed in the Old Testament is revealed much more plainly in the New. Now Jesus Christ, the incarnate Son of God, is engaged in open hand-to-hand combat with Satan. Demons and evil spirits appear on the scene in considerable numbers. Several incidents in the Gospels describe Jesus' battle, not against flesh and blood, but against these invisible rulers and authorities.

The text at the head of this chapter is not from any of the four gospels, but from the book of Revelation, which closes the New Testament. This passage seems to be the most suitable one in Scripture for summing up the present theme. The imagery at the beginning of Chapter 12 is quite clear. The woman clothed in the sun represents the church, the people of God. From the ancient church, the people of Israel, Jesus Christ sprang. He is the male child who will rule all the nations with the rod of iron, a picture taken from Psalm 2:9. And the dragon is Satan, the great adversary of God, who is poised to devour this child as soon as he is born.

THE TWO LINES: GODLY AND UNGODLY

What are we to understand by all this? Throughout the entire period of the Old Testament, Satan crouches before the people of God, a malevolent predator waiting to pounce on his prey at the first opportunity. This conflict is established in Genesis 3:15, where it is announced that there will be enmity between the offspring of the woman and the offspring of the serpent. But the offspring of the woman will ultimately prevail over the offspring of the serpent, crushing his head. For this reason the offspring of the woman can be called the "godly line," and the offspring of the serpent the "ungodly line."

The identity of the serpent and the dragon are one and the same, as is made clear in Revelation 12:9: "And the great dragon was thrown down, that ancient serpent, who is called the devil and Satan, the deceiver of the whole world." Indeed, the correspondence between this passage and Genesis 3 is apparent. They are like two symmetrical bookends that enclose the whole conflict. From Eden onward, the enmity between the two "lines" breaks out in the many crises that threaten the survival of the offspring of the woman. The godly line eventually culminates in Jesus Christ himself, who appeared in order to destroy the works of the Devil. Thus the war in heaven is played out in the arena of earthly history.

We should not overstate the imagery so as to imply that the dragon's "crouching" before the child suggests inertia on the devil's part. On the contrary, the devil is extremely active in the Old Testament, even though his actions are seldom attributed to him by name. After a single generation we see the ungodly line and the godly line represented by two brothers, Cain and Abel. Abel's faith in God arouses the evil jealousy of Cain, whose rage boils over into murder. Again and again this godly line is threatened: rivalry and enmity between siblings becomes a pattern in the generations that follow Abraham, with the threat of murder only just being averted in the cases of both Jacob and Joseph. The children of Israel, redeemed from Egypt—the land of bondage—seem to be sold out to the bondage of idolatry as they bow down to the golden calf, but Moses intercedes for them. Balak hires Balaam to curse these same people, but God turns the curse into a blessing. Every great conflict and crisis in Israel's history and, more particularly, every crisis and conflict that affects the line of promise, is an outworking of the enmity that was forecast in Eden.

And although explicit references to Satan and the demons may be somewhat limited in the Old Testament, their actions are nevertheless observable in places. The American theologian Wayne Grudem comments that "the people of Israel often sinned by serving false gods, and when we realize that these false 'gods' were really demonic forces, we see that there is quite a bit of Old Testament material relating to demons."[1]

SATAN UNMASKED

Nevertheless, when we come to the New Testament it is as though the masks and gloves are all removed. Just as the identity of the Seed of Abraham becomes fully disclosed as the person of Jesus Christ, so does the identity of the serpent himself—here is Satan, and with him are the demons, great legions of them.

But just who is Satan, and who are these demons? Where did they come from, and why are they evil? Holy Scripture observes sober restraint and reserve in addressing these subjects, not seeking to gratify any curiosity on our part that may be unhealthy. The Bible is a book for men, not for angels. It contains everything that man needs to know in order to glorify God and to be eternally saved. Consequently the Holy Spirit has chosen not to reveal certain details to us, and from this we can conclude that it is better if we do not know them.

We can infer that Satan is the head of a great company of angels who rebelled against God and lost "their first estate" (Jude 6 KJV). When Satan is among the "sons of God" in the first two chapters of Job, it is clear that he is presenting himself before God as one of the angels, albeit a fallen angel. Scripture is silent on the timing and circumstances of this angelic rebellion and fall. The precise nature and origin of the fall of Satan and of the demons, like the origin of sin itself, is kept concealed from us, and we need to pry no further.

It is the power and influences of Satan and his forces that are impressed upon us by the Scripture. As John Murray wrote, "Back of all that is visible and tangible in the sin of this world there are unseen spiritual powers."[2] Consequently the New Testament designates Satan with terms that underline this great power. He is "the prince of the power of the air, the spirit that is now at work in the sons of disobedience" (Eph. 2:2); he is, under the name Beelzebul, "the prince of demons" (Matt. 12:24); he is called by Jesus "the ruler of this world" (John 16:11); and Paul even refers to him as "the god of this world" (2 Cor. 4:4). This language is not hyperbole; it accurately describes the might of our great adversary.

And yet Satan's power is limited; he is tethered by the infinitely greater power of God himself. For this reason Satan tempted and tried Job no more than God permitted. John comforted his "little children" by reminding them that "he who is in you is greater than he who is in the world" (1 John 4:4). We do well to reckon Satan a great and mighty foe, but we do even better to acknowledge that God is greater and mightier than all else in creation, and that Satan and his leagues are created beings. Louis Berkhof summarizes: "He is superhuman, but not divine; has great power, but is not omnipotent; wields influence on a large but restricted scale . . . and is destined to be cast into the bottomless pit."[3]

THE CONTEST BETWEEN JESUS AND SATAN

So as we come to the four gospels, Satan himself is prominent, as are the many demons with whom Jesus comes into frequent contact. We need to see that the battle lines are being drawn. Our Lord's great adversary is marshaling his troops for the great showdown with the Son of God, the Seed of the woman. Now this Seed has appeared in Israel, his identity being testified by angels, by Simeon and Anna, by John the Baptist, by his own lips, and by the heavenly voice of God himself. The dragon is seeking to devour this child so as to falsify the prophecy made about his own doom in the Garden of Eden. Consequently he throws his heaviest artillery against Jesus, prosecuting his war all the way to Golgotha. Jesus will be bowed, bloodied, buried, and apparently beaten. Satan will look like the victor. But ultimately he will not and he cannot prevail. And because Satan cannot gain the ultimate victory over Christ, neither can he gain the ultimate victory over Christ's people. This is the great assurance and joy of every believer!

We will follow this conflict through, taking a look at some of the major confrontations. The image of the dragon seeking to devour the child finds the most graphic earthly fulfillment in the attempt of Herod the Great to murder the infant Jesus. Since that incident will be considered in the next chapter, we will leave it for the time being. So let us, in the present chapter, examine (1) the temptations Jesus faced in the wilderness, (2) the confrontation between Jesus and the demons, and (3) the accusation that Jesus was himself the prince of demons. Then, climactically, we will come to the cross itself and consider what it signifies in this spiritual conflict.

THE TEMPTATIONS IN THE WILDERNESS

Luke's account of the temptations of Christ, which is recorded in chapter 4 of his gospel, is preceded by clear signals that define the context of this battle. The mission of Christ is plainly set forth. Jesus, having been baptized by John in the

Jordan, is declared to be the Son of God by none other than the voice of the Father from heaven. This is accompanied by the visible descent of the Holy Spirit upon Jesus, the anointing he needed for his public ministry. We should not overlook this evidently Trinitarian emphasis, and neither should we miss Luke's emphasis on the work of the Holy Spirit throughout his gospel and throughout Acts. The presence and the fullness of the Holy Spirit empower Jesus' whole life and ministry; wherever Jesus goes he will be led by the Spirit. But why, we might wonder at this particular point, was Jesus being led by the Spirit into the wilderness?

Luke gives a clue to this question by providing a long genealogy, even longer than the one that begins Matthew's gospel. This genealogy is remarkable because it traces Jesus' ancestry all the way back to Adam himself, who is called "the son of God" (Luke 3:38). Adam was the "son of God" in the sense that he was created by God in his own image. Adam bore the very likeness of God, but he had a beginning in time and place. However, Jesus is far more than the duplicate of Adam. Adam was a created being who had his beginning in the Garden of Eden. Jesus eternally existed as the Son of God; he was never created.

When the first "son of God" was tempted by the devil he quickly succumbed to the temptations. So this is the burning question: will this "Son of God" succeed where his predecessor failed? The answer given—and it is an answer that should bring us the greatest comfort and joy—is that he will indeed prevail over Satan in circumstances much harder and harsher than those that Adam faced.[4]

Let us note the clear contrasts between the situations Adam and Jesus encountered. Adam was tempted in a garden of delights, with numerous fruit-bearing trees from which to choose, whereas Christ was tempted in a desolate wilderness where there was no food. Adam had no need to be hungry, whereas Christ had been without food for forty days. Adam had to face only one temptation, whereas Jesus had to face three. One more observation that could easily be overlooked: whereas Satan had never successfully tempted any human being before he came to Adam, by the time he squared up to Jesus he had enslaved every member of Adam's race. Satan came to that wilderness a wise and experienced adversary. He had never before failed in his temptations. He had a one hundred percent success record in getting people to sin. Here now was his most valuable prey; if he could obtain mastery over Jesus, then God's work of salvation would be forever undone.

In summary, the Spirit led the Son into an arena where he would be tempted to his ultimate capacity. Jesus had embarked upon a life of intense confrontation with the devil and his forces, and this test would display Jesus' true mettle as the Son of God.

How did Jesus resist Satan's temptations? He did so each time by quoting the words of Scripture. There is, of course, a plain application for every one of us here. Whenever we are tempted to sin we should use Scripture against Satan's devices. But that is not all. To return again to the contrast with Adam and Eve, we need to see that the key to their failure, and to Jesus' success, concerned their behavior in response to the word of God. For although Eve was able to *quote* the instructions she had received from the Lord, neither she nor her husband *obeyed* God's word to them. This is where Jesus succeeded. John Murray stated that obedience was "the unifying or integrating principle" in all that Christ did in securing our salvation.[5] He took on the form of a servant and did everything with the attitude of the Servant of the Lord. Therefore he came out of the wilderness with his obedience utterly intact.

We should note another important point about the wilderness temptation: the wilderness had a clear association with the people of Israel, who were there not for forty days but for forty years. As a generation, they failed spectacularly in the wilderness. From the beginning they grumbled against Moses and against

God. Rebellion and unfaithfulness characterized their attitude. Therefore that generation perished in the wilderness. It says dismally in Isaiah 63:10, "But they rebelled and grieved his Holy Spirit." Now, the same Holy Spirit led Jesus into the wilderness, and Jesus submitted and obeyed. He was "full of the Holy Spirit" when he was led into the wilderness, and he "returned in the power of the Spirit" from the wilderness (Luke 4:1, 14).

The first passage of Scripture that Jesus used against Satan was from Deuteronomy 8:3, which speaks of how the Israelites had to be humbled in order to learn this lesson: "Man does not live by bread alone, but man lives by every word that comes from the mouth of the LORD." He was succeeding here, not only where Adam failed, but where Israel as a whole failed. Jesus was embodying Psalm 33:18–19:

> Behold, the eye of the LORD is on those who fear him,
>   on those who hope in his steadfast love,
> that he may deliver their soul from death
>   and keep them alive in famine.

Unlike Israel, Jesus was trusting God to bring provision.

JESUS CASTS OUT DEMONS

Hard on the heels of Jesus' temptation in the wilderness was his first recorded encounter with a demon (Luke 4:33–37). This incident comes in the context of Jesus' teaching in the synagogue, which was characterized by authority.

Let us be satisfied that demon possession is quite simply not an archaic term for some kind of clinical insanity. Luke, a medical man, makes it clear that sometimes various maladies should be attributed to evil spirits, but that at other times they should not. In this case a real and distinct evil being exercised control over this man.

What does this demon say? "What have you to do with us, Jesus of Nazareth? Have you come to destroy us? I know who you are—the Holy One of God" (Luke 4:34). Note the extreme contrast. An unclean demon is in the presence of the Holy One of God. Consequently the demon expresses panic and alarm. "Why are we together in the same place? What do we have in common that you should want anything at all to do with us? Why don't you leave us alone?"

Notice that this demon was absolutely right in his theology. Unlike much of the human race, the demons had no difficulty in believing that there is one God—and they shuddered in doing so. More to the point, this demon had no doubt about the true identity of Jesus. What theological liberals shrink from affirming, this demon confessed with the greatest fear. Demons recognized the Holy One of God. What is more, they knew that for them there could never be any salvation or forgiveness, but only unending punishment. And indeed Jesus came into the world, from heaven, to destroy demons and all the power of evil. The demon in this synagogue accurately knew what the ministry of Jesus was all about.

By a single command Jesus rebuked the demon and it came out of the man. It was a strong, abrupt imperative, almost as if Jesus had said, "Shut up and get out!" In an instant the demon came out, throwing the man to the ground but not harming him. In the William Peter Blatty novel *The Exorcist*, which has been made into a film, Jesuit priests seek to exorcise evil spirits from a young girl, Regan MacNeil. The whole process is lengthy and exhausting and even results in the death of one of the priests. What a striking contrast is presented by Jesus' calm authority in this passage!

THE FINGER OF GOD

Let us next look at a specific accusation made against Jesus later in his ministry. The substance of it was that Jesus cast out demons by the power of Beelzebul, the prince of demons, and this is recorded in Luke 11:14–23. This followed an occasion when Jesus cast out another demon that had made a man unable to speak.

By this stage in Jesus' ministry a calculated plan was being put into action. It seems that spies were being sent out from Jerusalem to find out what he was up to and to try and stop him. During Jesus' ministry the attitude of the religious authorities toward him had mushroomed from curiosity, to annoyance, to rivalry, to envy, and now to bitter hatred. We can imagine a summary of their complaints. In their scheme of things Jesus broke the Sabbath by plucking and eating grain and by healing sick people. He gathered great crowds who loved to hear him, teaching by his own authority in a way that the scribes and Pharisees could not. He touched lepers, ate with tax collectors, and allowed women of dubious character to wipe his feet with their hair. With this bitter antipathy there arose a strong conviction—an illusion but a conviction nevertheless—that Jesus worked against them and against God and therefore was evil. By deduction, the miraculous powers he worked could not be from God, but from the forces of evil.

Observe carefully that this was the most malicious and poisonous accusation that could ever have been made against Jesus. It was a breathtaking claim. By "Beelzebul" the scribes and Pharisees meant none other than Satan himself. We read in 2 Kings chapter 1 of a local deity, Baal-zebub, the god of Ekron, whom king Ahaziah inquired of. By New Testament times the name Beelzebul was equated with the Devil, the prince of demons. The accusation was that Jesus, who had gone about Galilee doing mighty works of love and mercy, and had just performed such a work, was doing so by the power of Satan, the prince of demons, the Evil One. This kind of behavior can increasingly be observed among the Jews who opposed Jesus. They were horrible, wicked accusations of the most blasphemous kind. On three separate occasions in John's gospel they told Jesus that he was demon-possessed.

Notice that Jesus did not retaliate; he did not satisfy his enemies' longing to make him react. Instead he applied simple logic. A household or a country that is convulsed by war between its members will fragment and will be destroyed in the course of time. If they were right and Jesus was casting out demons by the power of Satan, then how could Satan's kingdom possibly have stood? If they were right, then Satan, working through Jesus, would always be undoing his own work. It is worth noting that Jesus accorded Satan the honor of having a kingdom. In fact, the accusation of Jesus' opponents was proof of the existence of this kingdom. Here were scribes and Pharisees, those who sat in Moses' seat, vehemently blaspheming the Son of God by telling him that he worked miracles by the power of Satan. What more compelling evidence could there be of the extent and scale of Satan's kingdom than these malicious allegations?

In Luke 11:21 Jesus paints a memorable picture of Satan. "When a strong man, fully armed, guards his own palace, his goods are safe." Here is a description of the Devil in all his strength, so apparently invincible and unassailable. He is not only very strong, but he is fully armed—as Hendriksen puts it, "armed to the teeth."[6] This strong man, Satan, guards his palace. He keeps the unbelieving world under lock and key. He is on the lookout for anyone who might rob him of his precious possessions—souls that he has duped and mastered. And while there is no one stronger than he, Satan keeps his goods in peace and safety. He has mastered and subdued every human individual who has ever lived—until one stronger than Satan comes and overpowers him.

The only strength that exceeds Satan's is not human, not even angelic, but divine. Here is proof, if one were needed, that Jesus is no mere man. To cast out demons, heal the sick, give sight to the blind, raise the dead, still the wind and waves—and to pronounce the forgiveness of sins—these are not human activities! Here is Jesus, disarming the weaponry of Satan and carrying off his spoils. Therefore Jesus tells his opponents that his casting out of demons is the exercise of "the finger of God" (Luke 11:20). This expression "the finger of God" points us back to the time of Moses when the people of Israel were still in Egypt, and to the third plague, the plague of gnats.

> Then the LORD said to Moses, "Say to Aaron, 'Stretch out your staff and strike the dust of the earth, so that it may become gnats in all the land of Egypt.'" And they did so. Aaron stretched out his hand with his staff and struck the dust of the earth, and there were gnats on man and beast. All the dust of the earth became gnats in all the land of Egypt. The magicians tried by their secret arts to produce gnats, but they could not. So there were gnats on man and beast. Then the magicians said to Pharaoh, "This is the finger of God." But Pharaoh's heart was hardened, and he would not listen to them, as the LORD had said. (Ex. 8:16–19)

The Egyptian magicians recognized that God was on the side of Moses and Aaron and that he was against Pharaoh and Egypt. This was no ordinary magic; this was not the kind of courtroom enchantment that ancient kings routinely witnessed. This could be explained only by the determined and direct intervention of God.

Now the finger of God had moved. Jesus Christ, the Son of God, had come, and he was mightier than Satan. He had demonstrated this right in front of these people on this very occasion. He had been doing so throughout his ministry. He had given full and unmistakable proof of his authority over the devil.

CLIMAX AND CONCLUSION

We have focused here on events in Jesus' ministry rather than on the circumstances that surrounded his death. It is clear that Satan was very active in the last days of Jesus' earthly life, in events that we will consider in more detail in subsequent chapters. We are told that Satan demanded to have Simon Peter, in order that he might sift him as wheat (Luke 22:31). Judas' determination to betray Jesus was due to the fact that Satan himself entered him (Luke 22:3; John 13:27). The appalling suffering of Jesus appears to speak of shame and defeat. There was his agonizing prayer, bloody sweat, and arrest, followed by the mocking, spitting, and beating, then the crown of thorns, the nails, the cross, and the cry of dereliction—it all looked as though the final and decisive victory belonged to Jesus' great enemy. It was indeed the hour of darkness.

But to consider Jesus' suffering as nothing other than darkness is to look at appearances only and fail to understand what was going on in the spiritual realm. Jesus' death on the cross was itself a triumph over the rulers and authorities (Col. 2:15). It was the public disarming of their powers. The resurrection of Jesus Christ and the glories that follow—his ascent to God's right hand, the giving of the Holy Spirit to the church, the proclamation of the gospel to the ends of the earth—all assert publicly that the Son of God has destroyed the one who holds the power of death, the Devil (Heb. 2:14).

We must always remember that Satan is Christ's defeated foe—and ours. His doom is utterly certain. And yet the final manifestation of his defeat awaits a future time. Satan's activity against the church, his war against the saints, will continue until heaven and earth witness his ultimate destruction. The comparison has often been made with the course of the Second World War after the Allied D-Day landings of June 1944. From that time onward, the defeat of the Nazis was practically certain. But they did not go down without a tremendous struggle. Some of the fiercest fighting of the war—for example, the Battle of Arnhem—took place during the eleven months before the final Nazi surrender.

But final victory will come. A day will dawn when Jesus Christ returns to earth in full and majestic power and glory. Paul's words at the end of his letter to the Romans need to be read as a comfort to Christians in every generation. "The God of peace will soon crush Satan under your feet." Therefore Paul adds with confidence, "The grace of our Lord Jesus Christ be with you" (Rom. 16:20).

3

HEROD THE GREAT

Then Herod, when he saw that he had been tricked by the wise men, became furious, and he sent and killed all the male children in Bethlehem and in all that region who were two years old or under, according to the time that he had ascertained from the wise men.
(Matt. 2:16)

THE FIRST ENEMY of Jesus Christ we encounter in the New Testament is Herod the Great. The designs of the predatory dragon that we considered in the previous chapter can be quickly discerned in the brutal, scheming actions of this king. No sooner has Jesus been born than the dragon is waiting to pounce and devour.

The chilling sound of Herod's name echoes down the centuries; I doubt whether anyone in recent times has had the heartlessness to name their child "Herod." Like "Sauron" and "Mordor" in the writings of Tolkien, the very name "Herod" has a portentous, baneful quality associated with it, at least for anyone familiar with the New Testament—and perhaps for many others familiar with nativity plays. Years ago, I attended a Christmas pantomime based on the events surrounding Jesus' birth. The villain, of course, was King Herod. When he appeared on the stage, everyone booed loudly—although like all good pantomime villains, he was the character the audience loved the most, and like all good pantomime villains, he engaged in frequent and joyous repartee with them.

But the Herod of the Gospels, and indeed the Herod of secular history, is not someone that people laugh or jeer at. He is the paranoid, frenzied megalomaniac who, confronted with the report that a new king had been born, responds with abominable infanticide that has become popularly known as the Massacre of the Innocents. This event has found its way into the Christian calendar, traditionally December 28th in the Western church, and has often been represented on canvas. The Flemish painter Peter Paul Rubens depicted a particularly harrowing scene. As we will see, this atrocity was entirely in keeping with what we know of the king's character. Were it not that two thousand years separated our times from those of King Herod, the portrayal of him as a character in a pantomime would be about as inappropriate as a depiction of Pol Pot, Idi Amin, or Mao Zedong.

TERRIBLE GREATNESS

Matthew is the only gospel writer who devotes any detail to Herod the Great, and all the information he provides is found in the second chapter of his gospel. Secular historians, especially the Jewish Flavius Josephus, are able to furnish us with a great amount of detail concerning Herod's background, character, life, and reign.[1] It is true that Josephus and other historians of the period do not speak of Herod's massacre in Bethlehem—but this is because his actions there might be considered "a drop in the ocean" by comparison with the many acts of carnage that he brought about. Yet not only does Matthew's account provide us with a portrait of Herod that is consistent with other historical records, but it brings Herod's life to its bitter end—and "bitter" is undoubtedly the most fitting word.

Secular history has accorded Herod the title "Great." In the New Testament he is simply referred to as "Herod the king" (Matt. 2:1, 3) or as "Herod, king of Judea" (Luke 1:5). The designation "Great" does enable us to distinguish him from several other rulers of the same name in his family, of whom he was the progenitor. There are two other men referred to as "Herod" in the Gospels: Herod Antipas, son of Herod the Great, who became tetrarch of Galilee and who beheaded John the Baptist and later mocked Jesus; and Herod Agrippa I, grandson of Herod the Great, whose imprisonment of the apostle Peter is recorded in Acts 12. But in addition to these two, many other members of Herod's family shared his name, which became a dynastic title.[2]

The English have shown typical restraint when it comes to bandying about designations like "Great." King Alfred, who died over eleven hundred years ago, is the only English monarch to have been so honored, and his greatness consisted of virtues that most would undoubtedly consider admirable. He was not only a noble and heroic warrior, but a true scholar and a wise legal reformer. But Herod's "greatness" was of the diametrically opposite kind. It was the brutal, terrible greatness of a Genghis Khan or an Attila the Hun. Wherever Herod went, he left a trail of blood and terror behind him, for he was utterly ruthless in his pursuit of power. In fairness it needs to be added that his "greatness" could also be seen in his marvelous building works; not only the enlarged and beautiful temple that he built in Jerusalem, but many other feats of architecture in that city and far beyond. A balanced treatment of Herod's character and reign would have to acknowledge these accomplishments. Nevertheless, it is as a man of violence and cruelty that Herod is remembered.

Anyone remotely acquainted with English history will be familiar with the reign of King Henry VIII, and in particular with his turbulent family life—six wives in succession, two of them divorced, two others beheaded—as well as his increasingly tyrannical grip on power as he grew older. But Henry VIII's record in the ranks of barbaric despotism, both within his family and in the context of political power, pales into insignificance alongside that of Herod. Among near contemporaries, the Roman Emperor

Nero might be reasonably compared to Herod in terms of his lust for blood and power—but Nero's life and evil deeds were mercifully cut short at the age of thirty, whereas Herod lived into his seventieth year.

What caused this man to react as he did to news arriving in Jerusalem from these strange travelers from distant lands? Why the craft and the deception, why the enmity toward an infant called Jesus whom he had never met, why the cold-blooded murder of so many baby boys in a nearby village called Bethlehem? We must remember that when Matthew wrote his gospel, "Herod the king" was still an immensely dominant figure in the memories of his readers. The sense of fear and alarm inspired by the name "Herod" would have been quite palpable. So let us now fill in some information that will enable us to see Matthew's depiction of Herod against a dark historical background.

BIOGRAPHY OF A TYRANT

The last century before Christ had been a time of immense military and political upheaval throughout the known world, and nowhere was this more evident than in Israel. The rivalries and intrigues that took place in Rome—by now the undisputed capital of the ancient world—had repercussions in every corner of the Mediterranean region, and indeed beyond.

In Israel the Hasmonean dynasty of kings had come to power in the previous century amid waves of glory, triumph, and expectation that at the time seemed messianic. The exploits of Judas Maccabeus and the rededication of the temple in Jerusalem in 164 BC, following the sacrilegious actions of the pagan king Antiochus IV, were permanently etched upon the patriotic hearts of the Jews.[3] This needs to be remembered in the light of what is about to be described.

All this high promise soon began to fade. The weak Hasmonean king Hyrcanus II was faced with the rebellion of his much more vigorous brother Aristobulus. Roman power, quite characteristically, exploited this volatile situation: the famous general Pompey, colleague-turned-rival of Julius Caesar, captured Jerusalem in 63 BC. Judea had now become a Roman protectorate within the larger Roman province of Syria.

At the same time, in the district of Idumea, a land whose name resembles that of the Old Testament land of Edom but in fact lay a little further south, a cunning and ruthless individual by the name of Antipater had emerged. Antipater had chosen to support Hyrcanus II in his dispute against his brother. It might seem that, with the Roman conquest, Antipater's hopes of real power had vanished. But he watched carefully for his opportunities, and when Julius Caesar defeated Pompey in 49 BC Antipater gave his allegiance to Caesar, which did much for his own personal prospects and the prospects of his two sons, whose names were Phasaelus and Herod. Now, at the age of twenty-five, Herod became the governor of Galilee. It was a significant first step, for just twelve years later he would become "king of the Jews."

Antipater was poisoned in 43 BC, the year after Julius Caesar was assassinated. Then the Parthians invaded from the east, and Rome itself was soon convulsed in civil war. But Herod turned each terrible event to his own interests, craftily siding with first one powerful figure, then another. Not only Pompey and Caesar, but also Antony and Cleopatra, and Octavian (subsequently known as the Emperor Augustus) were all players in this blood-drenched drama. By 37 BC, after many a plot and intrigue, Herod held Palestine and even some of the lands beyond in an iron grip, which he did not relinquish over the next thirty-three years. It was in the Roman Emperor's interests that such a ruthless, strong-willed ruler should be established in Palestine, a dangerous and troubled frontier region of the Empire.

The most significant fact of all about Herod, certainly in terms of the unfolding of the events of his reign, is that he was far from being a pureblood Israelite. His father Antipater was an Idumean, and his mother Cypros was a Nabatean, a member of a small Arab kingdom. Herod's ancestry meant that the designation "King of the Jews" was fiction in the eyes of the true Jews over whom he reigned, though he made use of this title whenever it seemed expedient. But his mixed lineage seems to have played very forcibly on Herod's own mind. During the course of his reign, Herod directly arranged the deaths of all the prominent members of the Hasmonean dynasty—about whose Jewish descent there could be no controversy—with cunning calculation. Herod had ten wives altogether, but the most important of them historically was the Hasmonean princess Mariamne, a direct descendant of the Maccabean kings. Over time, Herod killed Mariamne's brother Aristobulus,[4] her uncle Antigonus, and her grandfather Hyrcanus II. Then, in 29 BC, following rumors of adultery, Mariamne herself was executed. It does seem that Herod felt bitter self-recrimination after the death of Mariamne; the Jewish historian Alfred Edersheim noted that "the most fearful paroxysms of remorse, passion and longing for his murdered wife now seized the tyrant, and brought him to the brink of the grave."[5]

His bloodletting had not yet reached its fill, for the following year Mariamne's mother Alexandra became the next victim of Herod's sword. What was more, any children of Herod by Mariamne would have been heirs of the Hasmoneans, and in 8 BC, following highly complicated family intrigues, his two sons Alexander and Aristobulus were put to death.

This power-lusting ruler was possessed by a deep, dark, suspicious nature that led him to perceive enemies in every direction. The atrocities we have just described represent a tiny fraction of the bloodshed for which Herod was responsible throughout his life. Words written by Alan Bullock in his masterly study of Adolf Hitler could equally well be applied to Herod: "Remarkable powers were combined with an ugly and strident egotism. . . . The passions which ruled [his] mind were ignoble: hatred, resentment, the lust to dominate, to destroy."[6]

Much the same could be said of other tyrants from every era. This is what fallen human nature looks like when it seizes great power. It has rightly been said that "power corrupts, and absolute power corrupts absolutely." James tells us that "sin when it is fully grown brings forth death" (James 1:15). Tyranny results in the overthrowing of every restraint against sin, and inevitably death is multiplied.

A TALE OF TWO KINGS

Such is the "Herod the king" who we encounter as we turn to the second chapter of Matthew's gospel. Here in this passage we encounter the old despot in the declining months of his reign, by which time, according to Josephus, his mind and body were wracked with desperate torments. Now something happens that greatly agitates Herod. Odd and exotic travelers from the east—magi—suddenly appear in Jerusalem. This is not the place to speculate as to the precise identity of these magi; indeed our lack of certain information about them is in stark contrast to the wealth of material we possess with regard to Herod. We can be reasonably certain that they were not kings, contrary to popular tradition, and the number of them is unspecified. Though they sought signs from the stars in the heavens, it would be grossly unfair to lump them together with today's horoscope writers. Undoubtedly they were deeply cultured and educated men.

But it is the question they ask that awakens Herod's darkest suspicions: "Where is he who has been born king of the Jews?" (Matt. 2:2). We cannot be sure whether the magi make straight for Herod's palace. The likelihood is that if they had known anything about Herod's reputation, they would have acted with caution. At any rate, secrets cannot be kept from the king for very long. Word about these strange visitors and their inquiry quickly spreads throughout Jerusalem. We read that Herod is disturbed, and that spells trouble for Jerusalem, whose fearful citizens have known the outbreaks of the king's wrath on all too many occasions in the past.

"Herod the king" . . . "king of the Jews." Not only is there tension and rivalry here, there is also a clear literary design. Matthew is setting up a tale of two kings. Indeed he has been doing exactly that from the beginning of his gospel. He has already shown in the first chapter that Jesus is the son of David and that Joseph is descended from David. The second section of names in the genealogy, from David in verse 6 to Jechoniah in verse 11, lists fifteen kings who reigned in Jerusalem, even as Herod now reigned. A royal pedigree, at the very least, is suggested right at the beginning of Matthew's gospel. Now this royal theme is pushed up a notch as King Herod is spoken of, and it reaches extreme crisis point when the magi's question reaches Herod's ears. As we have seen, the king's intense jealousy easily displayed itself in bloodthirsty actions. Herod needs to do something quickly. He must suppress this threat immediately and starve this potential uprising of any opportunity. He needs to strangle it at birth and pull up this supposed "king" by the roots. Where can he find this king?

It should be understood that at this time Jerusalem and Judah are awash with messianic expectation. Consequently Herod automatically links the idea of "king of the Jews" with the concept of Messiah, of "Christ." So he summons the experts without delay. Indeed, he seems to call an extraordinary meeting of the whole Sanhedrin, the Jewish council. Perhaps we can picture the royal court, the king flushed with impatient rage and the poor flustered priests and scribes scurrying feverishly around with their scrolls, with shaking hands and stammering voices. There is a council of war in the throne room. But Herod gets the answer he needs: Bethlehem—that is what the prophecy of Micah says. A shepherd—and in Israel's understanding a shepherd represented a king—will come from Bethlehem, the city of the shepherd-king David, just six miles south of Jerusalem. Now

Herod shows all his craftiness and cunning. Concealing his well-practiced scheming from the magi—it is by a revelatory dream rather than their own suspicions that they will be warned—he interviews them, gains the necessary information about the time when the star first appeared, and requires them to report back to him once they have been to see this child.

GOLD FOR THE KING OF KINGS

What about this child? Matthew's account of the events surrounding Jesus' birth is thrilling, but it is a good deal sketchier than Luke's, whose first two chapters are roughly three times as long as Matthew's first two chapters. Matthew mentions no Roman census, no lowly manger, no angelic choir, no adoring shepherds, no devout Simeon or worshipping Anna. It is reasonable to assume that by the time the magi arrived, all these glorious scenes were firmly in the past; indeed, Matthew tells us that Jesus, Mary, and Joseph were now living in a "house" in Bethlehem (Matt. 2:11), presumably with Joseph's relatives.

Matthew has his own unique focus—the visit of these magi, the way they prostrate themselves in worship before this child, and the gifts they bring him. The Holy Spirit has chosen to show us what these gifts were; this is no mere embroidery or accidental detail. The child Jesus was presented with gold, frankincense, and myrrh. These would be unusual gifts to give a newborn baby today, but they would scarcely have been commonplace two thousand years ago. Surely the magi themselves did not know the full import of what these gifts signified. But armed with our Bibles we can see in each of them great lessons about the person, the office, and the work of the Lord Jesus Christ. It is only the first gift that we will consider here, that of gold.

When we look at the Old Testament, we see rather a lot of gold, its various uses both commendable and not so commendable. Gold was employed in the building of the tabernacle and the temple and in their various furnishings. Gold was used in the manufacture of jewelry, as it is today. Gold was also used, much more infamously, in connection with the calf that Aaron made and the two calves that King Jeroboam made in Bethel and in Dan, which became a sin for Israel (1 Kings 12:30). But what we see overwhelmingly in Scripture is that gold is associated with royalty. It symbolizes the power and wealth exercised by royal figures or those acting on their behalf. In Daniel's vision, reigning King Nebuchadnezzar is represented by a head of gold. King Ahasuerus extends to Queen Esther a golden scepter. King Solomon's wealth is dominated by the vast amount of gold he had. Gold is exceedingly rare as well as being so beautiful and noble a metal. Therefore it is a fitting gift for a king, and these magi, who are seeking the "king of the Jews," bring gold as the first of their gifts.

It is a gift that gave full expression to what lay within the magi's hearts. No human language could be more expressive of great, unbounded joy than what we read in Matthew 2:10, which could be literally rendered, "and seeing the star they joyed with joy great, exceeding." Here indeed is the fulfillment of Isaiah 66:10: "Rejoice with Jerusalem, and be glad for her, all you who love her; rejoice with her in joy." Their cup of joy was filled to overflowing. Here was the great hope of the nations; here was one who was born not only king of the Jews but king of the Gentiles, and High King over all the kings of the earth. The joy that the wise men knew progressed to adoring worship. They fell down to worship the child. They prostrated themselves before him. Though Jesus no longer lay in a manger, neither was he accompanied with the usual trappings of kingship. This child had no royal robes, no palace, no throne, no crown. But the magi adored Jesus with the eye of faith, rather than with the eye of flesh.

Thus John Calvin comments on this passage:

> They are convinced that he is divinely appointed to be a King. This thought alone, deeply rooted in their minds, procures

their reverence. They contemplate in the purpose of God his exalted rank, which is still concealed from outward view. Holding it for certain, that he will one day be different from what he now appears, they are not at all ashamed to render to him the honors of royalty.[7]

"Out of Egypt I Called My Son"

Let us see what Jesus' "exalted rank" means in terms of the unfolding events. It is only through the eye of faith that we can begin to understand how this child, with his mother Mary and her husband Joseph, could ever escape the clutches of Herod, who generally achieved everything he set out to do. While Herod in his throne room was making his plans, eagerly and impatiently waiting for the magi's report, heaven's throne room, through dreams given to Joseph and to the magi, ensured that the Son of God would be protected and preserved from the tyrant's schemes. Just as the infant Moses was sheltered among the reeds and rushes of Egypt, concealed in a basket and protected from Pharaoh's edict until his daughter should draw him out, so the child Jesus was withdrawn from the fury and rage of Herod until such time as the Father should draw his own Son out of Egypt. It is the Lord "who brings princes to nothing, and makes the rulers of the earth as emptiness" (Isa. 40:23). For "he does according to his will among the host of heaven and among the inhabitants of the earth; and none can stay his hand or say to him, 'What have you done?'" (Dan. 4:35).

And so the king's merciless actions follow, the episode of bloodletting in Bethlehem that would bring the mothers of that town into a state of "weeping and loud lamentation, Rachel weeping for her children; she refused to be comforted, because they are no more" (Matt. 2:18). Every house in Bethlehem becomes a scene of wailing and bitterness. But the house the magi visited is no longer occupied by the holy family; Jesus is out of Herod's grasp, kept by a power that Herod cannot control or oppose, and by which he himself is very soon to be summoned.

THE BLOODY AND BITTER END

And so Herod died—but only after one more act of jealous cruelty toward his family. It is wearying, as well as sickening, to relate that he had his eldest son, another Antipater, executed just five days before his own death. Josephus tells us that Herod's last days were marked by the most appalling physical and psychological suffering. A measure of the horrors he had inflicted upon so many others were visited upon him before he died. We have a modern-day parallel in Joseph Stalin to Herod's death in 4 BC. In 1953 Stalin died in desperate agony while choking on his own blood. The best doctors in the Soviet Union—the only people who might have been able to administer any kind of effective treatment—were locked up as part of the dictator's latest purge. Stalin was choking on his own blood, but it could have been the blood of his many victims, who numbered in the tens of millions.

Here then is a "tale of two kings," of two kings of the Jews. Spending some time comparing and contrasting them leads to conclusions that are not only fascinating but demanding of our most careful—and prayerful—reflection.

Herod achieved his title "king of the Jews" by force and intrigue, and clung to it jealously throughout the thirty-three years of his reign. Jesus lived on earth for about thirty-three years and never sought to be known as the "king of the Jews." Indeed at the end of those years a placard with the words "King of the Jews" was placed above his head, but it was put there in cruel irony. Herod sought and defended, at every cost, a worldly kingdom. Jesus said that his kingdom was "not of this world" (John 18:36). Herod shed rivers of blood—other people's blood—whenever he encountered opposition, or supposed opposition, from anyone. The only blood Jesus shed was his own. He did so to establish his kingdom, to redeem men and women who were by nature rebel sinners, transforming them into willing and faithful servants who bow their knees gladly to the eternal King of Kings. Herod died, his kingdom was divided among his sons, and within three generations his dynasty had expired. But when Jesus died, he did so that he might take up his life again, and by rising from the dead demonstrate the glorious and eternal future he has secured for all who put their trust in him.

"HIS KINGDOM STRETCH FROM SHORE TO SHORE"

In Jesus Christ alone are fulfilled the ancient prophecies of eternal kingship.

> May he have dominion from sea to sea,
>   and from the River to the ends of the earth!
> May desert tribes bow down before him,
>   and his enemies lick the dust!
> May the kings of Tarshish and of the coastlands
>   render him tribute;
> may the kings of Sheba and Seba
>   bring gifts!
> May all kings fall down before him,
>   all nations serve him! (Ps. 72:8–11)

As Isaac Watts wrote, and as we sing,

> Jesus shall reign where'er the sun
> Doth his successive journeys run;
> His kingdom stretch from shore to shore,
> Till moons shall wax and wane no more.

Nearly four hundred years after Herod there came a Roman Emperor who resisted the Lord Jesus Christ with all his might. He wanted to overthrow Christianity and turn the Romans back to their ancient paganism. His name was Julian, and he has become known to history as Julian The Apostate. He was killed on the battlefield, and legend has it that his last words were "Thou hast conquered, Galilean." It may be simply a legend, but it contains an important truth. No human power can prevail against the Lord Jesus Christ, the King of Kings. At the name of Jesus every knee will bow, both willingly and unwillingly.

Jesus says to all who will hear him,

> Come to me, all who labor and are heavy laden, and I will give you rest. Take my yoke upon you, and learn from me, for I am gentle and lowly in heart, and you will find rest for your souls. For my yoke is easy, and my burden is light. (Matt. 11:28-30)

Here is a King who sets his people free from their *every* enemy, even death, even the devil, even their own sinful and corrupt natures.

4

THE PEOPLE OF NAZARETH

And all spoke well of him and marveled at the gracious
words that were coming from his mouth. And they said,
"Is not this Joseph's son?" And he said to them, "Doubtless
you will quote to me this proverb, 'Physician, heal yourself.'
What we have heard you did at Capernaum, do here in
your hometown as well." And he said, "Truly, I say to you,
no prophet is acceptable in his hometown." (Luke 4:22–24)

WE MOVE FORWARD about thirty years and shift north-
ward from Jerusalem about seventy miles as we begin to look at
the enemies that Jesus faced during his adult public ministry.
The scene is a synagogue on a Sabbath morning in Nazareth in
Galilee.

It may be true that the events described here did not take
place at the very beginning of Jesus' public ministry. All the
wonderful narratives recorded in chapters 2 to 4 of John's
gospel almost certainly unfolded before this incident, as well
as the works referred to in Capernaum (Luke 4:23). In Luke's
carefully ordered scheme, this incident in the Nazareth synagogue marks the official inauguration of the work that Jesus
had been given to do. This is most appropriate, for it was the
Son of God's calling to spend the bulk of his earthly life in
the little town of Nazareth.

"CAN ANYTHING GOOD COME OUT OF NAZARETH?"

Nazareth! Some towns and cities are famed for their natural beauty, the grandeur of their architecture, or their importance in terms of commerce, transport, or history. Other towns have military and strategic importance. Still other towns are illustrious because of well-known individuals who lived there, or choice products that are manufactured there. In England, Stratford-upon-Avon is famous for its Bard, Cheddar for its Gorge (as well as its ubiquitous cheese), and Axminster for its carpets. But there are many towns of comparable populations, and some considerably larger, that apparently have little, or even nothing, to recommend them. Nazareth seems to have been such a place.

In Matthew 2:23 we read of how Joseph, with Mary and Jesus, settled in Nazareth in order that "what was spoken by the prophets might be fulfilled: 'He shall be called a Nazarene.'" Because our modern English translations put quotation marks around these words we suppose that this exact phrase must come from the Scriptures. But we look in vain in our Old Testament for this apparent quote, or indeed for any mention of "Nazareth" or "Nazarene" at all. Various explanations have been given. Might there be some significance in the way that the word *Nazareth* closely resembles *Nazirite*, a term that describes a male who was separated to the Lord from birth, as Samson was? There is no correlation between these two words, and neither is the idea of a Nazirite implied in Jesus' case; rather, it is the details given about John the Baptist that suggest that *he* might be in the category of a Nazirite (Luke 1:15). Others have suggested that the name *Nazareth* is related to the Hebrew word for "branch," *nezer*, which is found in Isaiah 11:1: "There shall come forth a shoot from the stump of Jesse, and a branch from his roots shall bear fruit." But this solution does not seem at all compelling.

The most satisfactory explanation is that Matthew, rather than quoting the precise words of any particular Old Testament prophet, is concisely summarizing what the prophets taught in general about the earthly circumstances of the Messiah. His lot would be that of the "Nazarene," meaning that in his earthly life and associations he would be scorned and despised by the people. Amidst all the glowing Old Testament prophecies of the reign and glory of the Messiah, there are many that speak of the modest and humble circumstances of his earthly life. The Servant of the Lord portrayed by Isaiah, in particular, is shown to be one "deeply despised, abhorred by the nation" (49:7), "despised and rejected by men" (53:3), who in his very death would be "numbered with the transgressors" (53:12). Psalm 22:6 speaks of the experiences of the Savior—"I am a worm and not a man." Psalm 69:7 gives expression to the rejection that the Messiah would know: "For it is for your sake that I have borne reproach, that dishonor has covered my face." Jesus' abode in Nazareth would fit in with all these details. The name of "Nazarene" was to be a term of opprobrium that stuck to Jesus, just as many of his followers have had similar names attached to them down the centuries. The titles "Puritan" and "Methodist" were first used as insults in the sixteenth and eighteenth century respectively, but to those who truly know their history and how God worked in their times, these designations have become badges of high honor.

But early in the first century AD, Nazareth was a small, despised town and its inhabitants were held in low esteem. There is no more eloquent indication of this than the response of Nathanael when he heard from Philip that Jesus, the one foretold by Moses and the prophets, had come from Nazareth. This seemed unthinkable; we can almost hear the incredulity in his tones. "Can anything good come out of Nazareth?" (John 1:46). There are other places in the Gospels where the words *Nazareth* and *Nazarene* are uttered with a similar kind of disdain. The servant girl who challenged Peter framed her words by saying, "You also were with that Nazarene, Jesus" (Mark 14:67). One can almost imagine her spitting out the words "that Nazarene." It may have even been that her disparaging remark hastened Peter toward his denial of Jesus.

Or Even Galilee?

What was true of Nazareth in particular could also be applied to the whole area of Galilee more generally. Although Isaiah had prophesied that "Galilee of the nations" (Isaiah 9:1) would be honored, this possibility seemed far from the minds of the religious leaders in Jesus' day, for whom anything of significance could happen only in or around Jerusalem. The people of Galilee were not highly regarded by those who lived in Jerusalem and its environs, that is, the lands allotted to the tribes of Judah and Benjamin.

Galilee was viewed as uncultured, unlearned, and pragmatic, a district of artisans rather than academics, and moreover a region where the purity of God's people was sullied with too much association with the Gentiles. Galilee was a remote northern outpost. Hence Peter, vigorously denying that he knew Jesus while he was in Jerusalem, would unmistakably have been identified as a northerner, rather like the broad Geordie on the streets of London before the days of steam—and perhaps today as well![1] The Messiah could not possibly come from Galilee. Everyone knew that Bethlehem, in privileged Judah, was to be the place from which the Deliverer would hail. When Nicodemus pleaded that Jesus might be given a fair hearing, he was rudely rebuffed; he ought to have known that no prophet came from Galilee (John 7:52). But this was one of a number of occasions when the Jewish leaders failed to know both the Scriptures and the power of God. Isaiah had prophesied seven centuries earlier that the land of the tribes of Zebulun and Naphtali, once brought into contempt, would be made glorious, and from then Nazareth would ever be celebrated as the home of the Messiah.

CHASTE SILENCE

Of Jesus' childhood and youth in Nazareth we know almost nothing, and this is for our good. We must guard against a kind of voyeuristic fascination that seeks to pry into details that the Holy Spirit (who gave us the Bible) has chosen not to disclose. This veil drawn over Jesus' childhood by the gospel writers is in the greatest contrast to what we find in sources—utterly untrustworthy sources—outside the Bible. The noted nineteenth-century church historian Philip Schaff comments that "when the legendary fancy of the Apocryphal Gospels attempted to fill out the chaste silence of the Evangelists, it painted an unnatural prodigy of a child to whom wild animals, trees, and dumb idols bowed, and who changed balls of clay into flying birds for the amusement of his playmates."[2]

Yet perhaps we can make one comment on this near-silence in regard to the first thirty years of Jesus' life. Can we not ascertain that Jesus' conduct during his childhood and youth, though exceptional and unique in its sinlessness, was not in any sense odd or freakish? Young Jesus of Nazareth took his place in the society into which he had been born. Luke 2:51 tells us that he was "submissive" to his parents. This submissiveness entailed a yielding up of the powers and rights that he could have exercised as the Son of God. In the full humanity with which he was clothed, he chose to be obscure until the appointed day came for him to be made known in Israel. What is more, this implies that a holy, reverent, God-fearing and parent-honoring upbringing was the accepted norm in first-century Israel. Heads in Nazareth did not turn when the child Jesus made his way down the street. His face fitted alongside all the others. Jesus, the sinless Son of God, would have stood out more if he had been raised in an irreligious and godless environment.

Jesus' growth and development was entirely in keeping with the human nature he shares with every one of us. Everything that is common to mankind, sin excepted, was true of Jesus in his childhood, youth, and manhood. Jesus, like any child, had to grow up. He had to mature physically, mentally, and emotionally. And so, after the occasion when the twelve-year-old Jesus stayed behind in Jerusalem after the Passover and was reproached by his mother for doing so, Jesus went back to Nazareth and lived in obedience to Mary and Joseph. This Jerusalem episode and its aftermath was a necessary means for the human Jesus to learn obedience. Jesus never sinned—his remaining behind in Jerusalem was not sin—but nevertheless all his human experiences taught him specific *human* obedience, fitting him perfectly for his role as Mediator and High Priest.

In the Synagogue

Let us return to our passage in the fourth chapter of Luke and to the synagogue in Nazareth. There is no mention of synagogues in the Old Testament; they came into being in the time of the exile in Babylon, six centuries before the New Testament era. At that time the Jewish people, being far away from Jerusalem, could not meet in the temple on the Sabbath or on feast days. In its place the synagogues became necessary meeting places for reading, for teaching, and for corporate prayer. When the people returned to the land of Israel, the practice of meeting in synagogues continued. By the first century AD, Jews had for some time been widely scattered throughout the Mediterranean world and, as we know from the Acts of the Apostles, they were meeting together in synagogues in all the cities where they were found.

On a Friday evening in Nazareth, as the shadows lengthened, the *Chazzan* or minister of the synagogue would have sounded a double trumpet blast, three times altogether. The people were being summoned to lay aside their work for the Sabbath. Then, early in the morning—almost certainly a good deal earlier than most Western Christians are accustomed to going to church buildings!—Jesus went to the synagogue. We will pass over a detailed description of what would ordinarily have taken place, but will note that the liturgical elements of the first-century synagogue service, as far as we can ascertain them, would not have been wholly foreign to a Christian worshipper from almost any era. Indeed, many aspects of synagogue worship passed over into church worship. The meeting would have begun with various prayers and readings, focusing on God's work in creation and his covenant with Israel, and above all the *Sh^ema* would have been recited with appropriate solemnity:

> Hear, O Israel: The LORD our God, the LORD is one. You shall love the LORD your God with all your heart and with all your soul and with all your might. (Deut. 6:4–5).

Many familiar faces would be in that Nazareth congregation, in which men and women sat separately. Jesus would have come forward at a certain point in the meeting with the approval of the synagogue authorities. It was the custom for different men to read and teach. There would have been scrolls on which the writings of all the Major Prophets (Isaiah, Jeremiah, and Ezekiel) were combined and others in which they were kept separate, as seems to be the case here. So he read this portion from Isaiah 61:1–2, which we find in Luke 4:18–19. After reading, Jesus rolled up the scroll, handed it back to the attendant, and sat down to teach. It was customary for the reading to be done from a standing position and the teaching to follow from a sitting position. So far, everything had been done decently and in order, and no feathers had been ruffled.

THE YEAR OF THE LORD'S FAVOR

Let us see what glorious words Jesus spoke to the people of Nazareth.

> The Spirit of the Lord is upon me, because he has anointed me to proclaim good news to the poor. He has sent me to proclaim

liberty to the captives and recovering of sight to the blind, to set at liberty those who are oppressed, to proclaim the year of the Lord's favor. (Luke 4:18–19)

Did Jesus comply with the designated reading for that particular day, or did he himself choose the passage from Isaiah 61? Of this we cannot be certain. Yet we can surely see that these words are a glorious summary of his mission to this world. They are an announcement of the character and purpose of Jesus' ministry. Sometimes this passage has been described as "Jesus' Manifesto." Political parties write manifestos before general elections. They make great promises that sometimes they are unable to deliver. By contrast, here is an announcement of what the Spirit-anointed Son of God was doing in Israel and what he has been doing infallibly ever since. It might even be boldly claimed that Isaiah 61:1–2 is the greatest "Christ passage" of the Old Testament. The Christ, the Messiah, is the Anointed One, and he has been anointed in order to bring relief, blessing, and mercy to his people. We rightly notice an allusion in verse 19 to the Israelite Year of Jubilee. The Year of Jubilee, like this passage, was all about liberty.

> You shall count seven weeks of years, seven times seven years, so that the time of the seven weeks of years shall give you forty-nine years. Then you shall sound the loud trumpet on the tenth day of the seventh month. On the Day of Atonement you shall sound the trumpet throughout all your land. And you shall consecrate the fiftieth year, and proclaim liberty throughout the land to all its inhabitants. It shall be a jubilee for you, when each of you shall return to his property and each of you shall return to his clan. (Lev. 25:8–10)

The Jubilee was a time of great rejoicing in Israel. But like so much in the Old Testament, it pointed to something much greater. There is a liberty that exceeds the social and the political.

And the ministry of Christ was all about proclaiming and obtaining liberty—spiritual liberty from every spiritual enemy. For Jesus tells them, "Today this Scripture has been fulfilled in your hearing" (Luke 4:21). We must not underestimate just what a striking and startling thing he was saying. The Jubilee stood there in front of his own people, incarnate in the synagogue in his hometown!

OUTRIGHT HOSTILITY

What did the congregation in Nazareth make of all this? Luke's report of their response shows a great deal of fickleness— all four seasons seem to have blown through the synagogue that morning. There was great admiration at the outset. Jesus' words, his "gracious words," caused the same astonishment as they had elsewhere. At the conclusion of the Sermon on the Mount we read that "when Jesus finished these sayings, the crowds were astonished at his teaching, for he was teaching them as one who had authority, and not as their scribes" (Matt. 7:28–29). Here was a teacher who spoke in such a way that everyone present was struck by his authority. He neither quoted the rabbinical sources nor presented his opinions of their latest pronouncements. He spoke with freshness, power, interest, and great persuasiveness.

Yet we can see how quickly admiration turned to amazement, amazement to incredulity, and incredulity to outright hostility. The congregation had their eyes fixed on him. To understand this heightened level of attention, we need to go back to verses 14 and 15. Jesus was becoming famous in Galilee and the people in the synagogues spoke well of him. His preaching and teaching had become popular and great crowds flocked to hear him. His earlier work in Galilee, Samaria, and Judea had all contributed to this. But it is only now that reality began to sink in all around the congregation, and the murmur arose, "Is this Joseph's son?" There were surely some in that synagogue who were only now making the connection: the exciting new teacher and miracle worker who people were raving about was one of Nazareth's own sons—Joseph's boy.

IS NOT THIS THE CARPENTER'S SON?

What caused the people's response to Jesus to become more hostile? Surely as he read about the coming messianic age they approved of everything he said, because talk of a golden messianic era was always guaranteed to win their rapt attention. But as he began to link this theme to himself, and the implications began to sink in, eyebrows were raised all over the synagogue. "The Spirit of the Lord is upon me." We can imagine their thoughts. "So just who does he think he is? He grew up here in this town, mixed with our children, came to this synagogue, and helped his father Joseph with the carpentry." Matthew, in what seems to be a parallel account of this incident, gives more details.

> Coming to his hometown he taught them in their synagogue, so that they were astonished, and said, "Where did this man get this wisdom and these mighty works? Is not this the carpenter's son? Is not his mother called Mary? And are not his brothers James and Joseph and Simon and Judas? And are not all his sisters with us? Where then did this man get all these things?" (Matt. 13:54–56)

But there is another, more important aspect to the attitude of the people. Jesus, knowing what was within the hearts of men and women, voices what they are thinking: "Physician, heal yourself." It was a well-known saying, more of a proverb than a parable. It meant something like this: "Physician, heal your hometown! We've heard that you did amazing miracles in Capernaum, and we deserve to get a piece of the action. This young fellow has done rather well for himself, and he's been doing all sorts of amazing things over in Capernaum. Get him to do the same back here in Nazareth!" A more applicable proverb from today would be "charity begins at home." If Jesus was such a great miracle worker and teacher, then he ought to have begun in Nazareth where he belonged. Should not they, the people of Nazareth, be entitled to some demonstration of the power that God had given him?

Observe that the people of Nazareth were not skeptical about the reports of miracles that they had received from Capernaum and elsewhere. It is interesting to note that as we read the Gospels, we do not find people disbelieving the miracles as many do today. First-century Jews seldom had intellectual difficulties with the existence of signs and wonders. This was the tragedy of the people of Nazareth—how parochial they were, how self-centered they were, how blind they were! They were neither able nor willing to ask what these signs and miracles meant; instead they were preoccupied with just one question: why on earth had these signs been performed in Capernaum rather than Nazareth? Now, with great boldness, Jesus tackles this issue head-on. He speaks his own proverb and introduces it solemnly with an "Amen." "I say to you, no prophet is acceptable in his hometown." Wherever a prophet may have honor, the last place he should expect it is in his own hometown. In a similar vein, we often say nowadays that "familiarity breeds contempt."

The Full Wrath of the Synagogue

It was Jesus' reference in Luke 4:25–27 to the two miracles performed by Elijah and Elisha—in which Gentiles, not Israelites, were blessed—that caused the full wrath of the synagogue to descend upon him. The words that Jesus had spoken about being unwelcome in his own hometown were confirmed. To compare a congregation of proud Jews to Gentiles was the most offensive thing Jesus could have done. The implication was that the people of Nazareth were less deserving than pagan Phoenicians and Syrians, and consequently the decorum of the service of worship in the synagogue soon became a riot.

Perhaps we can see the irony of the situation. Galilee was a despised region in Israel, Nazareth was a lowly town within Galilee, and now Jesus was not good enough for the people of Nazareth. A prophet who is false and leads the people astray must be put to death. So they try to rid the earth of this impostor. There is a steep cliff some forty feet high at the southwest corner of Nazareth. Below it are sharp rocks. Surely it was in this direction that they pushed Jesus, and it seems that they would have made an end of him—except that heaven would not allow it, and Jesus did not come to harm until the time of God's own choosing. We might even say that Psalm 91:11–12 was fulfilled here.

> For he will command his angels concerning you
>> to guard you in all your ways.
> On their hands they will bear you up,
>> lest you strike your foot against a stone.

He Came to Cast Fire on Earth

So much for the narrative of Jesus' Sabbath visit to the Nazareth synagogue. We now need to investigate the spiritual reasons for what took place. Does this enmity between Jesus and the people of Nazareth—even his own family members—find any explanation elsewhere in the Gospels?

In Luke 12:49–53, a passage in which he bared the inner thoughts of his heart, Jesus specifically addressed the subject of the division that his coming into the world would bring about. He began by saying, "I came to cast fire on the earth, and would that it were already kindled!" Many different explanations have been given as to the identity of this fire. Some have suggested that it is the fire that Jesus himself would endure on the cross. While it is quite true that the fire of judgment would fall upon Jesus at Golgotha, the fire spoken of here does not appear to be one that Jesus himself would face; rather he came to *cast* it. Another proposal is that this is the fire of the final judgment. The problem with this is that it appears to be something that Jesus has come to bring about in his own lifetime. The nineteenth-century Scottish commentator David Brown believed that this fire was "the higher element of spiritual life which Jesus came to introduce into this earth."[3] This may indeed be getting closer, but it does not seem to answer to the description of a fire.

John Calvin provides an explanation that fits well with the sense of Jesus' words and of the whole of Scripture. In his Harmony of the Evangelists, he wrote:

> The gospel is metaphorically compared to fire, because it violently changes the face of things. The disciples having falsely imagined that, while they were at ease and asleep, the kingdom of God would come, Christ declares, on the contrary, that there must first be a dreadful conflagration to kindle the world. And as some beginnings of it were even then making their appearance.[4]

"Violently changes," "dreadful conflagration"—he goes on to speak of "great commotions"—all of these take place when there is a fire. The lesson is that the kingdom of God is not going to come into this world without a great deal of upheaval, opposition, and persecution. It will be as Simeon had said to Mary—"this child is appointed for the fall and rising of many in Israel, and for a sign that is opposed" (Luke 2:34). What we particularly have here is an explanation of the rejection that Jesus faced and of the rejection that his followers everywhere face. It is an explanation of the existence of the suffering, persecuted church and of bitter division within families when one or a few members follow Christ and others do not. The enmity of the world that believers experience is the same enmity that Jesus himself knew.

Later in his ministry Jesus warned his disciples that this was exactly what they should expect. We read in John 15:18–20,

If the world hates you, know that it has hated me before it hated you. If you were of the world, the world would love you as its own; but because you are not of the world, but I chose you out of the world, therefore the world hates you. Remember the word that I said to you: "A servant is not greater than his master." If they persecuted me, they will also persecute you.

JESUS' FOLLOWERS SHARE IN HIS TRIBULATION

This division and persecution into which believers are thrust is our own participation in the sufferings of Christ. Now of course we must not paint a wholly depressing picture. The gospel of Jesus Christ brings peace to the soul who receives him—all the blessings of sins forgiven, fellowship with God, adoption as sons, everlasting life. The gospel brings peace to the church, who together know Christ and hear his voice. But nowhere are believers promised that if they embrace the gospel they will know peace in their relationship with the world. On the contrary, in this world Jesus' followers will have tribulation. They are promised it in the passages we have cited and in several others.[5]

The gospel message, which softens the hearts of God's people and brings them to salvation, is the same gospel that hardens those whom God will not save. The believer finds the gospel to be a sweet-smelling savor, the very savor of life, but to the unbeliever the gospel is the very stench of death. The unbelieving world hates the gospel now just as it hated Christ two thousand years ago. Therefore, to say that the people of Nazareth rejected Jesus simply because he was one of their own is an insufficient explanation. The real determining factor was their hardness of heart. The whole testimony of Scripture clearly brings this out.

In Psalm 69:7–8 David is foretelling the estrangement that his offspring, Jesus, would one day experience:

For it is for your sake that I have borne reproach,
  that dishonor has covered my face.
I have become a stranger to my brothers,
  an alien to my mother's sons.

Can we not see several instances in the life of Jesus in which he would have keenly felt this ostracization? On one occasion his own family was so perplexed and bewildered by Jesus' behavior that they went to try to seize him, saying, "He is out of his mind" (Mark 3:21).

Remember again the prophecy of Simeon. He went on to tell Mary that "a sword will pierce through your own soul also" (Luke 2:35). Perhaps we instinctively suppose that this sword would be fulfilled in the agony of watching her son die on the cross. There can be no doubt that this was an extreme moment of anguish for her, despite the comfort that Jesus himself provided through the care of the beloved apostle John (John 19:25–27). But another interpretation is at least possible: that Mary and all Jesus' earthly family would feel a sword of division throughout Jesus' years of ministry. His words would cut a swathe through the family in Nazareth. The fire and the sword of the gospel would be known in her own experience, and would indeed reach its bitterest extent at Calvary.

Many believers are caught up in a hostile and unbelieving environment. Many believers are the only Christians in their family. For them the words of Micah 7:6, which Jesus quoted in his ministry, are fulfilled: "For the son treats the father with contempt, the daughter rises up against her mother, the daughter-in-law against her mother-in-law; a man's enemies are the men of his own house." This should not be viewed as a surprise, as if something strange were happening to them; this is often the calling of the Lord's people in this world. Such an individual should continue to say with the prophet Micah, "But as for me,

I will look to the LORD; I will wait for the God of my salvation; my God will hear me" (Mic. 7:7).

Mother and father may forsake us, even husband or wife, but the Lord will take us in. All may be war around us, people losing their heads and blaming it on us, but we are at peace with God. The ostracization and estrangement that many believers experience, even from their nearest and dearest, is an experience that will, by God's grace, draw them toward one who is even nearer and dearer, for "there is a friend who sticks closer than a brother" (Prov. 18:24).

— 5 —

THE CLEANSING OF THE TEMPLE

In the temple he found those who were selling oxen and
sheep and pigeons, and the money-changers sitting there.
And making a whip of cords, he drove them all out of the
temple, with the sheep and oxen. And he poured out the
coins of the money-changers and overturned their tables.
And he told those who sold the pigeons, "Take these things
away; do not make my Father's house a house of trade."
His disciples remembered that it was written, "Zeal for
your house will consume me." (John 2:14–17)

I BECAME A CHRISTIAN at the age of twenty. Until this
time I had entertained an anemic and sentimental view of the
character of Jesus Christ that affected my entire understanding of morality and conduct. "Gentle Jesus, meek and mild"
was the totality of the impoverished portrait of Jesus that my
unconverted mind entertained. I was holding to an unhealthy
and unbiblical form of pacifism. My understanding of salvation
was non-existent; I thought that Jesus' death on the cross was
nothing more than an example of surrendering tamely to his
enemies' schemes, a Gandhi-like response of non-violence that
we should all seek to emulate. If we were successful in living in
this fashion, then surely God would count us worthy of heaven.
My convictions ran even deeper: no evil of any kind ought to
be resisted under any circumstances. To be a Christian meant

simply to absorb every kind of attack, and this maxim applied at every level of society. The husband whose wife was unfaithful had certainly been hurt, but his "Christian" obligation was to allow her to do as she pleased, certainly never to confront her. To demonstrate anger in the face of any kind of provocation was a denial of the character of Christ, which was what we should all seek to emulate.

It was when I began to consider the claims of Christ seriously that I first read C. S. Lewis, an author whom a number of Christians had recommended to me. Not everything that Lewis writes is good or helpful, and he would certainly not be the first author I would suggest to a young convert. It is quite incorrect to imagine that Lewis was an "evangelical" in the best and truest sense of that word. But some of his writings made a lasting impact on me. During a train journey, I was shocked to read these words in *Mere Christianity*: "It is, therefore, in my opinion, perfectly right for a Christian judge to sentence a man to death or a Christian soldier to kill an enemy."[1] It would be an exaggeration to say that my whole world was turned upside down, but I was roundly challenged; my tidy system of morality was thrown into disorder. For the first time I was confronted with the notion of righteous anger. To respond robustly to evil was presented as the Christian, even the Christ-like, thing to do.

JESUS THE REVOLUTIONARY?

Shortly afterward I remembered one of the passages in the Gospels about Jesus cleansing the temple and was reminded of a discussion that had taken place several years earlier in a lesson at school. The teacher had asked the class, most provocatively, "Did Jesus ever do anything *wrong*?" No one answered, so the teacher proceeded to tell us that when Jesus overturned the tables in the temple and drove out the money-changers and those who sold various animals, he was in fact "doing something wrong." This teacher was evidently guilty of holding the same inadequate caricature of Jesus to which I subscribed.

I have moved on since then and I have to say that now I find this episode one of the most adrenaline-inducing passages in the Bible. Here is the Jesus who was prepared to kick over the rotten "establishment" of his day. Here is the Jesus whose manhood was admirable and courageous. Yet we must not overplay the "Jesus was a revolutionary" type of slogan that has become popular in recent years. In 1999 the Church of England produced some posters with the caption *Che Jesus*, which attempted to liken Jesus to the iconic Cuban revolutionary Che Guevara. This was undoubtedly a step too far—though it was an attempt to react against the sickly presentation of Jesus similar to the one I formerly believed.

This episode might seem quite different from the others we are examining because here it looks as though Jesus was the antagonist. The sellers and money-changers in the temple were quite literally minding their own business, and it was Jesus who went in and started a great commotion. What so grieved the heart of Jesus that he so dramatically demonstrated anger, even violence?

A NOISY AND SMELLY LIVESTOCK MARKET

It is clear that there are two varying reports of Jesus cleansing the temple, one of which is reported in Matthew, Mark, and Luke, and which evidently took place during the last week of Jesus' earthly life.[2] John, by contrast, places his own narrative near the beginning of his gospel, although it too is connected with a Passover feast. My own clear conviction is that the cleansing of the temple that John records, though similar in some details to the one narrated by the others, is an earlier and quite distinct incident that took place at the beginning of Jesus' public ministry. In John 2:12 we see an evident relationship in time: "After this"—after the first of Jesus' signs, the changing of water into wine at the wedding feast in Cana—Jesus went to Capernaum for a few days, and the events at the Passover in Jerusalem soon followed.[3]

We should try to picture the scene. The seven days of the Passover festival in Jerusalem would have witnessed a great deal of animal sacrifice, vast quantities of blood being shed, and consequently the purchase of many animals for this purpose. It would not have been convenient for distant travelers to bring their beasts with them from far-off lands, and hence there was a frantic trade in animals for sacrifice in Jerusalem. When Jesus arrived at the temple and entered the outer court—known as the court of the Gentiles, because no Gentile could proceed beyond it—his senses would have been assaulted by a scene resembling a noisy, smelly livestock market.

Every worshipper was permitted, according to the law, to bring their own animals to sacrifice, provided they were "without blemish" (Num. 28:19). It was on this question, "without blemish," that the buying and selling became such a pointed issue. Who determined what "without blemish" really meant in practice? It does not take too much imagination to see how Jerusalem's cynical wheeler-dealers could exploit this situation. Perhaps we can imagine a typical exchange: "No, this bull won't do—don't you see this defect here that will disqualify it? But for a bit more money you can have this prize thoroughbred!" Here was an opportunity to get rich quickly—and the high priest and his cronies did little to discourage this practice, for much of the money gained filled their own coffers.

The money-changers would have been equally unscrupulous. Only the Jewish currency, the half-shekel, was acceptable as the temple tribute, so foreigners with their own money had to find someone who would change it. Today when you go into a bank or a post office to change your money from one currency to another, you will see a board on the wall proclaiming today's exchange rates for both buying and selling. Any commission that is charged will be stated and meticulously observed. Such regulations evidently did not apply in the temple courts. The money-changers would seize every opportunity to cheat and deceive their clients.

A DEN OF ROBBERS

When we understand the circumstances that prevailed in the temple, when we see the trafficking and the abuse that was going on everywhere, we see the applicability of the descriptions that Jesus gave it—that it was not only "a house of trade" (John 2:16) but a veritable "den of robbers" (Matt. 21:13). To this latter description we can instructively compare Jeremiah 7:9–12, where the prophet brings God's message of judgment to the Israelites in an earlier generation.

> Will you steal, murder, commit adultery, swear falsely, make offerings to Baal, and go after other gods that you have not known, and then come and stand before me in this house, which is called by my name, and say, "We are delivered!"—only to go on doing all these abominations? Has this house, which is called by my name, become a den of robbers in your eyes? Behold, I myself have seen it, declares the LORD. Go now to my place that was in Shiloh, where I made my name dwell at first, and see what I did to it because of the evil of my people Israel.

The reference to Shiloh is telling. It was in Shiloh in the latter, evil-spiraling days of the judges that Eli's sons practiced not only embezzlement and deception, but also blatant thuggery, seizing from worshippers what was unlawful, even when these same worshippers protested (see 1 Sam. 2:12–17). In response to this defilement of holy worship, the Lord pronounced a severe judgment against the house of Eli that was soon dramatically enacted. The tabernacle of the Lord had become a "den of robbers," and these robbers were swiftly expelled. God himself purged the evil out of his house. Now, in Jerusalem eleven centuries later, God the Son was doing exactly the same—indeed twice, as we have mentioned.

John records that Jesus made a whip out of cords, or of ropes made from rushes—of which there would have been a plentiful supply in a place with so many tethered animals—and then he began to drive out not only the animals, but also the people who were dealing in them. It was a wholesale purge of the temple courts that had been defiled. Jesus made a whip! He did more. Those strong arms that had been trained to build and fashion tables now turned these tables over, scattering coins in all directions, forcing the money-changers to leap back in amazement and alarm. The usual noises of bleating and lowing, the shouting and bargaining, were unexpectedly mixed with other sounds caused by the antics of this Galilean preacher who was creating mayhem in their midst: the lash of the whip, the angry cries of the indignant and retreating sellers, the crashing of overturned tables, and the commanding voice of the Savior himself saying, "Get these out of here!" (John 2:16 NIV). No one dared to oppose Jesus' authority.

GOD COMES TO HIS TEMPLE

No wonder Jesus' disciples, observing all that their Master did that day, called to mind the words of Psalm 69:9: "For zeal for your house has consumed me." We cannot be certain whether these words came to their minds on that day or subsequently, as they looked back over the ministry of Jesus. But we do need to see that Jesus was fulfilling a Psalm that is as abundantly messianic as any in Scripture, being quoted or alluded to many times in the New Testament. It paints the clearest picture of the suffering Jesus, not only in the torments of his body but in the anguish of his mind.

The disciples, noting this relationship between Jesus' actions and the words of the Psalm, were altogether wiser than the Jews who now asked Jesus to show a sign. For what could have been a more evident sign than what they had just witnessed? Here, indeed, was a direct fulfillment of what was promised in the book of Malachi, in the first three verses of chapter three.

> Behold, I send my messenger, and he will prepare the way before me. And the Lord whom you seek will suddenly come to his temple; and the messenger of the covenant in whom you delight, behold, he is coming, says the LORD of hosts. But who can endure the day of his coming, and who can stand when he appears? For he is like a refiner's fire and like fullers' soap. He will sit as a refiner and purifier of silver, and he will purify the sons of Levi and refine them like gold and silver, and they will bring offerings in righteousness to the LORD.

What a striking and graphic fulfillment of this prophecy was taking place! The Lord had, indeed, "suddenly come to his temple." And those who were sitting in the temple courts could not "endure the day of his coming," and neither could they "stand when he appears"! No, some of them were swept clean off their feet, not only by the force of Jesus' physical exertions but also by his supreme moral and spiritual authority.

We should be struck by the way Jesus called the temple "my Father's house" rather than "our Father's house." There is an echo here of his words to his mother when he was a twelve-year-old boy (Luke 2:49). As a boy, Jesus' delight was in his Father's house, and that delight had deepened and matured by the time he reached manhood. The temple in Jerusalem was the place where the God and Father of our Lord Jesus Christ had put his name. Therefore, the zeal that Jesus had for the house of his Father was a measure of the zeal that he had for the very name and honor of his Father. This designation, "my Father's house," is understood by Leon Morris to be a claim to deity.[4] Nowhere in John's gospel does Jesus speak of God as the Father of anyone but himself, with one sublime exception. This comes after he has been raised from the dead, and he speaks these gloriously inviting words with his disciples in mind: "I am ascending to my Father and your Father, to my God and your God" (John 20:17).

Why Was Jesus Angry?

We need to probe further: What exactly was Jesus objecting to? What was his zeal directed against? Was Jesus angry because the practice of animal sacrifice was being carried on in the temple of God? Evidently not, because animal sacrifice was commanded by God when the people of Israel were in the wilderness; they were to offer these animals at the altar until Christ himself came "at the end of the ages to put away sin by the sacrifice of himself" (Heb. 9:26). While it is true that the Lord desired mercy and obedience ahead of sacrifice, sacrifice was necessary because of the people's sin. The sacrifices offered under the old covenant were a rehearsal, a shadow, of Christ's own offering of himself. The prophet Malachi, who closes the Old Testament, spoke against the worship of God's people at his time, not because they were offering animal sacrifices per se, but because these animals were blind, lame, or sick (Mal. 1:8).

Was Jesus angry because of the sharp practices that were going on in the temple courts—the deceit and the swindling? Certainly this seems to have been the case in the account of the cleansing of the temple provided by the Synoptic Gospels, in which Jesus speaks of the way that these people have turned the "house of prayer" into "a den of robbers" (Matt. 21:13, Mark 11:17, Luke 19:46). But as we have already commented, these three evangelists are describing a separate cleansing of the temple that took place at the close of Jesus' ministry. And while the same abuses would surely have been taking place in the events described by John, this is not where our text points us.

Rather, we are led to the conclusion that Jesus responded with such zeal because his Father's house had become "a house of trade," or a marketplace. It was an abuse of the house of God.

The ESV accurately and helpfully translates the Greek by giving the word *house* twice in verse 16. It is not a house of *trade*, it is the house of *God*, the Father of the Lord Jesus Christ. I have already described the scene in the temple as a noisy and smelly livestock market. But it was not the presence of the animals that would have distressed Jesus; it was neither their noise nor their smell. It was the "market," not the "livestock," that offended Jesus. Jesus was angry because the temple was not being treated as holy. We need to examine just what this holiness meant, and then apply it to the present day.

HOLINESS

Holiness is the characteristic of God that marks him out as being distinct from everything else in all creation. Of course there are many respects in which this distinction can be seen. At the most basic and essential level, God is the uncreated Creator, whereas all else has been created. Certain truths follow: God is eternal, whereas all else is temporary; God is infinite, whereas everything else is finite; God is all-knowing and all-present, whereas everything and everyone else is restricted in knowledge and in space. In speaking of all this, we are speaking of God's holiness. Holiness properly belongs to God alone. His own character uniquely defines holiness.

But it is also right to speak of a holiness, albeit a derived holiness, that applies to God's *people*. God says to his people in every age, "You shall be holy, for I the LORD your God am holy" (Lev. 19:2; 1 Peter 1:16). Holiness is that "without which no one will see the Lord" (Heb. 12:14). How do men and women follow holiness? In his classic work on the subject, *Holiness*, Bishop J. C. Ryle puts it very succinctly: "Holiness is the habit of being of one mind with God, according as we find His mind described in Scripture. It is the habit of agreeing in God's judgement, hating what He hates, loving what He loves, and measuring everything in this world by the standard of His Word. He who most entirely agrees with God, he is the most holy man."[5] Holiness, as seen in men and women, arises from a heart that adores, knows, and longs to know evermore the greatness and glory of God. Holiness cries out with the psalmist, "My soul longs, yes, faints for the courts of the LORD; my heart and flesh sing for joy to the living God" (Ps. 84:2). Holiness must begin within us, deep within our souls.

GOD CALLS SOME THINGS HOLY

There is a specific aspect to God's holiness that needs to be seen in order to focus our understanding more sharply and guide our application. This is the need to appreciate that *God calls some things holy.* So much confusion arises because we are unable to perceive that some things are holy and others are not. To grasp this point is to understand the zeal that consumed the Son of God in his Father's house.

Perhaps we can imagine an objection being raised at this point. Was not one of the great outcomes of the Protestant Reformation, especially of Luther's work, the abolition of the distinction between the sacred and the secular? Was this not one of the great errors of the medieval church—that it elevated the "spiritual" people, the priests, monks, and nuns, above the laity? Surely the abolition of relics, holy places, and pilgrimages was a good thing! To these objections we must give a carefully worded reply. To be sure, the whole earth belongs to the Lord, the cattle on a thousand hills are his, and as the great Dutch theologian and politician Abraham Kuyper (1837–1920) famously said, "There is not a square inch in the whole domain of our human existence over which Christ, who is Sovereign over all, does not cry: 'Mine!'"[6] The Christian believer should therefore be strenuously laboring to bring everything in life under the lordship of Christ.

But however strongly we might emphasize Kuyper's maxim, we err when we fail to draw clear biblical distinctions between (1) those things God regards as holy—and, more to the point, *calls* holy—and (2) those good things that he has created and over which believers are to exercise godly stewardship, but are not holy as those in the first category are. *Holiness implies separateness; it indicates that something or someone is set aside and belongs to God in a singular way.* Holiness necessitates division and distinction. To say that "everything is holy" is to say that there are no such distinctions, but if there are no distinctions, then nothing can be holy and we have a clear contradiction.

Medieval Catholicism was right in its understanding that certain offices or practices in the church were holy, but wrong in the way in which it decided who or what was holy. Tradition became the guide rather than Scripture alone.

Let us begin at the beginning. It is particularly instructive that the first use of the word *holy* in the Bible is found in Genesis 2:3 and it deals with the Sabbath day. "So God blessed the seventh day and made it holy, because on it God rested from all his work that he had done in creation." What needs to be especially appreciated here is that there was as yet no sin in the world. Even before sin had entered, God set apart the seventh day as holy, for holiness does not depend on the existence of sin. The other six days were of course God-given; they were not and could not be inherently "sinful." But the seventh day was set apart from all the others, designated as holy. The holiness of the seventh day is a pattern, a theme, that is deeply embedded within the Scriptures. It is a weekly memorial to holiness itself, to the holy God who sanctifies his people. It surely follows that even before the fall, Adam and Eve would have observed the Sabbath day.

One great lesson being taught to the people of Israel in the wilderness was that the LORD called certain things holy. The area of land around the burning bush was "holy ground" (Ex. 3:5), and this was the first principle that Moses needed to learn. The concept of "holy ground" is systematically developed in Exodus and Leviticus. The camp of Israel was holy, but the tabernacle was especially holy. Within the tabernacle was the "Holy Place," but that was separated by a veil from the "Most Holy" (Ex. 26:33). Later the terminology of God's holy dwelling place was to be applied to the land of Israel, especially to Jerusalem, and most particularly to the temple. The people were a "holy nation" (Ex. 19:6) in distinction to all the nations of the earth, and at another level the priests were holy in a way that was not true of others.

The offerings that were prescribed by the Lord were holy, but those that God did not command were not holy. For that reason the unauthorized offering made by Nadab and Abihu, Aaron's sons, resulted in their destruction (Lev. 10:1–2). Certain animals were "clean," that is, set aside for the people of Israel to eat, whereas others were not. The picture is clear, as the Lord told Aaron in Leviticus 10:10–11:

> You are to distinguish between the holy and the common, and between the unclean and the clean, and you are to teach the people of Israel all the statutes that the Lord has spoken to them by Moses.

Even more succinctly, God told the people of Israel, "You shall be holy, for I the Lord your God am holy" (Lev. 19:2). The holiness of God necessitated the holiness of the people that he had taken into covenant with himself. The command to be holy is just as applicable to God's new covenant people—the worldwide, professing church of Jesus Christ—as it was to Israel under the old covenant; most emphatically so!

> As obedient children, do not be conformed to the passions of your former ignorance, but as he who called you is holy, you also be holy in all your conduct, since it is written, "You shall be holy, for I am holy." (1 Peter 1:14–16)

When Jesus came to the temple, then, he was not announcing the closure of the era in which holiness mattered. It mattered then, and it continues to matter now.

Where This Holiness Is to Be Seen

How is this holiness to be demonstrated in our present context? Notice that *the church of Jesus Christ is holy*. When the apostle Peter speaks of the body of believers as "a chosen race, a royal priesthood, a holy nation, a people for his own possession" (1 Peter 2:9) he is drawing all his language from Exodus 19 and the descriptions God gave to Israel. The exalted titles applied to the church by the New Testament writers— "God's field, God's building" (1 Cor. 3:9); "God's temple" (1 Cor. 3:16); "the body of Christ" (1 Cor. 10:16, 12:27; Eph. 4:12); and of course the bride of Christ (not that this actual expression is used in Scripture, but its suitability can be abundantly proved from Ephesians 5:22–33 as well as Revelation 21)—these all testify to the holy, glorious identity of the church of Jesus Christ. The "church" is not simply a convenient collective noun for Christians, as if we were speaking of a herd of cattle! It has been built by the Lord Jesus Christ; it is the dwelling place for his Spirit; it continues to be supplied by Christ with pastors, teachers, elders, and deacons, who are charged with responsibilities that pertain to it.

Notice that *the word of the Lord is holy*. So many trends in biblical scholarship for the best part of two centuries have undermined the inspiration, the accuracy, and the unity of Scripture. The trickle-down effect of these ideas has been devastating, robbing pulpits across the world of their authority. The human element in Scripture has been emphasized in place of the divine, assaulting the authority of both the Old Testament ("Thus saith the LORD") and the New ("Verily, verily, I say unto you"). Science, or more properly *scientism*, has shaken the confidence of many in the accuracy of biblical data, and consequently their confidence in the entire biblical record. Indeed, it might seem to many that there need not be such a category as "Holy Scripture" at all. The inclusion of certain ancient texts within a library called the "Bible" looks purely arbitrary.

The faithful church of Jesus Christ must stand firm against all this. God has spoken in his Word, and his people must answer to the description of Isaiah 66:2: "But this is the one to whom I will look: he who is humble and contrite in spirit and trembles at my word." We should tremble, and seek that others might tremble, at passages like Jeremiah 23:29: "Is not my word like fire, declares the LORD, and like a hammer that breaks the rock in pieces?" It is the word that brings life, that leads to salvation.

Notice that *the worship of the Lord is holy*. It has become an accepted truism today that for the believer, "everything is worship." A Christian is digging his garden, teaching a class, managing his business, or feeding her family, and that is regarded as worship. We need here to draw a clear distinction between "serving" God and "worshipping" him. Everything we do in this present life must indeed be a service to God, and we are right to underline the nobility of all work—not only paid employment, but all we do as stewards of God in this world. But there is a "worship" which is a distinct, holy activity. It is bowing down to almighty God; it is calling upon the name of the Lord and doing so in response and obedience to the revelation of himself that he has given. The first two commandments address the worship of God—that he alone is to be worshipped and that this worship is to be carried out in obedience to his own stated requirements. Failure to observe and understand these commandments, and to draw the appropriate conclusions from them, has led to a terrible downgrade of worship in so many churches.

Notice that *the name of the Lord is holy*. This is of course the substance of the third commandment. We must use the name of God with the greatest reverence, because his name is the very manifestation of his being.

The LORD, the LORD, a God merciful and gracious, slow to anger, and abounding in steadfast love and faithfulness, keeping steadfast love for thousands, forgiving iniquity and transgression and sin, but who will by no means clear the guilty, visiting the iniquity of the fathers on the children and the children's children, to the third and the fourth generation. (Ex. 34:6–7)

Let us teach our children to speak solemnly of "the Lord," not to talk casually and sometimes flippantly about "God" as though he might as well be the deity of any other religion.

Vincent Donovan was an American missionary living among the Masai tribe in Tanzania. He wanted to be on easy, familiar terms with these people, so he began using their personal names. But the Masai found this rude because they did not use personal names with the public and with strangers. Instead, they used titles or designations. One day a Masai man said to Donovan, "Do not throw my name about. My name is important. My name is me. My name is for my friends."[7] Is this not a striking illustration of the holiness of the name of God? "Do not throw my name about. My name is important. My name is me. My name is for my friends." Each of these statements could be taken and explored at great length.

It follows, as we come to the fourth commandment, that we should notice that *the Lord's Day is holy*. It might sound very plausible and even pious for a Christian to say that he regards all seven days of the week as being equally holy, but this is unbiblical as well as unworkable. The Christian Sabbath is God's gracious provision to his chosen people, the day on which they remember the resurrection of their Savior, the firstfruits of those who have fallen asleep. On the Lord's Day the church of Jesus Christ has a taste of the eternal, blissful rest that their Savior has purchased for the body. When it is understood in this way, any drudgery or supposed legalism connected to the Lord's Day will blow away like chaff in the wind.

Our church buildings are not temples, and our ministers are not sacrificing priests. But the gathering of the Lord's people is holy, as are the reading and preaching of his word and our responses in prayer and praise. How we need to pursue holiness in the house of God today!

6

THE PHARISEES

But woe to you, scribes and Pharisees, hypocrites! For you shut the kingdom of heaven in people's faces. For you neither enter yourselves nor allow those who would enter to go in. (Matt. 23:13)

WHEN THE IDEA of writing this book first occurred to me, it immediately became clear that the Pharisees would feature very prominently, surely more than any other individual or group of people. Of all the exchanges that took place between Jesus and his opponents, the most frequent and recurring were those with the Pharisees, although of course at various times the Pharisees are linked with the scribes and teachers of the law.

A careful survey of the four gospels reveals twenty-eight distinct confrontations between Jesus and the Pharisees. Matthew and Luke each record thirteen of them, Mark records seven, and John just five, although in John's case these five encounters tend to be reported at greater length.[1] Every one of them was marked by opposition, division, and growing enmity, with the possible exception of Jesus' interview with Nicodemus recorded in the third chapter of John. Nicodemus' problem seems to have been bewilderment rather than outrage.

WITHERING JUDGMENT

Perhaps the most striking of all the exchanges between Jesus and the Pharisees is the one we find in Matthew 23. Throughout Matthew's account the Pharisees are key players, powerful antagonists, taking every opportunity to oppose Jesus. In this chapter, which tellingly precedes the one that describes the forthcoming judgment against Jerusalem and Israel, the Lord Jesus sums up the divine case against the Pharisees. Although he has spoken against them on previous occasions, most notably in Matthew 15:3-11 where he addresses them as "hypocrites" (15:7), Matthew 23 is climactic. It is a chapter of solemn, authoritative, penetrating, and ultimately withering judgment, one of the great judgment passages in the whole of Scripture; seven woes uttered by the Son of God against these most prominent representatives of Israel's religion.

The chapter is paralleled, to some extent, in Luke 11:39-52. But on that occasion Jesus' woes—six of them rather than seven—are directed against the teachers of the law as well as the Pharisees—though, as we will see, there is overlap between these groups. In Matthew's account there is a more extended and devastating form of denunciation that appears repeatedly—"Woe to you, scribes and Pharisees, hypocrites!" And yet it is also a chapter that ends on a most poignant note, as Jesus laments over Jerusalem. He would have gathered them together as a hen gathers her chicks under her wings, but they were not willing to come, and for that reason their house is left to them desolate.

HISTORICAL BACKGROUND

Who were the Pharisees and how were they related to the other groupings described in the Gospels: the scribes, the teachers of the law, and the Sadducees? While some passages provide explanation of the practices of the Pharisees—note in particular Mark 7:3-4—they do not give an account of their origin. And although not every reader of the New Testament needs to become an expert in the sociology and culture of first-century Israel, a certain amount of background will undoubtedly help.

The famous Jewish revolt of Judas Maccabeus in 167 BC had been provoked by the atrocities of the Seleucid king Antiochus IV, known also to history as Antiochus Epiphanes. This pagan ruler had not only prevented the Jews from living and worshipping according to God's commandments, he had profaned the sanctuary in Jerusalem in the most appalling ways imaginable, dedicating the temple to Zeus and even sacrificing pigs there. Thus he became the fulfillment of the prophecy of Daniel 11:31: "Forces from him shall appear and profane the temple and fortress, and shall take away the regular burnt offering. And they shall set up the abomination that makes desolate." The revolt against Antiochus and the accession of Judas to the throne was therefore characterized by Jewish revulsion against all things Gentile, in particular all things Greek.

And the world had become predominantly Greek. Since the conquests of Alexander the Great, who died in 323 BC, Greek civilization had been in the ascendancy in Israel as it was throughout all the other lands conquered by Alexander. Greek language, Greek philosophy, Greek culture with such features as competitive spectator sports—all these were finding their way into Israel. This process, known as Hellenization (the Ancient Greek word for Greece was *Hellas*) was perceived by many Jews as a threat to their very distinctiveness, and this was felt most keenly by the group known as the *Hasidim*, or "holy ones." It seems likely that the Pharisees, as a distinct group, were a branch emerging from the *Hasidim*. Although we cannot be sure exactly when, they had certainly come to prominence by the middle of the second century BC.

The pure ideals of the earliest Maccabean rulers became increasingly compromised during the course of that century, and by its end both kingly and priestly power was concentrated in the hands of the same individual. Whereas the more worldly wise Sadducees were content to work within this arrangement, and indeed to perpetuate it, the Pharisees strongly resisted it. Thus it was that the political differences between these two parties were sharply set in place, and their beliefs and practices consequently diverged, as we see clearly in the New Testament.

During the reign of Alexander Jannaeus (103–76 BC), the process of Hellenization accelerated to breaking point. Judea was soon torn apart by civil war, and Josephus records that Alexander, bringing "rebels" to Jerusalem, "did one of the most barbarous actions in the world to them; for as he was feasting with his concubines, in the sight of all the city, he ordered about eight hundred of them [the rebels] to be crucified; and while they were living, he ordered the throats of their children and wives to be cut before their eyes."[2] It is likely that many Pharisees would have been among those who suffered.

By the time we reach the first century AD the Pharisees were well established in Israel, and the Roman forces that occupied Israel did not generally oppose them. The Pharisees were not regarded as a political threat, and although they longed for the day when the Roman yoke might be broken off, they did not agitate to achieve such a day. The Pharisees were not a sacred office in Israel, like the priests; neither did they constitute a professional body, like the scribes. They were instead a party from which were drawn many of the scribes and the teachers in the law.

STRICTEST SEPARATION

At the very heart of the Pharisees' creed was the need to maintain the strictest separation from anything that might be classed as defilement—the actual word *Pharisee* probably comes from a Hebrew root that means "to set apart." They searched the law of Moses in the greatest detail in order to work out how to apply its regulations to every area of life. They were concerned about religious conduct not only in and around the Jerusalem temple, but also in the synagogue and everywhere else across the land. From these practical concerns arose a great body of laws, the oral traditions, which we read about in the Gospels, as in Mark 7:3–13. These were seen as a "fence," the observance of which would maintain ceremonial cleanness.

It needs to be added that the Pharisees were the "men of the people"—the people of Israel, that is. It was the Sadducees who were the ruling elite, who were widely regarded as being out of touch with the common people. Though the actual number of Pharisees in Israel may have been few during the ministry of Jesus, perhaps around 6,000, they exerted an influence greater than their numerical strength. It is indisputable that they made the deepest impression upon the spiritual life of Israel. These men were viewed as the guardians of righteousness and purity in the land. Jesus' own striking words in Matthew 5:20 would have appealed deeply to this impression before challenging it: "For I tell you, unless your righteousness exceeds that of the scribes and Pharisees, you will never enter the kingdom of heaven." Everyone knew what the righteousness of the scribes and Pharisees looked like. In first-century Israel it was the gold standard that was constantly held up before the people, and it seemed impressive.

A "HOSTILELY EXAGGERATED" PICTURE?

On one occasion, having preached on the conflict between Jesus and the Pharisees, I was taken to task by a lady in the congregation (I was the visiting preacher). "You mustn't give the impression that the Pharisees were bad men," she said. "They were actually very *good* men." A number of New Testament scholars have maintained that the Pharisees have been harshly dealt with by the gospel writers, and by conservative theologians and preachers ever since. Raymond Brown, a Roman Catholic, represents this viewpoint when he claims that "the Gospels often portray the Pharisees as hypocrites and heartless legalists. Few doubt that this picture is hostilely exaggerated, reflecting later polemics between Christians and Jews."[3]

Statements of this kind need to be countered very robustly. They imply that contemporary New Testament scholars can speak on such matters with greater authority than the Scriptures themselves. We are being told that we need to filter out the prejudice of the early Christian community, a prejudice that is latent in the criticisms levied against the Pharisees. But if this were the case we would be unable to read the Gospels with a full persuasion that the Lord himself is speaking to us. The pronouncements of academic scholars, especially in dealing with issues surrounding first-century Judaism, must not be permitted to undercut the plain sense of the Scriptures. When Luke writes, for example, that the Pharisees were "lovers of money" (Luke 16:14) he is not, as a Gentile, taking a personal "dig" at the Pharisees. The Spirit of God has communicated this important truth about the attitude of the Pharisees so that we might better understand the passage. What is more, the content of Matthew 23 is none other than the very words of Jesus Christ himself. If Brown is right and the words recorded in the Gospels are fueled by "later polemics between Christians and Jews," might that not compromise the authenticity and accuracy of Jesus' words to the Pharisees in this chapter?

Let us be entirely clear: scholarship in the Scriptures, like every other form of scholarship, is to be pursued and not despised. Every student of the Bible must seek to become as competent as possible in understanding its contents. But biblical scholarship must be undertaken with genuine humility by those who tremble at God's Word (Isa. 66:2). When we approach the Scriptures we must come to them as the Word of God. We must seek the divine purpose in giving us the words of the Bible before we come to human considerations. An emphasis on the human aspect of Scripture—the time, circumstances, author, purpose in writing, and so on—is not to be neglected, but it is secondary to the infinitely greater matter of divine inspiration.

In what sense were the Pharisees "good men"? They certainly were in their own eyes, and they were the embodiment of righteousness in the eyes of most of their countrymen. Jesus himself did not doubt that the "outside of the cup" was very clean. We need to be entirely fair and note that among the Pharisees there were indeed certain good and honorable men. Some invited Jesus to eat with them, and we must suppose that their motivation was not always unfriendly. Nicodemus evidently became a friend of Jesus and the disciples as the crucifixion drew near, and it is most likely that Joseph of Arimathea, who was assisted in Jesus' burial by Nicodemus (John 19:38–40), was himself a Pharisee. We also read of the wise words of the Pharisee Gamaliel in Acts 5:34–39.

"Woe": An Expression of Terrible Judgment

Nevertheless, Jesus' discourse in Matthew 23, which summed up his judgment of the Pharisees, is marked by this repeated refrain: "Woe to you, scribes and Pharisees, hypocrites!" (23:13, 15, 23, 25, 27, 29). This climactic denunciation of the Pharisees is one of woe. This "woe" is an expression of grievous, horrified dread that effectively says, "How horrible it will be!" It is a word filled with the fearful anticipation of God's terrible judgment to come.

It finds Old Testament expression in Isaiah 5, and there seems to be an allusion to that passage in Matthew's gospel. In Isaiah 5:7 the prophet proclaims, "For the vineyard of the LORD of hosts is the house of Israel, and the men of Judah are his pleasant planting; and he looked for justice, but behold, bloodshed; for righteousness, but behold, an outcry!" Six woes are subsequently pronounced against Judah because of her wickedness, in particular her social injustice. Jesus' words at the Last Supper, words that were fulfilled in Judas Iscariot, spoke of woe. "The Son of Man goes as it is written of him, but woe to that man by whom the Son of Man is betrayed! It would have been better for that man if he had not been born" (Matt. 26:24).

What was the reason for these woes? It was the Pharisees' *hypocrisy* that poisoned their minds, their lives, and their work. Although the derivation of the Greek words for "hypocrite" and "hypocrisy" suggests stage actors, the usage of the words in the New Testament is morally loaded, just as in contemporary English.[4] A professional actor would not take kindly to being called a "hypocrite" today, any more than you or I would. The visitor to the theatre will not be surprised when a man walking around on stage pretends to be someone other than himself—after all, this is what he has paid to see—and he does not consider the actors to be hypocrites! Rather, the essence of hypocrisy is the intention to mislead; it is necessarily disingenuous. In Antioch Barnabas was led astray by the hypocrisy of the circumcision party (Gal. 2:13).

In short, hypocrisy is the enemy of genuine faith; it is the very antithesis of sincerity. Moreover, it is the inevitable fruit of human religion, religion which seeks the praise and acclaim of men. This may seem a rather bold and startling claim, so we need to examine it carefully.

THE EVIL OF HYPOCRITICAL WORSHIP

We can see how the Pharisees had perfected human religion. They had turned it into an art form of the highest sophistication. Their outward appearance of devotion to God and their detailed prescriptions of how to show that devotion—especially in the matters of ceremonial washing and of almsgiving—were striking, even impressive. But that is just what it was—an outward appearance—while their inner spirit was polluted, false, wicked, and greedy. Jesus exposes the great evil of hypocritical worship. Our Lord, indeed the whole Bible, demonstrates that what pleases God is worship that comes from the heart. Take, for example, the classic words of Micah 6:6–8, noting the conclusion in particular.

"With what shall I come before the LORD,
    and bow myself before God on high?
Shall I come before him with burnt offerings,
    with calves a year old?
Will the LORD be pleased with thousands of rams,
    with ten thousands of rivers of oil?
Shall I give my firstborn for my transgression,
    the fruit of my body for the sin of my soul?"
He has told you, O man, what is good;
    and what does the LORD require of you
but to do justice, and to love kindness,
    and to walk humbly with your God?

Likewise, "the sacrifices of God are a broken spirit; a broken and contrite heart, O God, you will not despise" (Psalm 51:17). Let no one begin to imagine that Old Testament faith was preoccupied with outward deeds and did not concern the inner motivations and desires of the heart.

Observe that in Matthew 23:17 Jesus calls these Pharisees "fools," indeed "blind fools." We should use a word like "fool" very sparingly; we are even warned about the danger of judgment if we employ it unadvisedly. Even the Lord himself uttered the word only occasionally—but he did so here. Of course this foolishness is not a lack of intelligence; it is far more serious than that. It is a moral failure, it is a sin—it is the obstinate refusal to see the truth.

Jesus draws a comparison and a contrast between the Pharisees themselves and their cups and dishes and shows them their sheer inconsistency. When they wash their cups and dishes, they want them to be clean on both the inside and the outside. It would be no good having a bright, sparkling tea set, with teapot, cups, and saucers pure and brilliant white, if they had never been washed on the inside and yesterday's tea stains were still there. But this is exactly what the Pharisees were like. They took the greatest care to wash their hands, to make their outward appearance as clean as possible. They were careful, so very careful, with their outward cleanliness, while neglecting the inward state of their souls. In doing so they were flying in the face of everything they ought to have known, of all human reason as well as all the testimony of Scripture. It is the *inward* state of a man that is of the greatest importance. The Pharisees were patching up the outside for all to see and applaud, while the inside was steadily rotting away into a state of greater and greater corruption. Could a more solemn and terrible description ever be pronounced than that which the Lord Jesus gave in verse 27? They were "like whitewashed tombs, which outwardly appear beautiful, but within are full of dead people's bones and all uncleanness."

Paying attention to the outside and neglecting the inside is always foolish and usually dangerous. We could imagine living in a house where the main reception room gradually develops dark patches which insidiously creep up the walls. They do not look very attractive to the people who come into our house, the people we want to entertain and impress. They might think we have a problem with our foundations or our walls. So we simply paint over these areas with white paint so that they look bright and clean. But all the time the house is being affected by rising mildew or some other problem. The longer we fail to attend to the root of the problem, the sooner the whole rotten structure will have to be pulled down, unless it falls down. It is foolish only to pay attention to symptoms of an illness, rather than the internal cause of the illness. If something is wrong with you—continual headaches, frequent infections, sores on the body, or other recurring symptoms—painkillers and plasters can mask the symptoms, but they cannot cure the inner disease.

Remember again those striking words of Jesus in the Sermon on the Mount, which we have already quoted: "For I tell you, unless your righteousness exceeds that of the scribes and Pharisees, you will never enter the kingdom of heaven" (Matt.

5:20). What a shock this would have been to Jesus' listeners! They would have considered the righteousness of the Pharisees, with all their detailed law keeping, ceremonial washing, and scrupulous tithing, and concluded that it was impossible for anyone to be more righteous. But as we read Matthew 23 we can understand what Jesus meant. Their religion and their worship cleansed the outside but left their wicked insides just as corrupt and evil as ever. In fact it only increased their evil. There was nothing they could do about it themselves. Job, in the course of his reflections, spells this out. "Who can bring a clean thing out of an unclean? There is not one" (Job 14:4).

The Kingdom of Heaven Shut in Men's Faces

But now we need to see the most terrible indictment of all. It was that they "shut the kingdom of heaven in people's faces" (23:13). Nothing could be a more appalling condemnation. This is the first of the seven woes that Jesus pronounces. The Pharisees were not only under a sentence of hell themselves, but by their actions they were dragging men and women there with them. This condemnation came upon these men who distorted God's truth and imperiled the spiritual well-being of God's people. These men were blind guides whom the Lord did not send, just as he did not send the false prophets in the days of Jeremiah.[5] It was man-made religion, not the true faith in God that the Lord himself had established. How did, and how does, this man-made religion shut people out of God's kingdom?

The teachers of the law were systematically making the worship of God into a grim, heavy, joyless duty, an endless series of rules and chores. We can see what kind of burdens the lawyers added. Many of them were in connection with the Sabbath. The rabbis drew up a list of thirty-nine principal works that were not permitted on the Sabbath, and each of these was subdivided into six sections. So they had a compendium of 234 forbidden Sabbath activities! They made it illegal to pick and rub grain on the Sabbath—this was seen as reaping and threshing, which was regarded as work. They told the man whom Jesus healed on the Sabbath, who picked up his bed and walked, that his actions were unlawful. They said the same when Jesus healed a man born blind on the Sabbath.

These burdens had been imposed because these men had lost their spiritual authority and had to find some kind of human substitute in order to create their desired effect. The teachers of Israel in the first century could not communicate to the people with the heaven-sent power and authority of Jesus. Lacking the spiritual understanding of the Scriptures, they resorted to man-made methods that kept the masses in subjection and thralldom. This is what happens when the spiritual worship of God degenerates into mere rule-keeping.

It begins when pastors and elders begin to lose sight of the gospel of God's free grace. In place of Christ-centered exhortation they substitute a set of psychological tools to make people obedient to the will of men. This can sometimes take the form of "heavy shepherding," in which an individual's conscience is taken over by a senior individual in the church rather than by the Lord himself. It is a form of manipulation of which the cults are masters, and which is the essence of the rites of Roman Catholicism and other degenerate forms of Christianity. But many an evangelical pastor and evangelical congregation have fallen prey to this tendency.

We need to see the extent and the irony of this tragedy. The purpose of these men, the Pharisees, scribes, and teachers of the law, was to understand the Scriptures, to unlock their meaning and make it known to the people. But the very opposite had happened. They had locked up the Scriptures and lost the key to them. They were unable and unwilling to understand them and consequently unable and unwilling to help others understand them. Their lives and their doctrine put a greater and greater distance between the people and the true knowledge of God.

Thus the people were left in a state of ever-increasing darkness and misery. The true knowledge of God, the new birth, the forgiveness of sins—the people of Israel were shut out from these treasures, and all the teaching of the Pharisees perpetuated this situation.

Here, then, is a terrible woe for those who claim to be Christians but who deny biblical, evangelical truth and steer souls into something grotesquely different, which does not save their souls from death and judgment but rather compounds their sin. False teachers, men who are charged with making known the truth but keep the truth from the people, face the greatest possible condemnation. The condemnation uttered in Jeremiah 23:1 applies to them. "'Woe to the shepherds who destroy and scatter the sheep of my pasture!' declares the LORD."

THE TRUE TREASURE OF THE CHURCH

The Pharisees and lawyers had buried the true knowledge of God under vast layers of human traditions, ceremonies, manmade rules, and practices. Human religion always does this. It substitutes the human for the divine. It always emphasizes something other than the precious, life-giving truth of the gospel. Martin Luther, contending with the idolatrous paraphernalia of the Church of Rome, wrote in the sixty-second of his famous Ninety-Five Theses: "The true treasure of the Church is the Most Holy Gospel of the glory and the grace of God." The Protestant Reformation that subsequently swept across Europe, transforming the lives and souls of untold millions, was nothing other than the rediscovery of "the true treasure of the Church."

When this treasure is taken away and false "treasure" is put in its place, the church perishes and souls are lost. This is what the Pharisees were doing. They worked ever so hard to build, rebuild, decorate, and maintain the tombs of the prophets. For the Pharisees the upkeep of these sites was an act of commemoration and devotion to their great heritage. It was the way they sought to honor the prophets. Here were worthy monuments to the great men of the past. But the Lord reinterpreted their actions. Their building of the prophets' tombs signified that they were continuing the work of their ancestors who killed the prophets. Their fathers killed the prophets and they, the sons, were building their tombs! Hence the Lord gave them an A and a Z of Old Testament persecution, from Abel to Zechariah, whose murder is recorded in 2 Chronicles 24.[6]

But history will continue to repeat itself in the New Testament. The sins of the fathers in killing the prophets sent to Israel of old will be duplicated in the sons, to whom God will send prophets and apostles. The judgment of God against the fathers will come against the sons because their deeds will be exactly the same. The story of the church of Jesus Christ, from the times of the Savior himself and his apostles, and indeed over the next two thousand years, is the story of persecution, of murder and bloodshed. Stephen became the first Christian martyr in Acts chapter seven. James, brother of John, was quickly killed. Peter would later be executed. John was exiled on Patmos. Paul and his companions faced persecution wherever they went.

This is where the Pharisees had gone wrong. They devoted themselves painstakingly to the upkeep of the prophets' tombs while rejecting the prophets' message and persecuting the true followers of the prophets. If they had wanted to honor the prophets they should have listened to what they taught and regulated their lives according to the words the prophets brought from God. The medieval church made much—and the modern Roman Catholic Church still makes much—of the tombs and relics of saints who have died. They claim to know the burial place of the apostle Peter in Rome. Thousands of pilgrims flock there daily. But is Peter's teaching, given to him by the Lord Jesus Christ, the Head of the Church, honored by those who pay such reverence to the tomb?

It happens in Protestantism too. Men like John and Charles Wesley are greatly commemorated in England today and rightly so. They were key instruments in a mighty work of God's Spirit that took place during the eighteenth century. In many towns in England there are plaques indicating that John Wesley preached or lodged in a certain spot. "Wesley Memorial Churches" have sprung up all over England. But if John Wesley visited many of these churches today and witnessed the content of the services, he would surely weep. Charles Wesley's hymns are sung—without understanding—in church buildings where the gospel preached by the Wesleys has not only been neglected, but denied. In many such places those who speak about the need for spiritual conversion and the new birth, who insist upon the authority of the Bible and the uniqueness of Jesus Christ, are silenced and ridiculed.

May God deliver his people from the downgrade whereby living and spiritual Christianity degenerates into a museum piece, a fossil, leaving us the lifeless husk of the gospel, while those who cling to the truth as it is in Jesus are a despised, laughable minority.

So the Pharisees were ripe for judgment, ripe for woe. The evil and adulterous generation to which Jesus was speaking had not taken to heart the truths God had sent to them through Moses and the Prophets. Thus they could not recognize the Savior when he came to them. They searched the Scriptures most diligently, believing that in them they would find eternal life, but they did not see that the Scriptures bore testimony to Jesus. So when he came they did not put their trust in him; instead they hated him.

THE END OF THE STORY?

That is almost the whole story, but not quite. There is another Pharisee who appears in the New Testament, whose name is not mentioned in the four gospels. We know nothing of his personal dealings with Jesus before Jesus' death and resurrection, if indeed there were any, But later in our New Testament we read of the encounter between the risen and glorified Jesus and this Pharisee who was as intent on destroying Jesus as any of the other Pharisees we have considered. I refer, of course, to Saul of Tarsus, also known as the apostle Paul. When we have understood the spiritual predicament of these Pharisees—when the devastating words of judgment uttered by our Savior have registered in our hearts and minds—then we can consider how the Lord worked upon this one-time Pharisee, the self-confessed chief of sinners, and we will marvel at the scale of God's grace.

— 7 —

THE CHALLENGE TO JESUS' AUTHORITY

*And they came again to Jerusalem. And as he was walking
in the temple, the chief priests and the scribes and the elders
came to him, and they said to him, "By what authority are
you doing these things, or who gave you this authority to
do them?" Jesus said to them, "I will ask you one question;
answer me, and I will tell you by what authority I do these
things. Was the baptism of John from heaven or from man?
Answer me." And they discussed it with one another, saying,
"If we say, 'From heaven,' he will say, 'Why then did you
not believe him?' But shall we say, 'From man'?"—they were
afraid of the people, for they all held that John really was
a prophet. So they answered Jesus, "We do not know." And
Jesus said to them, "Neither will I tell you by what authority
I do these things." (Mark 11:27–33)*

WE HAVE ALREADY reached the final week of Jesus' earthly
life and ministry, and the conflict between Jesus and his enemies
intensifies. He has ridden into Jerusalem on the foal of a donkey,
accompanied by loud shouts of "Hosanna" and the waving of
palm branches. He has done so intentionally in order to fulfill
the prophecy made about him by Zechariah: "Rejoice greatly, O
daughter of Zion! Shout aloud, O daughter of Jerusalem! Behold,

your king is coming to you; righteous and having salvation is he, humble and mounted on a donkey, on a colt, the foal of a donkey" (Zech. 9:9).

Jesus is coming into Jerusalem as King, and in the royal city he acts as King. The authority of Jesus dominates the ensuing scene. He has come to his people; he enters his temple; and all that he says and does speaks of his complete mastery of the situation, a mastery that will be sustained right up to the hour of his death.

REFORMATION IN JERUSALEM

Matthew, Mark, and Luke all record the way in which Jesus entered the temple and drove out the merchants and the money-changers.[1] This "cleansing of the temple," as we observed in chapter 5, was unlikely to have been the same one recorded by John, which took place at the beginning of Jesus' ministry. It is the aftermath of this second act of cleansing that we will consider in this chapter. But first of all we must see what motivated Jesus to do as he did.

Jesus' authoritative activities in the temple were not only acts of solemn judgment, but also deeds of gracious reformation. He was grieved by what he saw among the people of God and came in order to remove all that was displeasing to him, replacing it with what was right. Reformation always takes place when men and women, moved by the Holy Spirit, are stirred by abuses they see taking place in the church. Reformation always involves the Word of God being applied with divine authority to beliefs and practices in the church that have become degenerate.

We remember young Josiah, king of Judah, the rediscovery of the book of the law in Solomon's temple, and the great reforms that followed. We read that "when the king heard the words of the Book of the Law, he tore his clothes" (2 Kings 22:11). Even the godly King Hezekiah, Josiah's great-grandfather, had not presided over a reformation as thorough as this. Down came all the idols that had been erected all over Judah. Down came all the high places in the hills and the country. And he and the people celebrated the Passover Feast in a manner that had not been seen since the days of Samuel the prophet (2 Chron. 35:18).

Then perhaps we remember Martin Luther in Germany and the Indulgences controversy of the early sixteenth century. The people of Luther's day were deceived into thinking that God's pardon for sins could be bought with human currency. Luther understood that souls were being denied the true knowledge of the gospel and the grace of God, what he called the true treasure of the church. Grieved and provoked by what he saw, Luther was led upon a path that soon turned Germany, Europe, and the future course of world history upside down.

Christians need to be zealous and courageous. The spirit of reformation is always zealous. Today the English Puritans are often mocked, often by experts who function as guides around the great cathedrals of England. It was these gloomy Puritans, we are told, these killjoys without an aesthetic bone in their bodies, who emptied ancient medieval churches of all their beauty. But what was the true reason for their removal of images and altars? It was their zeal for God's holiness and their desire to worship God according to his own commandments in Scripture.

THE AUTHORITY OF THE PREACHED WORD

What is there in today's Western church that urgently needs reformation? Where can we possibly start? The safest starting point is surely to recognize that godly reformation must always be according to the Word of God. Here is a most basic consideration that lies at the very heart of the matter: *the authority of God speaking in his Word*.

The United Kingdom has witnessed a long decline in church attendance. According to a survey published by *WhyChurch*, the percentage of the population regularly attending a place of Christian worship fell from 11 percent in 1980 to just 6 percent in 2010.

Over the same period the average age of these congregations increased from 37 to 56.[2] What can we make of this? One view that has gained ground argues that the problem lies with the outdated concept of the "traditional" church service. A suggested way forward is to transform these churches into "caféchurches." If the people were seated around circular tables, in well-padded chairs, with coffee and other hot drinks readily available; if they felt free to get up and walk around; if, perhaps, there was some background music that helped them relax, then more people, and especially more young people, would surely come along. This would show them that Christianity is relevant. For what hope does the church have, in the twenty-first century, unless it learns to modernize and simply "chill out" a bit?

Something is not necessarily bad, nor is it good, simply because it is modern. And there is nothing particularly modern about coffee houses. But are there substantial objections to the implementation of such a practice to Christian worship? Most certainly there are. The heart of the matter is *whether such an atmosphere would tend to promote or to hinder the authoritative proclamation of God's Word*. Would the preached Word be heard with seriousness and solemnity if the overriding concern were to make people feel comfortable and at ease? It is hard to understand how the reverence of God would be found in such an environment.

J. C. Ryle observed this very point, demonstrating that there is really nothing new under the sun.

> [Jesus] would have us know that a reverence is due to every place where God is worshipped. The reverence He claimed for the temple, was not for the temple as the house of sacrifice, but as "the house of prayer." Let us remember this conduct and language of our Lord, whenever we go to a place of public worship. Christian churches . . . are places where God's word is read, where Christ is present, and where the Holy Spirit works on souls. These facts ought to make us grave, reverent, solemn

and decorous, whenever we enter them. The man who behaves as carelessly in a church as he would in an inn, or a private dwelling, has yet much to learn. He has not the "mind of Christ."[3]

"HANGING ON HIS WORDS"

Let us return to the temple in Jerusalem. Jesus, having driven out everything that was polluting it, has more or less taken up residence there; he is teaching there every day of that week, probably right up to Thursday. The chief priests could not get rid of him, try as they might. What is more, the people were "hanging on his words" (Luke 19:48). Here is a picture of true worship in contrast to false worship. This is the outcome of every true reformation: that the people come together and sit humbly and hungrily under the Word of God. The traders, the merchandise, the noise, has all gone. Here is the one flock under the care of the one Shepherd, striving to listen to his every word.

What is preaching? It is not one man standing up and stating his opinion on the Bible or current affairs or anything else. It is the authoritative proclamation of God's truth, in the name of Jesus Christ and by the power of the Holy Spirit. The one who preaches is under the authority of Christ and his Word just as much as the congregation is. Not only is that Word authoritative, but it has saving power. These are the considerations that need to be brought to our attention at the beginning of the twenty-first century, no less urgently than in 1969 when Martyn Lloyd-Jones said that "the greatest need in the Church today is to restore this authority to the pulpit."[4]

A DIRECT CHALLENGE TO JESUS' AUTHORITY

It is in this context that we come to the exchange recorded in Mark 11:27–33. All that took place—Jesus' triumphal entry into the city, the cleansing of the temple, and the crowd of listeners he subsequently gathered—greatly enraged the chief priests and scribes. Because of this they walked right up to him while he was teaching and challenged him face-to-face on the spot. There are three groups mentioned here: the chief priests, who were mainly Sadducees; the scribes, who were mainly Pharisees; and the elders, who were rulers of cities and towns. Together these three groups made up the Sanhedrin, the ruling council in Israel. The presence of them all demonstrates the almost universal opposition to Jesus that now prevailed among the leaders of the people. Their aim was to trap Jesus and condemn him. Their approach was direct. "By what authority are you doing these things, or who gave you this authority to do them?" (Mark 11:28).

It was undoubtedly clear to these leaders that Jesus was exercising rights that belonged only to God. He was acting with the prerogatives of the Lord himself, who comes suddenly to his temple (Mal. 3:1). Had not the whole course of Jesus' ministry pointed to his divine self-awareness: the proclamation of the forgiveness of sins, the raising of the dead, the giving of sight to the blind, the "I am" sayings, and so much besides?

We ought not to make the mistake of thinking that Jesus' opponents were honest inquirers approaching him with an open mind. They were coming with their own malicious agenda. They were plotting against him, being as clever as they could. They were trying to trap him. If Jesus said that his authority had come from God then he could be accused, condemned of blasphemy, and perhaps stoned to death. But if Jesus said that his authority had *not* come from God then he would look like a fraud and all the people would lose any respect for him. It looked as though it would be every inch a successful challenge.

Jesus has many clever opponents today. And like the groups who came to Jesus in our passage, they belong to groups who have little or nothing in common apart from their opposition towards Jesus. Some will be advocates of other religions like Islam. Some will be secular or scientific opponents of Christianity. Others will be enemies of any kind of "religion" because of their libertarian lifestyle preferences. Their aim is to outwit and trap followers of Jesus Christ.

JESUS AND JOHN THE BAPTIST

What does Jesus do in response to the question? He could have simply replied that "my Father gave me this authority," and in certain places he effectively did say that. In John 10:18 he said quite plainly, "No one takes it [my life] from me, but I lay it down of my own accord. I have authority to lay it down, and I have authority to take it up again. This charge I have received from my Father." Jesus could have said absolutely nothing, and when all sorts of false accusations were leveled at him a few days later, this is exactly what he did. But on this occasion Jesus replied with his own question. It was a brilliant example of his divine wisdom.

> I will ask you one question; answer me, and I will tell you by what authority I do these things. Was the baptism of John from heaven or from man? (Mark 11:29–30).

Was Jesus being evasive, like many a modern-day politician? He was not, because the question he asked had a great bearing on the question they put to him. Indeed his question addressed the core of the matter. By "the baptism of John" Jesus meant the whole ministry of John the Baptist. This is the question he was putting to his interrogators: was the recent John the Baptist phenomenon something which came "from heaven"; that is, was John a true prophet sent by God to fulfill his purpose? Or was it "from man"; was John self-appointed, or a representative of a merely human movement?

The point is that John's ministry and Jesus' ministry were indissolubly bound to one another. The great burden of John the Baptist's work was to prepare the way for Jesus and to point

Jesus out to those who came to him. John came not proclaiming himself, but proclaiming Jesus. We remember that a delegation of priests and Levites had been sent from Jerusalem to ask John about himself: was he the Christ, was he Elijah, or was he another prophet? John gave short and negative answers to each of these questions. So the religious leaders became exasperated and demanded that John give some explanation of who he was. He replied, "I am the voice of one calling in the desert, 'Make straight the way for the Lord'" (John 1:23 NIV).⁵ And he went on, "but among you stands one you do not know. He is the one who comes after me, the thongs of whose sandals I am not worthy to untie" (John 1:26–27 NIV). A little later he said of Jesus, "Behold the Lamb of God, who takes away the sin of the world!" (John 1:29). And later we see John speaking of Jesus as the bridegroom and of himself as the friend of the bridegroom who must fade away (John 3:29–30). If John's authority was from heaven, then so was that of Jesus because John constantly pointed people to Jesus.

Because of this, the religious leaders, having set out to trap Jesus, had now become trapped themselves. They were, as we say, caught between a rock and a hard place. We see their deliberations right here in the text. "'If we say, "From heaven," he will say, "Why then did you not believe him?" But shall we say, "From man,"?'—they were afraid of the people, for they all held that John really was a prophet. So they answered Jesus, 'We do not know'" (Mark 11:31-32). They were faced with the choice of either looking very foolish—a blow to their pride—or of risking their lives and perhaps being stoned to death. Indeed, they were in precisely the same corner into which they had sought to force Jesus! So they had to resort to dishonesty—for that is what it was. If they had said "we don't want to say," they would have been cowardly, though not dishonest. By saying they did not know, they were being both cowardly and dishonest.

THE CUL-DE-SAC OF UNBELIEF

The chief priests, scribes, and elders were evidently in the wrong. Their pride and self-importance meant that they could not admit it. But we all know from experience that there is nothing more foolish than to continue along a wrong path when it has been demonstrated to us that we *are* wrong! When you have committed an error, there is no way to correct yourself except by admitting that error and starting from the position you were in before the error was made.

When a student attempts to solve a mathematical problem and discovers that one of his calculations, at quite an early stage in his solution, was incorrect, there is absolutely no value in him continuing unless he goes back to that calculation and corrects it. When a man at home undertakes a Do-It-Yourself project and he finds himself drilling into electrical cables or gas mains, he needs to realize what he has done, stop his drilling immediately, deal with any damage, and begin again at the point before he began to drill. If a group of people are out walking in the hills and they realize that they are lost, there is no point in pressing on in the same direction. They have no option but to turn back, retrace their steps, consult a map, or ask a local expert for directions to their destination.

In each of these cases, the individuals concerned need to recognize that they are in a blind and dangerous alley, in a cul-de-sac. We use that word commonly to refer to a road with a dead end, a road that you can exit only by the way you entered. The mathematician, the handyman, and the hiker will incur grave difficulties if they attempt any other course of action.

But there is no more blind or dangerous cul-de-sac than the cul-de-sac of unbelief. There is nothing more perilous than being wrong about the identity of Jesus. And in particular, there is nothing more precarious than sticking stubbornly to being wrong about Jesus in the face of all the positive and compelling evidence.

RETRACING THE STEPS

The only way to exit a cul-de-sac is to do so via the entrance. That means retracing your steps, swallowing your pride, starting again with right assumptions. This applies, in fact, to every truth claim we might consider.

Someone who says that there is no such thing as truth will soon be trapped. "There are no facts, only opinions," he says. "Nothing is ultimately true—all is a matter of opinions and personal preferences." The trouble is that the speaker in his conversations relies upon the existence of truth and of trust. An atheist once said to a Christian, "Of one thing I am sure: that there is no such thing as absolute truth." "But are you *absolutely* sure?" the Christian replied. The atheist was as dumbfounded as the religious leaders in our passage. He was caught in the cul-de-sac of unbelief because the Bible teaches that God himself exists, he is true, and his word is truth. The atheist needs to go back to the beginning and question his initial assumptions.

Someone who believes wholeheartedly in the theory of evolution must eventually be tripped up. He believes in the survival of the fittest; that is his creed, and he believes that all life in this world operates on this basis. But he has an elderly and sick relative, and in his heart he knows that he must care for her. In fact he knows that he is being more humane, more human indeed, when he demonstrates care for the vulnerable and needy. His beliefs and his practice are clearly inconsistent. He too is trapped in the cul-de-sac of unbelief because the Bible teaches that mankind is made in God's image, to be like the God who "has pity on the weak and the needy, and saves the lives of the needy" (Ps. 72:13). The evolutionist has no option but to retrace all the steps in his thinking and start afresh, so that his theory and his practice will be coherent.

Then consider *someone who says that Jesus was a very good man, but he was not God.* He too is in an impossible position. How could he be "a very good man" when he spoke and acted as he did: pronouncing the forgiveness of sins, accepting worship from men and women, and proclaiming that he was "the bread of life," "the light of the world," "the resurrection and the life," and much more? These claims were clearly divine. If Jesus were not divine, then he would be an impostor, a false prophet, or perhaps a madman. Whoever says that Jesus is just a good man is in the cul-de-sac of unbelief because the Bible teaches that Jesus is the eternal, incarnate Son of God. And this was of course exactly the cul-de-sac in which these religious leaders now found themselves. What they ought to have done was to admit their error, indeed their great sin, and then cry out like Simon Peter, "You are the Christ, the Son of the living God" (Matt. 16:16).

"To the Crooked You Show Yourself Shrewd"

Mark 11:33, which concludes our passage, is a tragic comment on the spiritual condition of these men, and also on the condition of anyone who sets themselves against Jesus Christ. "Neither will I tell you by what authority I do these things."

The leaders of Israel came to Jesus with the stubborn refusal to believe that Jesus had come from God. Psalm 18:25–26 says,

> With the merciful you show yourself merciful;
>> with the blameless man you show yourself blameless;
> with the purified you show yourself pure;
>> and with the crooked you make yourself seem tortuous.[6]

On this day the latter part of this text was fulfilled in these men. They would not come to Jesus humbly; they came haughtily. Very well—Jesus will not reveal his true authority, his true glory, to these people who have taken up a position of enmity against him. Rather, Jesus closes the exchange with words of fearful condemnation. He will not reveal to them his true authority and nature, since they have closed their minds and their hearts to him.

I have used the description "cul-de-sac of unbelief," but to the stubborn unbeliever it is worse than this. Unbelief is not only a cul-de-sac; it is a blind alley—whoever stays in it too long will sooner or later find that there is no way to get out of it. In fact, the rebellious heart will become so hardened that such a person will not even want to get out—until it is too late and the last chance has gone. Those who stubbornly set themselves against the gospel of Jesus Christ will deny themselves the opportunity to hear that gospel. They imperil their souls. We will see this later in the case of Herod the tetrarch. One day the chance to repent and believe will have gone. The obstinate unbeliever will die and come face-to-face with God, or else the Lord himself will suddenly return. The unbeliever will be unprepared and terrified when he realizes his predicament. He will be like the five foolish virgins who had no oil and are shut out of the house. Darkness, the door in front of them barred forever, a voice saying, "I do not know you" (Matt. 25:12). Whoever resists the authority of Jesus Christ will find that almighty God is against him, and in the final day there will be no one with whom he can plead.

"To the Pure You Show Yourself Pure"

But let us finish this chapter with words of comfort and encouragement. Jesus Christ will never turn away the honest inquirer. For although Jesus does not give his opponents the answer to their question, that answer is plain enough to all who are willing to receive the word of God with humility. "To the faithful you show yourself faithful, to the blameless you show yourself blameless, to the pure you show yourself pure" (Ps. 18:25-26 NIV). Such people are like the crowds in the temple in Jerusalem, who hang onto every word of Jesus. Of such souls the Good Shepherd says, "My sheep hear my voice, and I know them, and they follow me" (John 10:27).

Who is pure? The one who renounces all pride, all guile, all hypocrisy, all opposition. We need to lay down our rebel arms. We need to submit to Jesus Christ gladly and totally. That means believing him, trusting him, and receiving his words and all the words of the Bible as the words of God himself.

8

THE SADDUCEES

Jesus said to them, "Is this not the reason you are wrong,
because you know neither the Scriptures nor the power of
God? For when they rise from the dead, they neither marry
nor are given in marriage, but are like angels in heaven. And
as for the dead being raised, have you not read in the book
of Moses, in the passage about the bush, how God spoke
to him, saying, 'I am the God of Abraham, and the God of
Isaac, and the God of Jacob'? He is not God of the dead, but
of the living. You are quite wrong." (Mark 12:24–27)

IN THE NEW TESTAMENT there is far less material dealing with the Sadducees than there is with the Pharisees. The
only exclusive encounter Jesus had with the Sadducees was the
one recorded in this text, which is also reported in much the
same form by Matthew, and in Luke's case has slight variations.
Though the Pharisees and the Sadducees are linked together in
a number of texts, most notably in Matthew 16:1–12 when they
came together to test Jesus, they should be seen as quite distinct
and very contrasting groups.

CONSERVATIVES AND LIBERALS?

The Pharisees and the Sadducees were both powerful parties
in Israel, both were strongly represented in the Sanhedrin, both

opposed Jesus, and both were the subjects of warnings that Jesus gave to his disciples. That is a good deal to have in common, but that is also where the resemblance ends.

The Sadducees were essentially an aristocratic party, jealous of their political power, whereas the Pharisees were a "popular" movement, in the sense that they gained their support from among the common people. One obvious reason why Jesus had more contact with the Pharisees was that they were dispersed throughout Israel, including Galilee, whereas the Sadducees were much more concentrated in their Jerusalem power base. This is because the Sadducees were closely associated with the priesthood, an office which had become heavily politicized since the time of the Maccabees in the second century BC. Indeed, the Sadducees were key protagonists in some of the bloody struggles that took place during the later Maccabean era. The high priests were generally drawn from the party of the Sadducees. The temple in Jerusalem, and the business conducted there, was largely under their supervision and control. It is quite likely that the Sadducees took their name from Zadok, the faithful high priest who ministered during the reigns of David and Solomon (2 Sam. 8:17; 1 Kings 1:34). But if they resembled Zadok in name, they were very different in character.

The contrast between the Pharisees and Sadducees can be seen sharply in one particular respect: whereas the Pharisees sought to distance themselves from all Hellenizing (Greek) influences, the Sadducees adapted to these foreign waves of thought because it was politically advantageous for them to do so. For this reason it is sometimes stated that the Pharisees were the conservatives of their time and the Sadducees were the liberals.

Labels such as *conservative* and *liberal*, whether or not the initial letters are capitalized, may not be especially useful in understanding the respective positions of the Pharisees and Sadducees. Adjectives like these are too likely to be conditioned by our own contemporary perceptions, in which religion, politics, and economics are often thrown into the melting pot together. What passes as a "conservative" in the United States, for example, is different from what the term might designate in Great Britain. The recent phenomenon of the "Tea Party" in the United States leaves many British people—even those of a more "conservative" leaning—bewildered. Moreover, comparisons between different eras are unhelpful. Anachronisms are bound to arise—we might just as well debate whether Augustine of Hippo was a Protestant or a Catholic, or whether Oliver Cromwell would have joined the modern Liberal Democrat Party in the United Kingdom.

Certainly, at first glance, the Sadducees might indeed be considered as today's "liberals" in terms of their doctrine, although the label "materialists" is less likely to be misunderstood. As is well documented in the New Testament, they did not believe in angels, spirits, or the resurrection, whereas the Pharisees held to the existence of these supernatural realities. The apostle Paul, of course, exploited these divisions to his advantage (Acts 23:8). The Sadducees also rejected any notion of God's providence in human affairs. In his *Antiquities*, Josephus says of them, "But the doctrine of the Sadducees is this: That souls die with the bodies; nor do they regard the observation of any thing besides what the law enjoins them; for they think it an instance of virtue to dispute with those teachers of philosophy whom they frequent."[1] As we see in the passage under consideration, the Sadducees were certainly fond of disputations; they could perhaps be described as boorish.

But in other senses the Sadducees were very much the "conservatives" of their day. They regarded only the written Scriptures of the Old Testament as authoritative, and they gave special place to the Torah (the five Books of Moses) without rejecting the rest of the Scriptures.[2] By contrast the Pharisees accepted not only the authority of all that we now call the Old Testament (the Law, the Prophets, and the Writings) but a whole body of—supposedly parallel—oral tradition. On this they based many of their distinctive and detailed legal requirements. It is noticeable too, that whereas the Pharisees were the key opponents of Jesus during his lifetime, the book of Acts has a great deal more to say about the opposition of the Sadducees. The reason is obvious: the apostles made the preaching of the resurrection a central pillar of their message, which brought about the Sadducees' anger and dismay.

RIDICULING THE RESURRECTION

Because the question that the Sadducees brought to Jesus concerned the resurrection of the dead, it was in their interests to approach him while the Pharisees were absent. Their essential motive was to debunk the whole notion of the resurrection of the dead, to expose it as a laughable myth, and to score a few points against the Pharisees as well as against Jesus. So they put together a story, certainly fictitious, about seven brothers who each, in turn, married the same woman and then died (Mark 12:20–23).[3] The woman herself died last of all. Having been married to seven different men, whose wife will she be in the resurrection?

Even though the Sadducees' scenario was a concoction, it was one that was founded upon Old Testament Law. In Mark 12:19 the Sadducees presented their case, citing Moses as their authority. The principle of what is sometimes termed "levirate marriage" is exemplified in Genesis 38:8–10 and given formal statement in Deuteronomy 25:5–10. In the first passage Onan, the second son of Judah and the younger brother of Er, whom the Lord had killed, was told, "Go in to your brother's wife and perform the duty of a brother-in-law to her, and raise up offspring for your brother" (Gen. 38:8). But he refused to carry out this duty, and consequently he too was put to death. In the Deuteronomy passage, the one to which the Sadducees were alluding, it is stipulated that if brothers live together and one of them dies, leaving a widow but no son, then his brother is to marry the widow in order to raise up seed, "that his name may not be blotted out of Israel" (Deut. 25:6). In the book of Ruth, Boaz's marriage to Ruth is a somewhat complicated version of the levirate marriage, though the same principle was applied.

However, we have no clear evidence that the practice of levirate marriage was being continued in Israel in Jesus' day. The Sadducees did not bring this problem to Jesus in order that he might help them solve a genuine, practical difficulty. They came to him with neither sincerity nor true scholarly interest. Rather, their actions sprang from "a frivolous desire to ridicule the doctrine of the resurrection."[4] They wanted to tie Jesus up in knots, and then to make sure that the Pharisees found out, so that they would be embarrassed. They wanted to get Jesus hung up on nice little details, try to detect inconsistencies in his argument, and therefore pull down what they saw as the fabrication of the whole idea of resurrection.

Although the Sadducees were trying to play games with Jesus, they had absolutely no idea of the weightiness of the subject they were touching upon. Their fabricated anecdote did not succeed in concealing their skepticism with regard to the subject of the resurrection. Jesus knew precisely what their motives were, and his response to them was quite devastating. He exposed their error in two respects. The first was that they did not know the Scriptures with which they so confidently affirmed familiarity; and the second, no less serious, was that they did not know the power of God, the mighty works he is able to do.

THE SCRIPTURES AND THE POWER OF GOD

Nevertheless, the way Jesus joined "the Scriptures" and "the power of God" is quite deliberate. The two are powerfully interlinked, though not inseparable. We can be certain that the testimony of history—both that of the Bible and that of church history—is that the power of God accompanies those occasions when the Word of God is spoken with authority and received with faith and humility. Conversely, the fount of all that we might call theological liberalism is the distrust of the Scriptures.

Let us consider this in a little more detail. The Scriptures are the revelation of a *speaking God*. God's first recorded words brought light into being—that is the measure of his power! It is well understood today that human speech is itself an act. Philosophers specializing in linguistics talk about "speech-acts." Our own speech is powerful; our spoken words produce results. How much more true is this of God! "By the word of the LORD the heavens were made, and by the breath of his mouth all their host" (Ps. 33:6).

More to the point, Scripture is God's supernatural revelation *to man*. God has intervened powerfully in human history by making himself known. This works in two ways. First, the power of God is abundantly displayed in his mighty works that Scripture describes—works that include the creation, the flood, the exodus, and all his great acts right up to the promised new creation. Secondly, God has revealed himself through all the Scriptures, which explain God's purposes in salvation through mighty works. This needs to be explored further.

When, in the history of the church, has the power of God been made known? The answer is, quite simply, when the Word of God has been preached, read, and heard with faith, understanding, and obedience. What is described in Acts 6:7 is nothing other than the manifestation of the power of God in the early church. "And the word of God continued to increase, and the number of the disciples multiplied greatly in Jerusalem, and a great many of the priests became obedient to the faith." The same applies when the power of God is made manifest in the church during any era, past, present, or future. In every true reformation and revival—and this is no crass generalization—the Word of God has always been central. Where living faith is found, God's Word will be at its heart. The words of J. C. Ryle are timeless. "The Protestant Reformation was mainly effected by translating and circulating the Bible. The Churches which are most flourishing at this day, are churches which honour the Bible . . . The godliest families are Bible-reading families. The holiest men and women are Bible-reading people."[5]

Here, however, is the great irony. Of course these Sadducees were Bible-reading people. But the tragedy was that they did not *know* the Scriptures. This may seem like a paradox: it is highly likely that each of the Sadducees present at this meeting could have quoted "the passage about the bush" (Mark 12:26) word-perfect, and yet not one of them really *knew* it. The possession of the Bible, a high view of the Bible, the regular reading of the Bible, and even a profound level of familiarity with the Bible, are no guarantees that the Bible will be rightly understood and used. On this subject, Professor Carl Trueman of Westminster Theological Seminary, who specializes in historical theology, makes reference to the Socinians, who were heretical opponents of the Protestant Reformation in the sixteenth and seventeenth centuries:

> The Socinians were very radical biblicists. They're often thought today to have been rationalists, but in actual fact, in their earliest incarnation they were radical biblicists. They were very much "Scripture alone" people; they interpreted Scripture very literally, and they ended up abandoning whole swathes of Christian orthodoxy: the Incarnation, the Trinity, the Atonement. It's a good example of how a bald assertion of Scriptural authority is not enough to guarantee or to generate orthodoxy. It's not enough only to hold Scripture as the supreme authority; one also has to *interpret* it correctly.[6]

All these descriptions could equally well apply to the Sadducees, if we substitute "resurrection, angel, and spirit" for "the Incarnation, the Trinity, the Atonement."

To delve deeply into the philosophical assumptions that underpinned the Sadducees' method of interpretation, let alone that of the Socinians, is beyond the scope of this study. We will content ourselves with one observation, which lies at the heart of this dispute: *the Sadducees were unable to raise their minds to consider transcendent realities.* They were boxed in by what they themselves could understand and experience in their own terms. This should become clear as we look at the dispute itself.

MARRIAGE AND WHAT IT POINTS TO

Jesus shows that the Sadducees' assumption about the nature of the resurrection was flawed to begin with. Of course they did not believe in a future resurrection, but allied to this unbelief was an inability to understand that the world of the resurrection would be quite different from this present one. Their question about marriage would simply not apply in the age of the resurrection. Marriage between one man and one woman is an ordinance given by God for this current age. It was ordained by God after the creation of the man upon the earth, and it belongs only to the earth in its present form.

In regard to marriage, men and women in the resurrection "will be like angels in heaven." We need to observe restraint here in case we extrapolate further than Scripture allows. The similarity to angels can go no further than this text states. Does Jesus imply that the differences between the sexes will be obliterated? The Bible never says that. When the Lord Jesus appeared to his disciples after the resurrection, he appeared as a man. There is not the slightest suggestion that his masculinity was compromised. Marriage will come to an end because the resurrected human race, in their immortality, will no longer need to reproduce and replenish the earth. But there is more that can be said. The institution of marriage in Genesis 2 points, not so much to procreation, but to mutual help and companionship as the first and greatest reason for marriage.

Paul's teaching in Ephesians 5:22–33 on marriage resembles two tightly-woven threads, both very beautiful. These two threads are (1) human marriage between one man and one woman, and (2) the love of Christ for his church, his bride. It is abundantly clear in these verses that although Paul is certainly giving practical directions to husbands and wives, he is also doing something transcendently greater. He is playing upon a theme that is sounded in other places in Scripture: that the covenant companionship of marriage finds its fulfillment in the eternal, blissful, and unbreakable covenant of love between the Lamb and the Bride. Isaac was comforted by Rebekah after the death of his mother Sarah (Gen. 24:67), but in the future state, all the comfort that redeemed humanity will ever need will come directly from God himself, who "will wipe away every tear from their eyes, and death shall be no more" (Rev. 21:4).

THE TRANSCENDENT POWER OF GOD

Anyone who has studied biblical hermeneutics, that is, the discipline of how to interpret the Bible, will have encountered allegorical methods of interpretation employed in the early and medieval church—especially those attributed to the Alexandrian church father Origen (185–254) and others who followed in his tradition. For several centuries the allegorical approach to Scripture became the standard one. This meant that every text in Scripture needed to be searched for spiritual, elevated meanings; the bare literal interpretation of the text was regarded as crude and unsophisticated. One has only to consider Origen's interpretation of the parable of the Good Samaritan to see this method at work.

> The man who was going down is Adam. Jerusalem is paradise, and Jericho is the world. The robbers are hostile powers. The priest is the Law, the Levite is the prophets, and the Samaritan is Christ. The wounds are disobedience, the beast is the Lord's body, the [inn], which accepts all who wish to enter, is the Church. . . . The manager of the [inn] is the head of the Church, to whom its care has been entrusted. And the fact that the Samaritan promises he will return represents the Savior's second coming.[7]

Nearly every modern reader of the Bible will (rightly) regard this explanation as fanciful, the product of an over-fertile imagination. The basic problem is that the central message of the parable—love your neighbor, even though he could be someone you regard as an enemy!—is entirely lost. I am not aware of many pulpits where the allegorical approach is commended or practiced today.

But is it possible that the pendulum swung too far in the opposite direction? Are we guilty of flattening the contours of Scripture so as to dumb down the spiritual and elevated meanings that God *intends* us to glean from the Bible? In seeking to promote *practical* Christianity, is it not possible to make preaching merely pragmatic and mundane?

The Word of God is vastly more than a handbook of ethics to help us deal with the issues that confront us in this world or a list of answers to satisfy the curiosities of our skeptical friends. It is a sure guide to heaven, a sure guide to Jesus Christ. It enables us to lift our eyes far above this present world and to see our eternal inheritance in him. To cite one of several possible examples, when Paul writes to the Corinthians about the experiences of the Israelites in the wilderness, he comes to the conclusion that "they drank from the spiritual Rock that followed them, and that Rock was Christ" (1 Cor. 10:4). The wanderings of the people of Israel did not constitute simply a self-contained national history. They had—and more to the point, they *have*—a typological value. This means that they point us to Jesus Christ, to whom men and women must come in order to be saved. Therefore Paul continues in 1 Corinthians 10:11: "Now these things happened to them as an example, but they were written down for our instruction, on whom the end of the ages has come." This is not speculative allegory, but biblical typology, illustrating for us the truth of Jesus' own words to his disciples: "everything written about me in the Law of Moses and the Prophets and the Psalms must be fulfilled" (Luke 24:44). When we see Christ in all the Scriptures of the Old and New Testaments, then it is that our minds have been opened to understand them. And then it is that the transcendent power of God has been at work in us.[8]

The poor Sadducees knew nothing of this transcendent power of God. They could not lift their eyes and their minds upwards; they were restricted to a two-dimensional view of existence, and this was and is a pitiable state to be in. But why were they in that state to begin with? Was it not that their simple reading of the Scriptures—of the Torah in particular—had led them to that conclusion?

EXODUS 3:6 AND THE RESURRECTION OF THE BODY

It is highly significant that Jesus went to the Torah in order to prove that the Sadducees were wrong. He met them on territory with which they felt familiar. We now reach an important question. Do the words of the LORD in this "passage about the bush" really clinch Jesus' argument in favor of the resurrection? When God said, "I am the God of your Father, the God of Abraham, the God of Isaac, and the God of Jacob" (Ex. 3:6), what did that have to do with a future state? Did the LORD not simply mean that he was the same God that these patriarchs had worshipped? And even if it were admitted that these patriarchs were among the living rather than the dead, does that imply anything about a resurrection body?

How we deal with questions of this kind reveals something of our attitude toward the authority of Jesus Christ himself. James Alexander made the observation that "this is not an argument at all, but an authoritative declaration of the truth."[9] We must not read these words as if Jesus were on a level playing field with the Sadducees, no more able than they were to understand and give expression to God's truth. The Lord Jesus has the authority to declare the true and full meaning of all the Scriptures, just as he did to the bewildered disciples on the road to Emmaus. New Testament believers, on whom the end of the ages has come, are to read the Old Testament in the light of all that Jesus Christ is and has done. This is what Peter explains in his first letter as he deals with the Old Testament prophets.

> Concerning this salvation, the prophets who prophesied about the grace that was to be yours searched and inquired carefully, inquiring what person or time the Spirit of Christ in them was indicating when he predicted the sufferings of Christ and the subsequent glories. It was revealed to them that they were serving not themselves but you, in the things that have now been announced to you through those who preached the good news to you by the Holy Spirit sent from heaven, things into which angels long to look. (1 Peter 1:10–12)

This means that the Old Testament must remain somewhat dark and obscure until the light of Christ in the New Testament shines upon it. The Lord Jesus Christ was and is the infallible exegete of every passage of Scripture, as he demonstrated to his disciples after his resurrection. On this occasion, at any rate, Jesus managed to silence the Sadducees. J. C. Ryle makes this honest and humble observation:

> Now if the Sadducees had not felt the argument convincing and silencing, they would not have submitted to it so quietly as they did. If we do not see the full force of the argument, the fault is evidently in ourselves. We do not see the fullness of Scripture as we ought to do. There is depth of meaning in many texts which we have not fathomed.[10]

SHEOL—"PALE AND JOYLESS EXISTENCE"?

But the question may still be asked: is the resurrection of the dead a doctrine that the Old Testament teaches? The New Testament scholar James Edwards observes that "the view that typifies the Old Testament understanding of the afterlife is not resurrection but Sheol, a netherworld characterized by a pale and joyless existence."[11] How did Old Testament saints view death?

What was the nature of this "Sheol" to which they so often refer? Any number of passages may be cited that appear to support Edwards's conclusion.

Jacob pleaded with his sons not to take their youngest brother Benjamin to Egypt with them: "If harm should happen to him on the journey that you are to make, you would bring down my gray hairs with sorrow to Sheol" (Gen. 42:38). Job seems to suggest that Sheol is a place from which there is no return: "As the cloud fades and vanishes, so he who goes down to Sheol does not come up" (Job 7:9). And in Psalm 6:5 David's statement seems conclusive enough: "For in death there is no remembrance of you; in Sheol who will give you praise?"

Sheol is a dominant and pervading theme in the Old Testament. Philip Johnston, in his fine and detailed study of this subject, comments that "there is no clearly articulated alternative to Sheol, no other destiny whose location is named, no other fate whose situation is described, however briefly. So the majority of Israelites may well have envisaged no alternative."[12] But he then continues: "And yet there seem to be some exceptions, a few texts which hint at or hope for some form of continued communion with God beyond death."[13]

What are these texts? It is a fascinating, rewarding, and heartwarming task for a believer to comb through the Old Testament Scriptures searching for these intimations of immortality.

INTIMATIONS OF IMMORTALITY

Genesis 5 begins with the observation that just as Adam was created in God's likeness, Seth, Adam's son, was begotten in the likeness and image of his father. But the rest of the chapter shows that this inherited image included unavoidable physical death. Though each of the men listed in this chapter, from Adam to Lamech, flourished and endured for several centuries, the mournful refrain is sounded—"and he died." There is, however, one exception to this rule: Enoch. Of him it is said, "Enoch walked with God, and he was not, for God took him" (Gen. 5:24). The lack of detail here is tantalizing, but the writer to the Hebrews helps us further by telling us, "By faith Enoch was taken up so that he should not see death, and he was not found, because God had taken him. Now before he was taken he was commended as having pleased God" (Heb. 11:5). Death indeed reigned from Adam to Moses, but in the case of Enoch we are given a glimpse of the immortality that the righteous will inherit.[14]

In Psalm 16 David seeks his refuge in God. Does the deliverance of God last only for the duration of this life? As he nears the end of the Psalm he speaks of his soul not being abandoned to Sheol, and not seeing corruption. On the contrary, he praises God, saying, "You make known to me the path of life; in your presence there is fullness of joy; at your right hand are pleasures forevermore" (16:11). Psalm 49 goes further in drawing a distinction between "those who have foolish confidence," who go down to Sheol and remain there, and the psalmist himself: "But God will ransom my soul from the power of Sheol, for he will receive me" (49:13, 15).

There are also clear references to the body living again. Job, as he plumbs the bitter depths of his despair, also soars to dizzying heights and cries out,

> For I know that my Redeemer lives,
> and at the last he will stand upon the earth.
> And after my skin has been thus destroyed,
> yet in my flesh I shall see God,
> whom I shall see for myself,
> and my eyes shall behold, and not another. (Job 19:25–27)

In Isaiah 26:19 we read a prediction that seems crystal clear. "Your dead shall live; their bodies shall rise. You who dwell in the dust, awake and sing for joy! For your dew is a dew of light, and the earth will give birth to the dead." Johnston comments on this verse: "The imagery clearly envisages the personal resurrection from death of at least some Israelites. Foreign oppressors will definitely not rise, but God's people clearly will. The application may be national, but the imagery presupposes a concept of individual resurrection."[15] We could not very well omit quoting Daniel 12:2 at this point: "And many of those who sleep in the dust of the earth shall awake, some to everlasting life, and some to shame and everlasting contempt."

It is nonetheless true that when we search the Old Testament Scriptures for clear and unmistakable references to immortality, or to a bodily resurrection, there is perhaps not as much material as we would like. All we have are glimpses and intimations. Yet this should really not surprise us. The Old Testament is partial and incomplete without the New. It awaits fulfillment; it awaits "our Savior Christ Jesus, who abolished death and brought life and immortality to light through the gospel" (2 Tim. 1:10).

What is the ultimate answer to the Sadducees' doubts? It is the resurrection of the Lord Jesus Christ himself. His own body would die and be laid in the tomb, but then he would come forth in a far more glorious resurrection body. Christ's resurrection is fruitful because by its power, he has secured the resurrection of all those who are in him. Hence what may *seem* to be lacking in the Old Testament is made more plain in the New Testament. The resurrection of Jesus Christ is the crowning climax to all four gospels. It is the great subject of apostolic preaching in the book of Acts. Psalm 16:11, referred to above, is demonstrated to be fulfilled in Jesus Christ (Acts 2:25–32). And Paul devotes one of the most thrilling chapters in the whole of Scripture to the subject of the resurrection, proving that Christ's own resurrection from the dead is the firstfruits of all who are united to him (1 Cor. 15).

"Frankly Supernatural"

B. B. Warfield (1851–1921), the scholar of Princeton Seminary, began one of his greatest, most magisterial works, *The Inspiration and Authority of the Bible*, with these magnificent words: "The religion of the Bible is a frankly supernatural religion."[16] It is precisely this that the Sadducees needed to hear. A denier of the Bible is a denier of the existence of supernatural realities. For the whole of Christianity, from beginning to end, is indeed "frankly supernatural."

Is it possible that the Christianity practiced by many of us is tainted with the doctrines of the Sadducees? Are we too earthbound? Are we characterized by somberness and doubt; are we generally burdened with a spirit of heaviness? Why might this be? Is it due to our failure to give any time at all to meditating on heaven? To set our minds on things above is no escapism, no burying of our heads in the sand. We ought not to believe those who say that "he's so heavenly minded he's of no earthly use." This is the slogan of a Sadducee. To be mindful of what lies ahead, in glorious, heavenly immortality, is the joyful privilege of Christian obedience.

I conclude with the words of Richard Baxter (1615–91), the great English Puritan, who underwent varying degrees of physical pain for the last forty years of his life. It made him more aware of the brevity of life and the certainty of death. From the age of about thirty-five he began a habit of meditating for half an hour each day on the glories of heaven, the results of which are seen in his great spiritual classic, *The Saints' Everlasting Rest*.

> Consider, a heavenly mind is a joyful mind: this is the nearest and the truest way to comfort; and without this you must needs be uncomfortable. Can a man be at the fire, and not be warm; or in the sunshine, and not have light? Can your heart be in heaven, and not have comfort? . . . What could make such frozen, uncomfortable Christians, but living so far as they do from heaven; and what makes others so warm in comforts, but their frequent access so near to God?[17]

9

CAIAPHAS THE HIGH PRIEST

So the chief priests and the Pharisees gathered the Council and said, "What are we to do? For this man performs many signs. If we let him go on like this, everyone will believe in him, and the Romans will come and take away both our place and our nation." But one of them, Caiaphas, who was high priest that year, said to them, "You know nothing at all. Nor do you understand that it is better for you that one man should die for the people, not that the whole nation should perish." He did not say this of his own accord, but being high priest that year he prophesied that Jesus would die for the nation, and not for the nation only, but also to gather into one the children of God who are scattered abroad. So from that day on they made plans to put him to death. (John 11:47–53)

JOHN'S GOSPEL is a journey marked by seven "signs," specific actions of Jesus in which his great purposes were unfolded. They begin at the wedding feast in Cana, where we are told that Jesus "manifested his glory. And his disciples believed in him" (John 2:11). The manifestation of the glory of Jesus Christ, and the faith of those who observed his works, were the purposes of these seven signs. Thus we see the Lord turning the water to wine, healing the official's son, causing a crippled man to walk, multiplying the loaves and fishes, walking on the waves of Galilee, restoring sight to a man born blind. Each of these displays the glory, the person, and the work of the Son of God, and each is given in order that men and women should put their trust in him.

THE RAISING OF LAZARUS AND ITS AFTERMATH

The seventh and last sign takes place in Bethany, just a few miles from Jerusalem, and probably only two or three months before Jesus' final entry into that city. In the raising of Lazarus from the dead, the great mission of the Savior is most clearly demonstrated—he has come to make known his power even over death. Jesus delays coming to Bethany for two days so that by the time he arrives, Lazarus has been in the tomb four whole days. This detail is significant, not only because his body is evidently decomposing, but because of the superstitious idea that "the soul of a deceased person hovers around the body for three days in the hope of reunion."[1] It is not that the Lord himself submits to this opinion, but the raising of Lazarus on the fourth day clears away any doubts from the minds of those who might have clung to this belief. Beyond controversy, Lazarus has been raised from the *dead!*

The occasion of this great seventh sign coincides with that majestic saying of Jesus to Lazarus' sister Martha:

> I am the resurrection and the life. Whoever believes in me, though he die, yet shall he live, and everyone who lives and believes in me shall never die. Do you believe this? (John 11:25–26)

The seven signs are preserved in John's gospel as the evidence that accompanies the seven "I am" sayings. Here are the mighty works of Jesus Christ; here are his mighty words. Do you believe this? This is the key question.

As we consider both the sign and the saying we are nearing our ultimate destination. The raising of Lazarus is our nearest approach to the empty tomb in the garden in Jerusalem a few months later—until we actually arrive there! The sign (Lazarus being raised from the dead) resembles the thing that is being signified (the resurrection of Jesus Christ himself from the dead) more than any sign that has previously been shown. What is more, the loud cry of Jesus, "Lazarus, come out," anticipates the day "when the dead will hear the voice of the Son of God, and those who hear will live" (John 5:25).

Understanding the gospel of Jesus Christ, understanding Jesus himself, depends on being able to read the signs accurately. The spiritual ability or inability to do so marks out the difference between Jesus' friends and his enemies.

UNDERSTANDING THE SIGNS

For this reason John gives a great deal of attention not only to the sign itself, but to the responses that accompanied it. The signs of Jesus typically resulted in a clear division between two groups of people—those who believed in Jesus and what he claimed, and those who did not. Examine the aftermath of some of the other signs and you will observe the same pattern.

It is important to see that *the skepticism toward Jesus did not center on the reality of the miracles themselves.* Our current age is still largely influenced by the modernism that denies the supernatural, but this was evidently not true of first-century Jews. This becomes obvious when we consider the actions of the five thousand who were fed by Jesus. The great majority of them came back the next day for more of the same. They had witnessed this miracle and had no difficulty in believing it. But Jesus shows most plainly that their interest was merely carnal and not spiritual. "Truly, truly, I say to you, you are seeking me, not because you saw signs, but because you ate your fill of the loaves" (John 6:26). That is, they witnessed the outward *miracle*, but they did not perceive the *sign*. Any human onlooker could have tasted of the bread and fish, and could have gone home and told his neighbors what he had eaten. But to observe the *sign*—that these actions demonstrate a great truth about this man Jesus Christ and a reason I must put my trust in him—was only possible for those who had spiritual eyes to see.

Some people today are agitated about the question of present-day miracles. Do they still occur, and if they do, why do they not occur more frequently, especially in our own experience? Underlying these questions is often an assumption that is quite mistaken. It goes something like this: "If my unbelieving friends and family saw a miracle, then they'd all become believers." The rich man in the parable in Luke 16:19–31 fell into this category. He wanted Lazarus to be sent back from the dead to warn his five brothers about the terrible place of torment in which he now found himself. But the great lesson of the parable is that even such a great miracle, in and of itself, does not generate faith. "If they do not hear Moses and the Prophets, neither will they be convinced if someone should rise from the dead" (Luke 16:31). Seeing miracles needed to be mixed with faith in the promises of God found in Scripture, or it accomplished nothing. The same is true today.

This is how we can understand what John goes on to say in 11:45–46.

> Many of the Jews therefore, who had come with Mary and had seen what he did, believed in him, but some of them went to the Pharisees and told them what Jesus had done.

The division between Jesus' friends and his enemies witnessed here is the outworking of Simeon's prophecy made when Jesus was an infant. This is "the fall and rising of many in Israel." Jesus is "a sign that is opposed" (Luke 2:34). There are many whose faith and trust in Jesus Christ has been strengthened by the raising of Lazarus. But let us not underestimate the bitterness of his opponents. One miracle too many has now taken place; this is the last straw. The ill will of Jesus' enemies is seen in this:

they go to the Pharisees to tell them what has happened. With this development, the final plot to destroy Jesus of Nazareth is now well and truly underway. A great meeting of the Sanhedrin is called.

THE SANHEDRIN AND THE HIGH PRIEST

The word *Sanhedrin* is Greek in origin and could be used to refer to any court of justice. There were "sanhedrins" in various Greek cities, such as Athens and Sparta, in the centuries before the birth of Christ. But in first-century Israel it was usually applied to the "Great Sanhedrin," the highest Jewish tribunal of all, which was composed of seventy-one members. In its first-century form it was of comparatively recent origin; the tradition that it was first founded by Moses and then reorganized by Ezra is not at all well established. The Sanhedrin in Jesus' day was fundamentally an aristocratic body, and it was composed of the high priest, who was its head, former high priests, members of high-ranking families from whom high priests had been drawn, as well as elders and scribes. It was made up of both Pharisees and Sadducees but, as we have seen, the real power in the Sanhedrin belonged to the Sadducees, from whom the high priests were chosen.

The office of high priest was, of course, one with an ancient and biblical pedigree. God himself had instructed Moses to anoint Aaron as Israel's priest, and his sons were to follow him. When we read what Aaron was instructed to do, we are reading the detailed stipulations that applied to the office of high priest. It is evident that the high priest of other Old Testament texts was the one who followed in Aaron's line. Hebrews 8:3 reminds us that "every high priest is appointed to offer gifts and sacrifices." It was the high priest alone who was permitted to go into the Most Holy Place on the annual Day of Atonement. It was Hilkiah the high priest who found the book of the law in the temple during the reign of godly king Josiah (2 Kings 22:8). And after the captives returned to Jerusalem from Babylon, the high priesthood was reinstated. Joshua the son of Jehozadak was high priest in the time of Haggai and Zechariah (Hag. 2:2–4).

But as the centuries went by, the office of high priest became an increasingly compromised political position. During the Maccabean period (164–63 BC), the high priest had been closely identified with the royal line. In the time of Herod the Great, unsurprisingly in view of that tyrant's paranoid character, the king sought to minimize the potential rivalry of the high priesthood by appointing men who "were of no eminent families, but barely of those that were priests."[2] When Judea passed into direct Roman rule after the deposition of Herod Archelaus in AD 6, the situation began to change and the Sanhedrin became a much more potent force in Israel. Josephus tells us that "the high priests were entrusted with a dominion over the nation" that effectively lasted until the siege of Jerusalem in AD 70.[3] As we encounter the Sanhedrin in the Gospels, then, we see it at the peak of its power, and the high priest was at the peak of the Sanhedrin. Annas was the first high priest appointed under the new jurisdiction. He was in office from AD 6 to 15. We know from John 18:13 that Caiaphas, the subject of this chapter, married Annas' daughter. It was a typical example of keeping the power of the high priesthood contained within one family.

CAIAPHAS

How much do we know about Caiaphas, the high priest who presided over this particular meeting and would later accuse Jesus of blasphemy and send him to Pontius Pilate? The answer is that there is little we can ascertain about him outside the New Testament itself. In 1990 a limestone ossuary was discovered bearing the simple inscription, in Aramaic, "Joseph son of Caiaphas," but its authenticity has been questioned.[4] Josephus says relatively little about Caiaphas. John mentions three times that Caiaphas was high priest "that year"

(11:49, 51; 18:13). Some have therefore drawn the conclusion that the high priesthood rotated from year to year, but this is incorrect. In fact Caiaphas was appointed high priest by the Roman governor Valerius in AD 18, and he was deposed from his position eighteen years later by another governor, Vitellus. All that John intends to say is that during this particular year, this most momentous of all years—probably AD 29 or 30—Caiaphas was the high priest.

But what about Annas? In John 18:19 he is himself referred to as the "high priest." Were there two competing claimants for that office? Any confusion can be cleared up by considering that according to strict Jewish law, Annas would indeed have been considered the legitimate high priest—it was an office which continued until death—but that Caiaphas had been appointed to that office by the ruling Roman authorities.

Caiaphas' personality, as depicted in the Gospels, was well suited to the political power play that characterized the functioning of the Sanhedrin in general, and the high priest in particular. His brusque and terse words to the Sanhedrin recorded in our text—"You know nothing at all" (John 11:49)—convey something of the abrasive, bullish character of the man. He was a man who was used to getting his own way. The arrest of Jesus was carried out by "a great crowd with swords and clubs" who had come from the chief priests (Matt. 26:47). When Jesus was before Annas, one of the officers struck him savagely, an action that was repeated when the apostle Paul was before another high priest a generation later. The whole trial of Jesus, of course, was to be a setup, a "kangaroo court," with the desired end being to accuse and condemn Jesus of blasphemy. And when that end was reached, Caiaphas tore his robes in a display of mock grief and sorrow (Matt. 26:65).

But what caused the Sanhedrin—this combination of chief priests, who were mainly Sadducees, and also some Pharisees—to meet in such a frenzy as they did after the raising of Lazarus?

POLITICAL ALARM

The answer is that all these men felt deeply threatened by the miraculous works and the consequent popularity of Jesus. They knew that they could not allow this "Nazarene" to keep performing signs, in case the whole nation rose up and followed him. The signs of Jesus, as we have already noted, provoked a great deal of controversy among these leaders. The Pharisees were scandalized when Jesus healed the man who was born blind, and all the more so at the suggestion that they, the Pharisees, were the ones who were truly blind (John 9:41)! The Sadducees surely would have been shaken by the raising of Lazarus and the implications in terms of a future resurrection—see the previous chapter—but this was not their main concern here.

Their anxieties would have been more political than theological. What kind of a stir would Jesus provoke among the Jewish people? Already in John's gospel there has been a report of an attempt to make Jesus king by force (John 6:15), in the aftermath of the feeding of the five thousand. So their fears were certainly not groundless. If the Roman authorities got wind of what was going on, if they feared that this Galilean preacher was at the head of a Jewish rebellion, then the precarious position of the Jews in Palestine would soon collapse utterly. The taking away of the "place" in John 11:48 surely refers to the temple in Jerusalem, which was first-century Judaism's center of gravity.

A little knowledge of subsequent Jewish history reveals that the Sanhedrin rightly gauged the political climate even though they were utterly unable to grasp Jesus' mission. The province of Judea was a hot spot in the Roman Empire throughout the first century, up to the terrible events of AD 66–70, which were an eventual fulfillment of the Sanhedrin's prophetic fears. The Jewish rebellion against Rome culminated in the siege of Jerusalem, the destruction of the temple, and the scattering of Jews in all directions. It is possible that over a million Jews were slaughtered at this time. Sixty years later, in 132, the Romanization of Jerusalem would be complete: the emperor Hadrian renamed the city *Aelia Capitolina*, and Jews were forbidden to enter it.

JESUS' KINGDOM NOT OF THIS WORLD

We need not ask whether the zealots in Israel, those who tried to make Jesus king by force at an earlier date, might have attempted to do so again. By God's providence this was never permitted to take place. What is absolutely clear is that Jesus himself never gave the remotest support to the view that he was a political agitator of this kind. He disavowed all suggestions of this kind when he was standing before Pontius Pilate and told him plainly, "My kingdom is not of this world." And then he went on to expand on this: "If my kingdom were of this world, my servants would have been fighting, that I might not be delivered over to the Jews. But my kingdom is not from the world" (John 18:36).

This is not the place for a detailed treatment of Jesus' relationship to earthly politics, still less for a study of the Christian attitude toward politics. We will comment a little more on this subject in Chapter 11, with Jesus' words to Pilate. It is enough for the time being to make a few general observations.

Both Paul, in Romans 13:1–7, and Peter, in 1 Peter 2:13–17, teach that every authority instituted among men has been established by God. Jesus himself both practiced submission to these authorities and taught others to do the same. When he was confronted with a question about the rightness of paying taxes, he acknowledged that Caesar, the supreme earthly ruler, was indeed owed revenue.[5] When the question of the half-shekel temple tax was raised, Jesus told Peter that in an absolute sense, the sons of the kingdom of God are free. Do sons ordinarily pay tax to their father the king? But Jesus provided for both himself and Peter to pay this tax, so as not to give any offense to those who were collecting it (Matt. 17:27).

The eternal Son of God humbled himself as he came into this world, and that involved being submissive to all human authority, though he himself was and is Lord of all. He calls upon his followers, themselves citizens of heaven, to emulate him in this regard. The whole course of Jesus' earthly life, especially the last days and hours, continually demonstrates this submissive attitude. When the appointed time came and he was arrested in the garden of Gethsemane, he went with his captors without struggle or complaint. Though he chose to remain silent throughout most of his trial, he answered Caiaphas when he adjured Jesus, by the living God, to say if he was indeed the Christ, the Son of God. He gave his back to those who struck him, and his face to those who pulled out his beard; he did not hide his face from shame and spitting. "When he was reviled, he did not revile in return; when he suffered, he did not threaten, but continued entrusting himself to him who judges justly" (1 Peter 2:23).

Thus it is entirely inconceivable that Jesus would ever have endorsed an armed struggle against the Roman authorities. He told Peter to put away his sword, for example, when he was arrested. The kingdom he had come to establish was spiritual, not earthly. But we can see that there were those in Israel who entirely misunderstood his mission, and therefore from the perspective of Caiaphas and the Sanhedrin, some degree of alarm was not surprising.

A MAN FOR ALL THE PEOPLE

So what was the best course of action for the Sanhedrin? It is in the midst of the ensuing commotion that Caiaphas spoke his abrupt, rough, and yet—as we shall see—prophetic words. "You know nothing at all. Nor do you understand that it is better for you that one man should die for the people, not that the whole nation should perish" (John 11:49–50). We need to ask what it was that Caiaphas intended by these words before we go on to consider their vastly broader, more momentous and eternal significance.

Caiaphas felt certain that the action of putting Jesus to death would stave off the danger of the Roman authorities clamping down on the Jews in the event of a rebellion. Leave Jesus alive, and the hysteria of those who follow him would reach fever pitch and foment all kinds of unrest of the kind to which Judea was prone. Put Jesus to death, and it should all quiet down. In the following chapter it becomes clear just how far the chief priests were prepared to go in order to quell such unrest. They made plans to put Lazarus to death as well, a man who had become an overnight celebrity and a living token of the power of Jesus! Hear the despairing cries of the Pharisees: "Look, the world has gone after him" (John 12:19).

But beneath the thin veil of this observation there was a seething mass of envy toward Jesus. Patriotism and national security may indeed have featured high in the religious leaders' minds. Yet surely it is also possible to see the root of bitter jealousy that drove them on toward their ultimate aim. Caiaphas and the members of the Sanhedrin—whether Sadducees or Pharisees—loved their own exalted position, the popularity and the praise of men. Here was a young man who drew vast crowds with his astonishing signs and teaching. Quite simply, the Sanhedrin could not bear this, and Caiaphas found a way to articulate this position in a manner that sounded reasonable: "it is better for you that one man should die for the people, not that the whole nation should perish" (John 11:50).

Caiaphas' plotting is reminiscent of the way King Saul schemed to get rid of his great rival, David son of Jesse. The king was inflamed with envy and sought all manner of ways in which to have David killed. The song of the women of Israel galled Saul and provoked this great malice. They sang, "Saul has struck down his thousands, and David his ten thousands" (1 Sam. 18:7). In a similar fashion, the Sanhedrin were provoked to murderous hatred by the crowds that followed Jesus everywhere.

Were Caiaphas' words in John 11:50 accurate—that is, in the sense in which he stated them? For although the Jews would continue to live in their national homeland for another forty years, their dwelling place, and Jerusalem in particular, would then be subjected to the most appalling destruction at the hands of the Romans, as we have already considered. The best we can say of Caiaphas' intention is that it might seem to buy the people, the whole nation, a little more time. In point of fact, however, the rejection and murder of Jesus by his own countrymen brought the wrath of God upon them (see Matthew 27:25). There will be further comment on this subject in chapter 15.

But who indeed are the "people"? Who are the "whole nation" of whom Caiaphas spoke? This leads us to consider the hidden, prophetic meaning of the high priest's words. Caiaphas knew exactly what he wanted to say, and he said exactly what he wanted to say. And yet he did not understand the full import of what he said, for the Lord, by his own overruling, invested Caiaphas' words with a meaning far above and beyond his comprehension. The words of Caiaphas were words of prophecy.

IS CAIAPHAS ALSO AMONG THE PROPHETS?

There seems at first glance something quite incongruous about this particular high priest, Caiaphas, engaged in the act of prophesying. Instinctively we associate prophecy with men (and women) of the Old Testament who truly stood in God's counsel, who knew God. We remember prophets of old who delivered their utterances, whether of promise or of judgment, in a spirit characterized by the love and the fear of God. Moses, Samuel, Elijah, and Jeremiah are four outstanding examples. Caiaphas, we would surely agree, does not appeal as a natural successor to such illustrious names.

However, the God who chooses to make his mind known by prophecy is not restricted in the individuals he chooses to use. What is more, although we have seen much that was ungodly and corrupt about Caiaphas' character, the fact remains that he was the high priest in Israel, and in this capacity he was divinely appointed and publicly recognized as one who stood between God and his people. When John speaks of Caiaphas' words as "prophecy," he is not employing a figure of speech. The God of Israel, who had instituted the office of high priest centuries before, while Moses and Aaron were in the wilderness, continued to make himself known through the same office, hideously compromised as it had become.

Caiaphas spoke of the need for Jesus to die, and his words sprang from motives that were calculatingly coldblooded. There was no sense in which his mind was elevated to some higher plane so that somehow he was given insight into the cosmic saving purposes of God through Jesus Christ. But those who know the saving work of God's Spirit, and who read Caiaphas' words in the Scriptures, are able to perceive the deeper meaning of the high priest's prophecy.

Yes, Jesus was about to die for the nation—and not only for that nation, but in order to gather into one people the scattered children of God. The stark difference between Caiaphas' intended meaning and the true meaning of the prophecy really hangs on the definition of the words *nation* and *people*. Caiaphas, with the great majority of the Jewish leaders, could think only in political terms. The "people" were national and political Israel. The Scripture, on the other hand, links the "nation" with the "children of God" who were "scattered abroad." In particular, throughout John's gospel, the "children of God" have been defined as those who believe that Jesus is the Christ, the Son of God. Together these two groups—the children of God belonging to the "nation," who were Jews, and the children of God who were "scattered abroad," the Gentiles—would form one spiritual body, the body which Jesus would bring into being by his death.

In short, the death of Jesus would result in the gathering of the worldwide church. Thus his own words would be fulfilled: "I have other sheep that are not of this fold. I must bring them also, and they will listen to my voice. So there will be one flock, one shepherd" (John 10:16).

A little further inquiry into biblical history will reveal that Caiaphas, a man with wicked intentions who functioned as the mouthpiece of God, was by no means unique. The most obvious parallel in the Old Testament is Balaam, who was hired by Balak, king of Moab, to curse the people of Israel. The great multitude had been marching through the wilderness, defeating Sihon, king of the Amorites, and Og, king of Bashan. Their military triumphs surely had to be halted before Moab fell prey to them, and thus Balaam the enchanter was pressed into service. It was with the greatest confidence that Balak called upon Balaam, for he said to him, "I know that he whom you bless is blessed, and he whom you curse is cursed" (Num. 22:6). But these words, which are so ironically similar to the words God first spoke to Abram when he called him, were to be overturned. God spoke to Balaam and told him, "You shall not curse the people, for they are blessed" (Num. 22:12). When at last Balaam opened his mouth to speak—having been hindered by the angel of the Lord and by his own donkey, which spoke to him!—he could not utter curses, only blessings, prophecies of the glories that God would bring to his people Israel. Balaam could do no other.

It was likewise with King Saul, as he was pursuing David like a "dead dog," like a "flea" (1 Sam. 24:14). In 1 Samuel 19, Saul's murderous attempts were foiled, first by Jonathan's counsel, then by Michal's deceit. Saul found out that David was staying with Samuel at Naioth, and he sent messengers to finish David off. But something strange happened: when these messengers reached Samuel they saw that he was with a company of prophets, prophesying, and these messengers were, in a manner which we cannot really understand, constrained to prophesy. After two more attempts, Saul himself came to Naioth, and . . . exactly the same phenomenon happened to him! "Is Saul also among the prophets?" (1 Sam. 10:11–12) Just how it was that the Spirit of God worked upon Saul's mind and emotions we are unable to tell. Neither do we know precisely what this prophesying meant, nor its content.

CONCLUSION

The wrath of man shall praise God, and even unregenerate, wicked men can be mouthpieces of the Lord. The most important point to notice is the invincible sovereignty of God, who will bring about events just at the time of his own choosing, and using his own appointed means. God would keep and shield his anointed servant from all the attacks of his enemies, until the time had come. And then the death of Christ would be the means by which all God's scattered children would be gathered into one body, the church of the Savior.

Jesus' enemies were now set firmly upon their course—this man must die. We now turn to look at the individuals and groups who played a key part during those busy and intense hours from Gethsemane to Calvary.

Judas Iscariot

Then when Judas, his betrayer, saw that Jesus was condemned, he changed his mind and brought back the thirty pieces of silver to the chief priests and the elders, saying, "I have sinned by betraying innocent blood." They said, "What is that to us? See to it yourself." And throwing down the pieces of silver into the temple, he departed, and he went and hanged himself. (Matt. 27:3–5)

THE BETRAYER is Judas' timeless and changeless epitaph—if indeed it is fitting to apply an "epitaph" to one who died as Judas did, for the scene of his departure became known as the "Field of Blood" (Matt. 27:8, Acts 1:19). The name of Judas will ever be associated with only betrayal and treachery. When someone acquires a nickname of "Judas" there can be no doubt as to what is being insinuated. The gospel records themselves, whenever they speak of Judas Iscariot, invariably refer to his identity as the betrayer of Jesus. The lists of the twelve apostles, which we find in Matthew 10:2–4, Mark 3:16–19, and Luke 6:14–16, each begin with the name of Simon Peter and each finish with the name of Judas Iscariot, the one who betrayed Jesus and became a traitor. There is a fourth list of the apostles in Acts 1:13, but by this stage, of course, Judas was no longer numbered among them. We are subsequently told that his camp became desolate and another filled his office. The betrayer had gone to "his own place" (Acts 1:25) and we hear no more of him in the remainder of the New Testament.

We might even go so far as to say that the words *Judas* and *betrayer* are virtually synonymous. I would not have known what the word *betray* meant had I not first encountered it in connection with Judas, and I suspect the same may be true of many other readers. Likewise, the meaning of the word *denial* was perhaps first made known to us through the account of Simon Peter's denial of Jesus.

The words *betray*, *betrayed*, and *betrayal* can be used in a variety of different contexts. We might, for example, say that someone's shaky and uncoordinated manners betray their nervousness. Or we may speak about the betrayal of a confidence, which might be inadvertent. But in the case of Judas, "betrayal" is a deliberate act of disloyalty and treachery. What makes Judas' actions so heinous is that he was a disciple, indeed a chosen apostle, of the one he betrayed. What makes his actions yet more appalling is that it was the Lord Jesus Christ, the one Judas called "Rabbi," whom he betrayed to his enemies.

Who was this betrayer, this traitor, this son of perdition? How did he ever become an apostle of Jesus in the first place? What clues to his character can we find as the gospel records unfold? And what lessons can we draw from his life—and his death?

Clues from His Life

The name *Judas* was common enough in Israel, being the name of one of the other apostles—the Judas (not Iscariot) of John 14:22. This particular apostle is referred to in the Synoptic Gospels as "Thaddeus." *Judas* is simply the Greek form of *Judah*, and we should not be surprised that this was a favorite name in Israel. After all, was not David descended from the tribe of Judah, from whom the scepter would never depart? The surname *Iscariot* is from the Hebrew "man of Kerioth." The exact location of Kerioth cannot be ascertained with any great certainty, though it probably corresponds to the Kerioth-hezron mentioned among the towns of Judah in Joshua 15:25. We know that Judas' father was named Simon (John 6:71; 13:26), but that is all we can specify about his family background.

Matthew and Luke deal with Judas' final end, but it is John alone who furnishes us with various glimpses of Judas at certain points in Jesus' ministry. The other gospels supply a record of Judas' call to be an apostle but do not mention him again until he approaches the chief priests in order to betray Jesus. We will consider a little of John's material because it provides necessary and fascinating insights.

The sixth chapter of John's gospel consists for the most part of a long discourse by Jesus that followed his fourth and fifth signs, respectively the feeding of the five thousand and his walking on the Sea of Galilee. A new day has dawned, and a great crowd has gathered to him, seeking more of the same. But to their great disappointment he does not repeat the miracle or entertain their nationalistic hopes as to the kind of prophet he is. Rather he speaks to them about his own identity as "the living bread which came down from heaven" (John 6:51).

SPIRITUALLY BLIND

The great majority of people there are spiritually blind to what Jesus is saying. They shake their heads in disbelief and confusion, and their earthbound hopes are dashed. His closing words to the crowd are these:

> It is the Spirit who gives life; the flesh is of no avail. The words that I have spoken to you are spirit and life. But there are some of you who do not believe. (John 6:63–64)

Then follows the remarkable explanation: "For Jesus knew from the beginning who those were who did not believe, and who it was who would betray him" (v. 64). Therefore it is quite clear that

Jesus had Judas Iscariot in mind as he spoke these words. Judas was unspiritual, carnal, a man who did not believe in Jesus as the Messiah.

The chapter closes with what we might call a "reverse exodus" of many one-time followers of Jesus. Like their forefathers in the wilderness, they are dissatisfied with "the bread that came down from heaven"—for Jesus himself is that bread (John 6:41). They are effectively turning back to Egypt. Judas could have gone back with these crowds—that would have been quite fitting—but he remains. Twice more Jesus effectively gives Judas an opportunity to leave. The Twelve are asked, quite openly, "Do you want to go away as well?" (John 6:67). In passing we might note that few people today would advocate an evangelistic technique like that!

Then, following Peter's wonderful profession of faith in Christ, Jesus tells them that one of the Twelve is a devil (6:70–71). Does Judas know that this description applies to him? Yet he chooses to stay with the disciples. What made him decide to do so? Pure and spiritual motives, the desire to deny himself and follow Jesus by carrying the cross, must be ruled out.

Another episode involving Judas provides further clues. At the beginning of John 12 the scene has shifted to Bethany, the home of Mary, Martha, and Lazarus, all of whom are mentioned in this account. It is just six days before the Passover feast, during which Jesus will be tried and crucified, and a dinner is being held. Martha, true to form, is serving the meal, while Mary, still sitting at Jesus' feet, anoints them with a fragrant and expensive perfume. Judas is outraged—what an irresponsible waste of such a precious commodity! This could have fetched three hundred denarii and that money could be given to the poor. To our ears, Judas' objection may smack of plausibility. Many today are still trying to "make poverty history." But he is shown to be a fraud, his protestations of concern for the poor to be a hypocritical sham. As the keeper of the disciples' purse, Judas had slippery fingers. He was motivated by selfish greed to the point of dishonesty, which of course goes a long way toward explaining his actions in betraying Jesus.

Quite incapable of genuine spiritual affection toward Jesus, even at this late hour in his ministry, Judas is moved only by carnal, self-centered considerations. Therefore he can only look on with incredulity as Mary of Bethany carries out her act of devotion to Jesus. He shakes his head in bewilderment and disbelief, and Jesus' subsequent words about his own burial leave Judas quite cold.

SON OF DESTRUCTION

It is clear that Jesus knew of Judas' character and treachery long before the actions of betrayal took place. We have seen this in the express declaration that one of the chosen Twelve was a "devil." What is more, Judas' betrayal of Jesus is shown to be a specific fulfillment of prophecy. In John 17, in what is widely known as Jesus' High Priestly Prayer, he speaks thus of his twelve apostles: "While I was with them, I kept them in your name, which you have given me. I have guarded them, and not one of them has been lost except the son of destruction, that the Scripture might be fulfilled" (John 17:12). In this verse we see the only shadow that darkens this brilliant chapter, and yet even this is a key link in the chain of God-ordained events during which Christ's work of salvation will be executed.

The word for *destruction* can be variously understood as "perdition," "ruin," or even "hell." That Judas was the "son of destruction" is a typically Jewish way of saying that Judas was destined for destruction, that his character and purpose were directed toward that end.[1] The same description, "son of destruction," occurs in 2 Thessalonians 2:3, where Paul speaks about the "man of lawlessness" who will be revealed at the last time. As to the precise identity of this later figure we are necessarily uncertain. But it is striking to consider that Judas partakes of the same essential character—ruin and destruction. Just what Scripture did the Lord Jesus have in mind as he uttered the words of this verse? There is no accompanying explanation in the immediate context, as there often is elsewhere, to the effect that these words fulfilled a specific prophecy of the Old Testament.

However, we do not need to look far in order to find one. Back in 13:18 Jesus, having washed his disciples' feet and spoken about the blessedness that the disciples will themselves know in doing the same, adds this warning: "I am not speaking of all of you; I know whom I have chosen. But the Scripture will be fulfilled, 'He who ate my bread has lifted his heel against me.'" Most evidently Jesus is alluding to Psalm 41:9: "Even my close friend in whom I trusted, who ate my bread, has lifted his heel against me." This Psalm, written by David, speaks of the eventual triumph of God's anointed servant, but before this time comes he is surrounded by enemies on every side. Wicked men plot his ruin and delight to anticipate his end, but the bitterest enmity is that which comes from a familiar friend, a sharer in table fellowship. C. H. Spurgeon says of this lifting up of the heel, "Not merely turned his back on me, but left me with a heavy kick such as a vicious horse might give. Hard it is to be spurned in our need by those who formerly fed at our table."[2]

It was the intention of God's providence that Judas Iscariot should not slink away with the crowds when so many others did after the discourse about the bread that comes down from heaven. Rather, God purposed that Judas stay with the disciples, in order that he might deliver this savage final blow against his Master, so that the Scripture might be fulfilled. Indeed, we must conclude that Judas was first chosen as one of the Twelve for this precise purpose. That is why he is always referred to as the betrayer, the traitor. This betrayal had to be carried out by a close friend, a table companion of Jesus.

Nevertheless, it should be absolutely understood that Judas Iscariot acted as a free agent in his determination to hand Jesus over to the chief priests. Matthew, in his account of the anointing at Bethany, mentions neither Mary's name nor Judas'. It is the disciples, mentioned collectively, who are recorded as having shown indignation at the apparent waste of the perfume. But it is interesting to note that the very next section of Matthew's gospel (26:14–16) recounts Judas' clandestine meeting with the authorities. It was there that the payment to be given to Judas was not only agreed, but actually transacted—thirty pieces of silver. The mutual understanding was that Judas would betray Jesus at the most convenient opportunity, and that he would do so soon.

The chief priests must have been surprised and delighted by the approach of Judas. The intention to lay hands on Jesus and seek to condemn him to death had been in his enemies' minds from an early stage in his ministry. Who could be a better informer than an insider, one of these twelve privileged disciples! They must have felt that it was safe to pay Judas before the deed was committed; he would scarcely back out if the transaction had taken place and the money was in his pocket. The value of the "thirty pieces of silver" cannot easily be reckoned in today's money. The precise amount is specified because this detail was also a fulfillment of Old Testament prophecy, in this case Zechariah 11:12–13. However, it was also the price set upon a male or female slave gored by an ox (Ex. 21:32). Judas took his pay with him; these thirty coins meant more to him than his Master, with whom he had spent the last two or three years.

Why did he do it? Was it simply greed for "filthy lucre," the most appalling exhibition of the depth of evil into which the love of money can lead a man? Was there, in Judas' mind, a sense of disappointment that Jesus did not prove to be the type of messiah that the people of Israel were awaiting? Was he jealous because Peter, James, and John seemed to be the privileged ones while he,

Judas, seemed to have no chance of attaining membership in that favored inner circle? Was he afraid of the impending persecution that Jesus had frequently promised for those who follow him? All these motives may well have played a part. Regarding his greed, we have seen the clear evidence from the Gospels.

"And It Was Night"

But there is a more fundamental explanation. The bottom line was that Judas had a heart that was untouched and unmoved by the grace of God. What appeal would a *spiritual* Messiah have to such a man? Why would Judas, hard-hearted as Pharaoh, have any desire to take up his cross and follow Jesus to a life of suffering and rejection by the world? Luke and John probe even deeper and tell us that Judas' decision to go to the chief priests was as a result of the specific activity of Satan (Luke 22:3; John 13:2, 27). A "devil" as he had been for some time, now Judas was entered by the Devil himself. John's account is particularly poignant: the departure of Judas from Jesus and the other eleven is signaled by the comment "it was night" (13:30). It was indeed the hour of darkness, the hour of apparent triumph for Jesus' enemies.

In passing, notice that Judas left the company of disciples just as Jesus was about to take the other disciples into what Charles Ross calls *The Inner Sanctuary*.[3] That last, most exalted discourse of Jesus, which drew back the curtain to allow the disciples to view the glorious mysteries of the Holy Trinity itself and culminated in the High Priestly Prayer of Jesus, was uttered in the absence of Judas the traitor. Judas went about the business of the night, while the disciples in the upper room basked in glory and brightness hitherto unseen on earth.

It is as the instrument of Satan, a man in whose heart is spiritual midnight, that Judas procures a band of soldiers from the chief priests and makes his way over the Kidron Valley into the garden of Gethsemane. It is with the most devastating irony and hypocrisy that he identifies Jesus with a kiss. It is the uttermost pretense of true love and affection, when he is poised to deliver Jesus over to his enemies. Such irony has a good deal of precedent in the Scriptures. Cain had invited his brother Abel to go out into the field with him before he killed him; Absalom invited his half-brother Amnon to a feast, wining and dining him before ordering his murder; Naboth was set at the head of the people before he was slain by the order of wicked Queen Jezebel.[4] Evil often masquerades as kindness; it is of the very essence of evil to assume an innocent appearance, as it was from the beginning. Judas' kiss was the most galling episode of duplicity that has ever taken place.

UNBEARABLE PAIN

We read nothing more of Judas in any of the gospel accounts, until we come to the concluding, chilling episode of his life. Matthew and Luke (in Acts 1:15–26) record his final end. Of course there are differences between these two accounts, but the differences have sometimes been exaggerated. I can recall how, as a new believer, fresh, hungry, and excited at university, I was somewhat crestfallen when an older student told me categorically that the two accounts are evidently contradictory! But there is really no such difficulty. The money that Judas threw on the floor of the temple was later taken by the priests for the purchase of the field, as Matthew describes, but in reality this was Judas' purchase, as Luke states in Acts, because the money had been paid to Judas. As regards the way in which Judas died, there is nothing implausible about him hanging himself and then, subsequently, the rope being loosed and his body falling to the ground, with the unpleasant consequences described in Acts 1:18.

Over the course of that long, dark night, Judas underwent an about-face—yet, as we shall see, he fell short of genuine repentance. At what point did his mind change; when did his conscience begin to accuse him? It was at the very point when he realized that Jesus had been condemned and led away from the Sanhedrin to Pontius Pilate. It is impossible to say with certainty whether the possibility of condemnation and death had really registered with Judas before this point. His own greed and selfish scheming had surely blinded his mind to that potential outcome. Here is another example of the deceitfulness of sin. It says in Psalm 36:2 of the wicked man that "he flatters himself in his own eyes that his iniquity cannot be found out and hated." When sinners are set upon a wicked course of action, as in the case of David with Bathsheba and Uriah, the consequences they might face seem remote. Sin, especially greed and lust, makes a man intoxicated with the immediate reward that he perceives to be waiting for him.

But now, in the cold light of day, Judas became horribly aware of what his actions had caused. He had been carried along upon a wave of vicious excitement but had never soberly anticipated the endgame. Now plagued with regret, he came back to the chief priests and informed them of his change of mind. Was it those final words of Jesus to him, "Judas, would you betray the Son of Man with a kiss?" (Luke 22:48), that tormented him the most? Perhaps when they were first uttered they meant little to Judas, but now, as the horrifying import of what he did loomed large upon his conscience, the pain became unbearable.

WORLDLY GRIEF AND GODLY GRIEF

It is very instructive to note that we are not told that Judas ever repented. The verb used in Matthew 27:3 implies that there was regret, a change of mind and intent, but the usual Greek word for repentance, *metanoia*, and other related words are nowhere present. There is such a thing as a deep and agonizing sorrow that does not result in godly, spiritual repentance. The actions of Judas in throwing down the money and then going to hang himself surely indicate that he was not performing a charade. He was a desperately broken, anguished, tortured individual, as surely as are so many other people who choose to take their own lives. Furthermore, it is clear that Judas sorrowed over his own sin. Does he not say so? "I have sinned by betraying innocent blood."

Yet the experience of feeling acute pain and grief because of sin—not merely the *consequences* of sin, but the sin itself—is not necessarily the prelude to true, evangelical repentance, where the sinner is brought through the darkness to see the light and glory of God's free grace in Jesus Christ. In 2 Corinthians 7:10 Paul concisely summarizes the distinction between sorrow that leads to repentance and sorrow that does not. "For godly grief produces a repentance that leads to salvation without regret, whereas worldly grief produces death." Paul's own letter to the Corinthian church had made the people grieve; however, it was not grief alone that Paul sought, but a grief that became the springboard to true repentance.

In his *Pilgrim's Progress* John Bunyan describes how Christian, having entered the House of the Interpreter, encounters the man in the Iron Cage, an individual whose spiritual experiences have been much discussed. This wretched soul cries out thus: "I am now a Man of Despair, and am shut up in it, as in this Iron Cage. I cannot get out; O, now I cannot."[5] Many readers of Bunyan have been puzzled and alarmed by this description. Can a sinner ever be in such a desperate state that he is literally beyond redemption, having sinned away his day of grace? Is it possible for someone in that state to speak as this man did? We must remember, of course, the allegorical character of Bunyan's writing, and there are other details applied to the Man in the Iron Cage that do not apply to Judas Iscariot.

Nevertheless I believe we can answer these two questions. Yes, a sinner can be in such a state that he is beyond God's saving grace; but no, someone in such a condition would not be able to say, as this man did, "God hath denied me repentance; his Word gives me no encouragement to believe."[6] To understand this correctly we need to appreciate the difference between human history, lived and experienced, on the one hand, and allegory that seeks to describe a reality that the person himself could not express, on the other. To put it more simply, it was quite true that the Man in the Iron Cage had been denied repentance. But no historical, living person in that condition would ever actually say this!

Judas was evidently in this condition, being designated for destruction. There were pain, sorrow, and grief, but these did not lead to the repentance that would in turn lead to restoration. The substance of his agony was his own terrible, overwhelming sin that engulfed him.

I write these things in case there are souls reading this book who have become genuinely troubled and alarmed. Trouble and alarm, at some point in our experience, are normally necessary experiences in order that we will flee to Jesus Christ for safety. This is the question that such people need to answer: in your pain and distress, do you realize that God, in Jesus Christ, is gracious to every sinner who repents? Worldly grief, which leads to death, was as far as Judas ever travelled. But godly grief, which leads to repentance, is what the Scriptures direct us toward. Worldly grief looks inside our own sinful, guilty souls and can see no way out. But godly grief, having looked inside—and shuddered—goes further and sees God's glorious and gracious provision for all sin in the blood of Jesus Christ.

JUDAS AND PETER: A CONTRAST

The example of Simon Peter will help to bring this out more clearly. There are clear parallels between Peter and Judas that we can observe. The narratives of Peter's denial of Jesus and Judas' betrayal, in all four gospels, are closely intertwined. Is this not deliberate on the part of the Author? Both are predicted by Jesus; in both cases Jesus' prediction meets with intense dismay on the part of the disciples. Both took place in the cold, dark night. Both were sinful actions, and both led to intense pain and regret on the part of the two disciples who were responsible.

The more we investigate, however, the more contrasts we find. Judas acted with a "high hand," in cold blood, in calculated treachery, whereas Peter's terrible lapse was a case of sheer cowardice in the face of danger, following his earlier bravado. His spirit capitulated to the weakness of his flesh. Judas had been scheming for some time, allured by the possibility of material reward. Peter panicked when caught in the headlights; his blurted-out words being in some ways reminiscent of his unknowing speech on the Mount of Transfiguration.

But there are deeper, far more important contrasts between these two men, and they have to do with the divine purpose being worked out with each of them. The grace of God in Jesus Christ worked mightily upon Peter, whereas the same grace was not operative in Judas. Jesus told Peter that Satan was asking to take him and sift him like wheat. He would be the designated target of a specific attack from the Devil. So too, of course, was Judas, as we have seen. But the Lord tells Peter, even before he has committed these denials, that he had already prayed for him to be restored and ultimately strengthen the brothers (Luke 22:31–32).

What grace from the Savior, and what gracious timing as well! Thus it was, as Luke alone tells us, that "the Lord turned and looked at Peter" after the third denial (Luke 22:61). It was a look of reproach that caused Peter to retreat into the darkness and weep longer and more bitterly than he ever had before. And yet it was surely also a look that must have reminded Peter that his Master's love and grace had not been taken from him. Did that lessen the extent of Peter's grief and pain? Clearly not, but throughout this dark and terrible season of Peter's soul, the loving-kindness of his Savior was never relinquished. We see it, most movingly, in the words of the angel on resurrection morning. Peter was singled out from all of the disciples—the great and glad tidings were to be relayed especially to him (Mark 16:7). And, of course, we see it in that most touching of all biblical narratives, the exchange between the Lord and Peter on the shores of Galilee (John 21:15–19).[7]

As for Judas, no words of grace had been spoken to him, neither was a comforting look directed toward him in his darkest hour. Judas' terrible remorse is marked by the absence of Jesus. He cannot find a gracious Savior. There is only hopeless despair, and so it is that Judas takes his own life and goes to "his own place" (Acts 1:25).

What is "his own place"? In the words of James Alexander, "various efforts have been made to escape from the obvious but fearful sense of these words."[8] Do these brief words refer to the field that Judas bought with his own money? Do they refer, not to Judas himself, but to Matthias, Judas' replacement, who took Judas' "own place"? These two explanations are respectively evasive and confusing. It is clear that Judas *went* somewhere, to a place where the other apostles did not go. As we have seen before, this disclosure of the Savior in the upper room was made in Judas' absence. In particular, the "place" that Jesus was going to prepare for the eleven disciples—and, surely, countless others from all generations and lands—was not to be Judas' own place. Judas' place would be one where the hopelessness and despair of his last hours would be perpetuated for all eternity.

PREDESTINATION OR FATALISM

Some readers may well struggle to accept the implications of all this teaching. Did Judas have no choice in this matter; was he merely fodder for destruction? Was he the King's pawn thrust out into the fourth rank, into the thick of the fighting, just as Uriah was sent by David? Was he simply programmed by his Creator to carry out the treacherous act of betrayal, after which he would quickly be hastened on to self-destruction?

In dealing with this subject, we must not confuse the sovereign decree of God, his predestination, with an impersonal fatalism. What is the difference between them? The chief answer, as far as we are concerned, is that *fatalism overlooks personal responsibility*. It effectively says *Que sera sera*. But the Christian understanding of God's decree takes into account, most carefully and soberly, the free and willing actions of the creatures whom God has made. The Westminster Confession, in the first paragraph of its third chapter, "Of God's Eternal Decree," puts this magnificently:

> God from all eternity, did, by the most wise and holy counsel of His own will, freely, and unchangeably ordain whatsoever comes to pass; yet so, as thereby neither is God the author of sin, nor is violence offered to the will of the creatures; nor is the liberty or contingency of second causes taken away, but rather established.

The second part of this statement illustrates the clear difference between impersonal fate and the biblical doctrine of the divine decree. To put it a little more simply, Judas was entirely responsible. He was not moved against his will. His actions were entirely free insofar as he chose to do just as he did.

The biblical teaching on divine predestination is not supplied in order to furnish material for scholarly speculation. It is given for the comfort and assurance of God's own people. For in his great prayer Jesus stated that "the son of destruction" would be the only one of the disciples who would not be kept and guarded by him. The other eleven disciples, hearing this, would have been confirmed in the security of their standing; they were indeed those whom the Father had given to the Son. All of God's elect rejoice because they know that from first to last, the author of their salvation is the triune God alone.

Thus with the greatest wisdom and insight, the Westminster Confession goes on to say, in the final paragraph of the same chapter, that the doctrine of this high mystery of predestination is to be handled with special prudence and care, that men, attending the will of God revealed in His Word, and yielding obedience thereunto, may, from the certainty of their effectual vocation, be assured of their eternal election. So shall this doctrine afford matter of praise, reverence, and admiration of God; and of humility, diligence, and abundant consolation to all that sincerely obey the Gospel.[9]

PONTIUS PILATE

*Jesus answered, "My kingdom is not of this world. If my
kingdom were of this world, my servants would have been
fighting, that I might not be delivered over to the Jews.
But my kingdom is not from the world." Then Pilate said
to him, "So you are a king?" Jesus answered, "You say
that I am a king. For this purpose I was born and for this
purpose I have come into the world—to bear witness to
the truth. Everyone who is of the truth listens to my voice."
Pilate said to him, "What is truth?" (John 18:36–38)*

SOONER OR LATER we had to come to Pontius Pilate. After
all, he was the Roman governor who was ultimately responsible
for the crucifixion of Jesus. But is it wholly fair to label Pilate
one of Jesus' "enemies"? The testimony of two thousand years
of history has provided no clear unanimity on this question, for
various sources and traditions give widely diverging responses
to the part played by Pilate in Jesus' condemnation.

The Apostles' Creed and the Nicene Creed, venerable documents of the ancient church, both specify that Jesus suffered
under Pontius Pilate. On initial reading this may seem to give the
impression that Pilate was chiefly responsible for the crucifixion
of Jesus. However, these creedal statements also serve another
purpose, namely to emphasize that Jesus suffered physical death

at a certain time in history, at the hands of a specific Roman governor. The genuine humanity of Jesus and his actual death at a certain point in time and space are thereby established. This was an important truth to affirm in the early centuries of the Christian era, when various forms of Docetism—the heretical teaching that Jesus only *appeared* to be human—needed firm rebuttal. Nevertheless, Pilate's name remains inscribed upon these documents as it were in letters of red, so that his central part in Jesus' death is recited by people around the world every week. Without Pilate's command, Jesus could not have been crucified.

In sharp contrast, the Ethiopian Orthodox Church went so far as to declare, in the sixth century, that Pilate was a saint, and they even assigned him his own saint's day, on June 25.[1] However, this assessment of Pilate is largely based upon an apocryphal book that has been known variously as the *Acts of Pilate*, the *Gospel of Pilate*, and even the *Gospel of Nicodemus*; the contents are evidently a fanciful and imaginative embellishment of the scriptural record and can safely be dismissed.

THE RELUCTANT ENEMY

Where are we to place Pontius Pilate? The Lord Jesus himself seemed to go some way toward exculpating him when he told him that "he who delivered me over to you has the greater sin" (John 19:11). Surely Jesus is referring here to the high priest Caiaphas, who pronounced him guilty of blasphemy and sent him to Pilate. Later, when Peter addressed the crowds in Solomon's Portico, after the healing of the lame man, he appeared to draw a distinction between the lesser guilt of Pilate and the far greater guilt of the Jewish authorities. He told them, "You delivered over and denied [Jesus] in the presence of Pilate, when he had decided to release him. But you denied the Holy and Righteous One, and asked for a murderer to be granted to you" (Acts 3:13–14). The malice and murder directed against Jesus had come from his own countrymen.

It is Pilate's hesitation, his terrible crisis of conscience, that makes it difficult to decide what to do with him. We should certainly allow that he was a most reluctant enemy of Jesus. Like several other characters in the Bible, he is one of the "nearly men." Herod Antipas—whom we will discuss much more in the following chapter—could have become a hero by renouncing his foolish oath and refusing to behead John the Baptist. Felix trembled when he heard the apostle Paul, and King Agrippa, before the same prisoner, seems to have come close to being persuaded of the Christian faith. These men *nearly* made it, but in the end they fell short. The same is true of Pilate. What would have happened, for example, if he had responded robustly to his wife's dream or to the fear that seized him when he heard that Jesus had "made himself the Son of God" (John 19:7)?

Speculation is fascinating but seldom profitable; we must deal with the record of what really took place, rather than what might have taken place. We will look first at the background of Pilate himself, and the most important fact about Pilate was that he was a Roman.

ROMAN GOVERNOR OF JUDEA

At the time in question, the Roman Empire was well on its way to achieving its greatest physical extent, most memorably described by Edward Gibbon as "the fairest part of the earth, and the most civilized portion of mankind."[2] True, Britain had not yet been conquered, but in those days she was a chilly, drizzly, fairly inconsequential outpost on the northwest frontier. For over two centuries Rome had been the dominant power throughout the Mediterranean world. The youthful days of the Roman Republic had passed; now the descendants of the great Caesar presided as emperors. Although the moral fiber of the Roman world—not least the families of the Caesars themselves—was already rotting to the core, there was no hint in anyone's imagination that the proud, majestic empire might one day collapse. The great Roman roads, together with the rule of the sea, permitted Rome's commercial activity. Above all, the power and efficiency of the Roman armies had secured their apparently impregnable position. The celebrated *Pax Romana* seemed to be not only an aspiration, but something approaching reality. The noted church historian Philip Schaff writes, "The Romans from the first believed themselves called to govern the world." And then, "having conquered the world by the sword, they organized it by law, before whose majesty every people had to bow."[3]

But how did Rome manage to cause the zealous, religious, troublesome people of Palestine to bow before their might and majesty and keep rebellion in check? For many years the answer to this question was simply the name and the power of one man, Herod the Great, whose brutal story is told in chapter 3. After the death of Herod, which must have occurred in or around 4 BC, the situation changed at once. His kingdom was divided into four territories, and consequently the ruler of each of these was given the title "tetrarch," meaning one of four rulers. However, the apparent simplicity of this setup was considerably complicated—as one would expect when dealing with Herod's line—by various considerations of history and politics. There were in fact only three rulers: Herod's son Archelaus ruled over Idumaea, Judea and Samaria; Archelaus' brother Herod Antipas was given Galilee and Perea; and their half-brother Philip received Ituraea and Trachonitis.[4]

Archelaus proved to be no less cruel than his father—early in his reign he massacred almost three thousand Pharisees—but he was less durable. When the Jews complained about his brutality to the Roman Emperor Augustus, Archelaus was deposed. This took place in AD 6, and from that time direct Roman rule was imposed on Judea. Four governors followed in relatively quick succession, the accumulated length of their ascendancies amounting to twenty years. They governed Judea, not from Jerusalem but from Caesarea on the Mediterranean coast.

Then came Pontius Pilate in AD 26. The contemporary authors Philo, Josephus, and Tacitus refer to him in their writings, but as with several other characters in our study, much about Pilate's origins still remains obscure. The name *Pontius* suggests that his lineage was from the people group known as the Samnites, who held territory in south-central Italy until the Romans overcame them early in the third century BC. Gaius Pontius, who resisted Roman aggression around this time, is referred to in connection with the so-called Battle of the Caudine Forks (321 BC) and was quite probably an ancestor of Pontius Pilate.

As for "Pilate" itself, opinion is rather more uncertain. The name may be derived from the Latin word *pileus*, which denotes a cap worn by a freedman; that is, a one-time slave who had been freed. So it is possible that Pilate himself was descended from a freed slave, but if this theory is true then it is likely that this ancestor was removed from him by several generations. Pilate is clearly portrayed as a Roman of exalted rank; the governorship of Judea was no minor undertaking. Indeed the extent of Pilate's authority was considerably greater than that of the governors who preceded him. Whereas their responsibility was largely fiscal, Pilate exercised full military and judicial authority in Judea.

With the rise of liberal biblical scholarship in the nineteenth century came a certain amount of skepticism surrounding the historical existence of Pilate, despite the testimonies of the contemporary historians listed above as well as the records in all four gospels. Then, in 1961, as so often in the twentieth century, archaeology silenced many critics of the Bible's reliability. Some Italian archaeologists, excavating the ancient theater in Caesarea, found the damaged remains of a limestone block containing a Latin inscription. Although the content of the entire inscription must remain uncertain, there is no doubt that it contains a dedication to Tiberius Caesar from "Pontius Pilate, Prefect of Judea." Since that discovery, quite unsurprisingly, doubts concerning the authenticity of Pilate have largely been silenced.

That title "Prefect," in Latin *praefectus*, was extremely common in the ancient Roman world, and it designated senior Roman officers in a variety of ranks and responsibilities. Another Latin term, *procurator*, is often used to designate the office Pilate held. But that title seems to have been more commonly used at a later date, and in any case the more familiar word *governor* is the preferred translation in English versions of the Bible.

CRUELTY AND CONSCIENCE

What can we say about the character of the man? The Gospels say nothing of Pilate's actions before the morning of the crucifixion, with one important exception. We read in Luke 13:1 that certain people told Jesus "about the Galileans whose blood Pilate had mingled with their sacrifices." This rather gruesome report suggests that Pilate had ordered the massacre of some Galileans whom he suspected to be seditious, and that the bloodletting had taken place while the Galileans were engaged in the very act of temple-worship. This atrocity, comments Alfred Edersheim, was "not mentioned by the Jewish historian Josephus, nor in any other historical notice of the time, either by Rabbinic or other writers. This shows, on the one hand, how terribly common such events must have been, when they could be so generally omitted from the long catalogue of Pilate's misdeeds against the Jews."[5]

Pilate was undoubtedly capable of very great cruelty, as would be expected of a Roman governor in an area of great political volatility. But he seems also to have had a penchant for trampling upon the religious sensibilities of the Jews, provoking them to extreme anger and then threatening violence if they failed to submit to his demands. Josephus records one such incident in the eighteenth book of his *Antiquities of the Jews*:

> Pilate, the procurator of Judea, removed the army from Caesarea to Jerusalem, to take their winter quarters there, in order

to abolish the Jewish laws. So he introduced Caesar's effigies, which were upon the ensigns, and brought them into the city; whereas our law forbids us the very making of images; on which account the former procurators were wont to make their entry into the city with such ensigns as had not those ornaments. Pilate was the first who brought those images to Jerusalem, and set them up there; which was done without the knowledge of the people, because it was done in the night time; but as soon as they knew it, they came in multitudes to Caesarea, and interceded with Pilate many days that he would remove the images; and when he would not grant their requests, because it would tend to the injury of Caesar, while yet they persevered in their request, on the sixth day he ordered his soldiers to have their weapons privately, while he came and sat upon his judgment-seat, which seat was so prepared in the open place of the city, that it concealed the army that lay ready to oppress them; and when the Jews petitioned him again, he gave a signal to the soldiers to encompass them routed, and threatened that their punishment should be no less than immediate death, unless they would leave off disturbing him, and go their ways home.[6]

However, Josephus goes on to say that

they threw themselves upon the ground, and laid their necks bare, and said they would take their death very willingly, rather than the wisdom of their laws should be transgressed; upon which Pilate was deeply affected with their firm resolution to keep their laws inviolable, and presently commanded the images to be carried back from Jerusalem to Caesarea.[7]

This incident is well worth noting because it resonates somewhat with what we read of Pilate in the gospel records. Here was ruthless intent tempered by a nagging conscience, and perhaps by a certain degree of superstition. With this in mind, we now turn to Pilate's dealings with the Jewish priests who brought Jesus to him, and with Jesus himself.

"What Accusation Do You Bring against This Man?"

Although Pilate would usually have resided in Caesarea, the Jewish feasts, especially the Passover, witnessed vast crowds in Jerusalem with the potential for considerable unrest, so Pilate removed his headquarters there. The likelihood is that Pilate would have resided in Herod the Great's palace, while the Roman military presence was stationed at the nearby Antonia Fortress.

It was very early in the morning when Pilate was met by Jesus' accusers. In view of his tendency to despise the Jews and their customs, it is significant to read that he agreed to venture out of his headquarters to meet them, on account of their desire not to contract ceremonial defilement on the day of the Feast (John 18:28–29). Presumably Pilate had learned, by experience, that refusal to comply would only have stalled the problem. We may also detect the signs of wariness on Pilate's part; if there were a crisis that had the potential to develop into a full-blown drama, then it needed quelling at the earliest opportunity.

Nevertheless, the exchange that followed between Pilate and the chief priests reveals the differences in the way the two parties operated, and something of the mistrust between them. Pilate wanted to know what specific charge was being brought against Jesus. There is no doubt that he was well aware of Jesus and his followers and of the great stir that was taking place in Jerusalem. The arrest in the garden of Gethsemane could hardly have taken place without Pilate's knowledge, or even without his permission. He knew very well that the chief priests regarded Jesus as a troublemaker, but in order to conform with Roman law, he had to determine the precise nature of the charge against Jesus.

The chief priests did not specify any details at this stage; their accusation was rather vague. Basically, this Jesus was a troublemaker as far as they were concerned. We can sense their impatience; would they have brought a man to Pilate unless they themselves were convinced of his guilt? Pilate, anxious to be involved as little as possible, responded rather curtly, "Take him yourselves and judge him by your own law" (John 18:31).

Now the controversy really heated up, because the priests were determined that Jesus had to die, and in order to achieve their end they needed to secure the consent of Rome—indeed of Pilate himself. It would be to their great advantage if Rome were to be seen as ultimately responsible for Jesus' death. Nothing could be a more certain seal and vindication of their own pronouncements about Jesus. More pointedly, only the Roman governor could authorize death by crucifixion. The subsequent baying of the mob, "Crucify him!," surely indicates that Jesus' accusers had this particular accursed death in mind. It would be the most fitting judgment upon a blasphemer, "because anyone who is hung on a tree is under God's curse" (Deut. 21:23 NIV). Indeed, peering a little more deeply into John's gospel, we can see that "death by crucifixion would fulfill what Jesus had indicated would take place" (John 12:32, 3:14).[8] The Son of Man had to be lifted up from the earth.

The question Pilate puts to Jesus, "Are you the King of the Jews?," is recorded in all four gospel accounts, and this great question really takes us to the heart of the matter.

THE TWO KINGDOMS

Pontius Pilate is a perceptive, streetwise fellow. He has not reached his position of authority without having a certain amount of gumption. It has always been clear to him that the Jewish leaders handed Jesus over to him out of envy (Mark 15:10). Luke details some rather specific charges that they have brought against Jesus: that he leads the nation astray, that he forbids the payment of taxes to Caesar, and that he calls himself Christ, a king (Luke 23:2). Pilate surely knows, as do we, that these accusations have been maliciously distorted. He can see that Jesus in and of himself presents no threat to Roman rule and law. This

Galilean is completely harmless. Yet Pilate is intrigued by this particular matter of kingship. What exactly does Jesus mean?

The ensuing conversation is the most fascinating episode in the whole Pilate narrative. It is here that the two great concepts of kingship—the worldly and the spiritual—come into sharp contrast. The theme of Jesus as king, in particular the "King of the Jews," recurs throughout the proceedings that follow. It is by this title that Pilate refers to Jesus publicly, again and again. It these terms that the soldiers used to revile him so cruelly, with purple robe, crown of thorns, and mocking charades of reverence. It was the substance of the written charge that Pilate ordered to be set above Jesus' head on the cross, to the consternation of his accusers.

Would that this conversation between Pilate and Jesus had gone on longer, and that Pilate—instead of dismissing Jesus with an irritated, shoulder-shrugging "What is truth?"—had been able to inquire more deeply into the meaning of his words! Notice how the Lord himself, though he is officially "in the dock," is clearly determining the direction of the conversation. Furthermore, notice that Jesus, who maintained silence with the chief priests and with Herod, is quite prepared to speak to Pilate.

To Pilate's direct question, "Are you the King of the Jews?," Jesus does not immediately give a direct reply. He wants to know whether the governor's question arises out of his own concerns, or out of those of the Jewish priests. Pilate's impatience is not hard to detect; he wants to get quickly to the root of the charge. Just what has Jesus done that has led the chief priests to request the death penalty?

Now, for the first time, Jesus refers to his own kingdom. His initial description of his kingdom is a negative one. His kingdom is not of this world (John 18:36). Its origin and character are wholly different from every earthly kingdom, every type of kingdom that Pilate has ever heard of. It is for this reason that William Hendriksen preferred the word "kingship" to "kingdom" in his own translation.[9] Jesus' kingship is not earthly or "political" in the commonly understood sense. Every earthly king has a number of men under him, to guard him and wage war against his enemies. If Jesus had been such a king, then he would have marshaled his disciples against the Jews. But the very reverse had happened. When Peter drew his sword against Malchus, the high priest's servant, and cut off his ear, Jesus rebuked him and told him to put his sword away (John 18:11).

A short digression may be called for here. The kingdom of God is not to be identified with or confused with any earthly kingdom. Whenever this key distinction has not been observed, great harm has been done to the cause of the gospel. The church of the first three centuries knew that the Roman emperor, like all governing authorities, was appointed by God, and therefore they were subject to him (Rom. 13:1). They would render to Caesar what belonged to Caesar, out of reverence to God, as we have already seen in chapter 9. But Caesar had no authority in the church of God. The secular realm and the spiritual realm were kept quite distinct, and for that reason the early church continued in relative moral and spiritual purity during these centuries. The accession of Constantine to the throne of the Caesars, followed by his fabled conversion in 312, changed everything. From that time on the church and the state became increasingly identified with one another. From that confusion sprang the abuses and tragedies that beset the medieval church, including the Crusades and the papacy. Even the Protestant Reformation did not wholly deal with this issue. The concept of "Christendom," in its various guises, has still not been shaken off today.[10]

Let us return to the matter at hand. Pilate needs to press on with the interrogation. Jesus' description of his own kingdom has puzzled Pilate, but he needs to make absolutely sure that he has the answer he needs. "So you are a king?" Now it is time for Jesus to explain, positively, what his kingship is all about. It is a spiritual kingship, made up of those who know and love the truth—or those who worship God in spirit and truth (John 4:24). Truth is one of several key ideas in John's thinking: Jesus has come from the Father, "full of grace and truth" (1:14). He is the faithful witness who, having been in the bosom of the Father from all eternity, bears full testimony to God's own truth—specifically the truth of how man can be put right with God. In Jesus is all truth; so his subjects, bowing to his kingship, receive that truth from him and are delivered from every lie.

We can sense the tone of Pilate's brief response, "What is truth?" It is not the honest inquiry of a true seeker, but the dismissive exclamation of a skeptic. And we need to appreciate the considerable irony of the situation. About twelve hours earlier Jesus had told his disciples that he himself was "the truth" (John 14:6). So then, Pilate—what *is* truth? This man standing in front of you is truth! As we will see, Pilate is not without a conscience and he is certainly not without superstition. But above all he is a pragmatist, and he has a decision to make, quickly. So he returns to the Jewish leaders who were waiting outside and tells them, effectively, that the case is dismissed.

FIVE STEPS TO CALVARY

But Pilate's work is not over; it has only just begun. He now has to reckon with the persistent accusations of the chief priests and the whipped-up ferocity of the fickle crowd. Since we will deal with each of these groups in future chapters, we will comment only briefly on their words and actions and will focus more on how Pilate repeatedly sought to clear Jesus but eventually felt forced to capitulate. Five specific episodes draw our attention.

First of all, Pilate seeks to make use of the popular custom that he would release one prisoner to the Jews at every Passover Feast. Evidently, by this stage, the number of people assembled outside Pilate's headquarters has grown considerably. Which prisoner should he release—Jesus or Barabbas? The portrait of Barabbas painted by the Gospels is a vicious one. He is a "notorious prisoner" (Matt. 27:16); a rebel "who had committed murder in the insurrection" (Mark 15:7) and also a robber (John 18:40). Surely the crowd, having cried out "Hosanna" to Jesus just five days earlier, could not turn against him now in favor of Barabbas. Pilate's plea to them seems to anticipate that they would ask for Jesus. But both Matthew and Mark report that the chief priests and elders did their utmost to poison the crowd's minds against Jesus. They shouted that Jesus should be crucified. Pilate is utterly taken aback by this. What evil has this man done? Do they really want their king to be crucified?

Second, if we read the gospel accounts carefully, we see that it was at this point that Pilate's wife sends word to her husband, warning him to leave Jesus well alone because of the distressing dream she had suffered. Pilate's wife, who has been traditionally known as Claudia Procula, has also been canonized like her husband—one might say with a little more reason, but maybe not much more! [11] The controversial 2004 film *The Passion of the Christ* assigns her a larger role than Scripture does. Far more important is that the report of her dream must have rocked Pilate to the core, at the very time when passions in the crowd were boiling over. It may even have been that this announcement caused a break in proceedings, which the chief priests and elders used to their own advantage to spread their malicious propaganda.

Third, witness the desperately barbaric scourging that Jesus received, followed by the cruel mockery of the Roman soldiers. We will pass over the gruesome details here, as Scripture does. The point is that after the scourging Pilate was still determined to release Jesus if he could. The crowd had been baying for blood; were they not satisfied now? The oft-quoted cry of Pilate, "Behold the man!"—the Latin is *ecce homo*—was calculated to fix the crowd's eyes upon a vision of blood and gore. Isn't this enough now? It wasn't enough; the demands for his crucifixion grew ever more frenzied.

Fourth, we see that at this point Pilate in his exasperation is prepared to hand Jesus over to the chief priests, that they themselves should crucify him. Both Pilate and the chief priests know full well that this scenario is impossible; therefore the priests bring a fresh accusation with a new dimension. "We have a law," they insist, "and according to that law he ought to die because he has made himself the Son of God" (John 19:7).

What is noteworthy here is the growing fear that seizes Pilate. We have already commented on his superstition. The Roman world of Pilate's day was, perhaps, not as "religious" as it had been some two hundred fifty years earlier, when the gods of Rome, largely adapted from the Greek pantheon, were greatly honored. Increasingly it was the emperors who assumed divine titles for themselves. But there is enough awareness of higher powers in Pilate's mind to cause his alarm to surge at the point when he hears the claim that Jesus is "the Son of God." When this startling revelation is allied to the dream that has come from his wife, he feels compelled to speak to Jesus. This situation is far beyond his experience and even further beyond his comfort. His initial question, "Where are you from?," receives no answer, but it evidently implies that Pilate's personal interest has been heightened since his first interview with Jesus.

Pilate presses Jesus further. Does the Nazarene not understand the nature of the authority that Pilate possesses—that according to his own will he can either crucify or release Jesus? Does this need to be spelled out to him? Once more we see the Lord Jesus Christ in utter control as well as in full composure. As the apostle Peter was to write about thirty years later, Jesus "continued entrusting himself to him who judges justly" (1 Peter 2:23). All authority in earth is granted by the one who reigns in heaven. But Pilate was less culpable than the high priests, especially Caiaphas, who had handed Jesus over to Pilate with such wicked determination. This is why Jesus replies as he does: "You would have no authority over me at all unless it had been given you from above. Therefore he who delivered me over to you has the greater sin" (John 19:11). What does Pilate make of Jesus' response? Surely he is confirmed in his original belief that Jesus had done no wrong. From this point Pilate is continuously seeking a means to release Jesus. The endgame has now been reached—but it is the Jews who force checkmate.

Fifth and finally, Pilate has to face a devastating challenge from the men who have brought Jesus to him. We read that the Jews "cried out"—note the intensity—"If you release this man, you are not Caesar's friend. Everyone who makes himself a king opposes Caesar" (John 19:12). The deplorable threat lurking beneath this statement is very thinly veiled. How on earth can Pilate continue in his position as governor if his absolute loyalty to Tiberius Caesar, son of the Divine Augustus, appears to be compromised? Pilate's great fear is undoubtedly mixed with loathing for the Jews. He knows that they forced him into his current position and that he now has no room to move. He knows that their profession of loyalty to Caesar is hollow and dishonest, but that if he does not give in to their demands, the consequences might well destroy him.

Who Put Jesus on the Cross?

It is when we step back and view the situation from a distance that we see that Pilate's designs were completely overruled. Ultimate authority does not belong to him, as Jesus had told him, but to heaven itself. On several occasions he uttered the words, "I find no guilt in this man," or something to similar effect. The riot that seemed to be developing persuaded him that he could do nothing other than give in to the demands of the crowd. Indeed, he might have reasoned that if he let Jesus go, the mob could have set upon him straightaway. He is acting under unavoidable compulsion. The washing of his hands, recorded in Matthew 27:24, would have conveyed deep significance to the watching audience. "I am innocent of this man's blood; see to it yourselves." We will consider the ominous response of the crowd in chapter 13.

But of course, Pilate must not be absolved of all responsibility. In the final analysis, his last actions are those of a coward. He feared the people of Jerusalem more than he feared God; for, as we have seen, much had happened to Pilate that made it quite clear that Jesus had come from God, however Pilate might have understood this. He would rather save his own skin than his own soul. Pilate himself had to issue the sentence of crucifixion. He was also responsible for placing the written charge, "This is the King of the Jews," above Jesus' head. It was Pilate whom Joseph of Arimathea turned to when he wanted to bury Jesus' body. And it was Pilate whom the chief priests and Pharisees sought when they wanted to make the tomb as secure as possible. Pilate may have washed his hands, but he could not shake off the consequences of what he had done with Jesus.

But our final conclusion must be this. Pilate, though he was governor of Judea, could not control the situation he faced. The course of action that he intended—to release Jesus, having found no guilt in him—was overturned. So does that mean that the chief priests won the day, that they were in ultimate control? No, for as Jesus himself told Pilate, "You would have no authority over me at all unless it had been given you from above" (John 19:11). The early Christians, having faced the opposition of the same enemies, summarized the entire situation in the following words.

> For truly in this city there were gathered together against your holy servant Jesus, whom you anointed, both Herod and Pontius Pilate, along with the Gentiles and the peoples of Israel, *to do whatever your hand and your plan had predestined to take place.* (Acts 4:27–28)

So who put Jesus on the cross?

Yet it was the will of the LORD to crush him;
    he has put him to grief;
when his soul makes an offering for sin,
    he shall see his offspring; he shall prolong his days;
the will of the LORD shall prosper in his hand.
Out of the anguish of his soul he shall see and be satisfied;
by his knowledge shall the righteous one, my servant,
      make many to be accounted righteous,
      and he shall bear their iniquities (Isa. 53:10–11).

— 12 —

HEROD ANTIPAS

*When Herod saw Jesus, he was very glad, for he had
long desired to see him, because he had heard about him,
and he was hoping to see some sign done by him. So he
questioned him at some length, but he made no answer.
The chief priests and the scribes stood by, vehemently
accusing him. And Herod with his soldiers treated him
with contempt and mocked him. Then, arraying him in
splendid clothing, he sent him back to Pilate. And Herod
and Pilate became friends with each other that very day,
for before this they had been at enmity with each other.*
(Luke 23:8–12)

WE SAW IN THE PREVIOUS CHAPTER that Pontius
Pilate was determined to evade the responsibility of dealing
with Jesus. This he continually sought to do until the relentless
pressure of the situation caused him to capitulate. Luke alone
tells us, however, that the trial before Pilate was interrupted by
Jesus' brief appearance before Herod.

Now why is this interesting and possibly rather important
information recorded in only one gospel? Why did not Matthew, Mark, and John also give some space to describing the
trial before Herod? These other accounts all seem to read as if
Pilate's dealings with Jesus were carried on seamlessly. Another
objection might be raised: surely a considerable amount of time

would have been taken up in securing an audience with Herod and with escorting Jesus backwards and forwards? Could this appearance before Herod, as described by Luke, really have taken place in the allotted time? These questions must be dealt with.

DID THIS REALLY HAPPEN?

First, observe the relative lack of importance of Herod's role in connection with the eventual condemnation and execution of Jesus. His part was not nearly as significant as that of the chief priests and elders, nor indeed as weighty as Pilate's final decision. Indeed, our passage emphasizes that the brief involvement of Herod added nothing of material significance to the charge against Jesus. Jesus was sent back to Pilate and proceedings continued precisely where they had left off. The Roman governor said as much when he resumed speaking to Jesus' accusers.

> You brought me this man as one who was misleading the people. And after examining him before you, behold, I did not find this man guilty of any of your charges against him. Neither did Herod, for he sent him back to us. Look, nothing deserving death has been done by him. (Luke 23:14–15)

Pilate, to his undoubted chagrin, was "back to square one" with this troublesome case.

Why then does Luke mention this episode with Herod at all? The reason is that it ties in with the "orderly account" which he is endeavoring to set before his friend Theophilus and before us all. We must never forget that the gospel of Luke is the first volume of a two-volume series, and that in the Acts of the Apostles he will go on to his sequel. A considerable amount of space in Acts is taken up in describing the persecution that the early church faced, and in chapter 4 we are told that this persecution is seen as the fulfillment of the Second Psalm.

"The kings of the earth set themselves,
   and the rulers were gathered together,
      against the Lord and against his Anointed"—

for truly in this city there were gathered together against your
holy servant Jesus, whom you anointed, *both Herod and Pontius
Pilate*, along with the Gentiles and the peoples of Israel, to do
whatever your hand and your plan had predestined to take
place. (Acts 4:26-28)

So why did Luke include the Herod account? In order to demonstrate that the Scriptures had been fulfilled.

Secondly, what about the time and the distance involved?
This is not really a problem. The consensus of most archaeologists and historians is that Herod would have been staying in
the Hasmonean Palace on the northern side of Jerusalem, which
was itself part of a much larger complex of huge buildings. This
would have included the palace of Herod the Great, where Pilate
resided when he was in Jerusalem. The point is that Jesus, along
with his accusers, would not have to travel very far from Pilate
to Herod and then back again. Proceedings would no doubt have
been hurried along by the urgency of the chief priests and scribes,
by Herod's initial desire to see Jesus, and then by his eventual
disgust, which would have caused him to send Jesus away quickly.

SHEER EXPEDIENCY

How was it that Herod was caught up in this business? The
chief priests, in the course of their accusations against Jesus,
told Pilate that he "stirs up the people, teaching throughout all
Judea, from Galilee even to this place" (Luke 23:5). Their mention of Galilee immediately made Pilate's ears prick up. If this
man were a Galilean, then could not Herod, tetrarch of Galilee,
be helpfully brought in? Hendriksen comments that "Pilate,
consistent with his purpose almost to the very end of the trial,

saw in this link between Jesus and Galilee the very opportunity he was looking for to get rid of this annoying case."[1]

Pilate certainly did not refer the case to Herod because of deeply held convictions concerning legal or procedural principles. If Pilate desperately wanted to get rid of a man who happened to be in Judea, he would have taken swift action without bothering to inquire which province he came from or whose jurisdiction he came under.[2] After all, he had not scrupled to refer the Galileans of Luke 13:1 to Herod's judgment! No, the speed with which Pilate sent Jesus to Herod was a measure of how eagerly he wanted to "pass the buck" to someone else. In short, this was sheer expediency on Pilate's part. A long shot perhaps, but just maybe he might see this case dismissed. It may also be that the superstitious fear that we have already noted was beginning to affect his decisions.

So we turn our attention now to Herod himself, and will start by clarifying his identity. In the New Testament he is sometimes referred to as "King Herod," sometimes as "Herod the tetrarch," but usually he is simply "Herod." We will designate him in this chapter as "Herod Antipas," the title by which he has generally been known to history, although nowhere in the New Testament is the name "Antipas" used with reference to him. The only place where that name is found is in Revelation 2:13, which speaks of a completely unrelated individual, Christ's "faithful witness" in Pergamum who was put to death.

There are forty references in the New Testament to someone who is called "Herod." It needs to be remembered that the name was passed down through his dynasty so that most of his male descendants were distinguished with it—or perhaps not quite so distinguished! The name is applied to three different individuals in the New Testament, as well as to several others not mentioned in Scripture. The reader who wishes to know more about the Herod dynasty should consult the appendix at the end of this book.

A Downsized Version of His Father

At one point Herod the Great had intended to make Herod Antipas the sole heir of his entire kingdom, but in the dying days of his life he changed his mind and partitioned his territory between his three sons: Philip and Archelaus, in addition to Herod Antipas, as we have seen. Predictably, this resulted in a feud between the three heirs that necessitated a formal judgment from Augustus Caesar, upholding Herod the Great's final will.

In several respects, Herod Antipas was like a downsized version of his own father. His power and influence never approached that of Herod the Great, though his reign (4 BC to AD 39) was somewhat longer. Like his father he was a prolific builder, founding the city of Tiberias—named in honor of the Roman Emperor Tiberius—on the western shore of the Sea of Galilee, from where he ruled over that province. A child of an extremely dysfunctional family, Herod Antipas indulged his own sordid extramarital interests. Being a "fox" (Luke 13:32), he was a crafty, cunning schemer, prepared to stoop to acts of foul cruelty. He never caused bloodshed on the scale that his father had, but that was because his own power was considerably more limited. It was bad blood between Herod and his relatives that eventually caused his own end. Herod Agrippa I, his nephew, conspired against him and his allegations were upheld by Caligula, the notoriously corrupt successor of Tiberius as Emperor. In AD 39 Herod Antipas was exiled to Gaul, probably to what is now Lyons, where he died shortly afterward.

What do we know of Herod from the gospel records? The longest and most detailed account we have describes the events that led up to the execution of John the Baptist and can be read in Mark 6:14–29. It is well worth reflecting on this episode at some length because it goes a long way toward explaining Herod's subsequent behavior when he was confronted with Jesus.

HEROD AND JOHN THE BAPTIST

We need to remind ourselves of the history between Herod and John and the reason for the conflict between them. John had been preaching fearlessly against Herod, who by marrying Herodias, Herod Philip's wife, had acted in clear violation of God's law.[3] The details of this unlawful union are recorded by Josephus.[4] Herod, on a visit to Philip in Rome, had become infatuated with Herodias. But Herod had already been married for many years to Phasaelis, daughter of Aretas IV Philopatris, king of the Nabateans.[5] When Herod sent Phasaelis away, Aretas used this as a pretext to send his armies against Herod, who suffered a considerable defeat.

The question may well be asked: which eventually caused Herod more grief, the armies of Aretas or the preaching of John the Baptist? The reader may decide for himself! Herod was even further from being a pureblooded Israelite than his father, but that did not deter John from preaching against him and denouncing him as a lawbreaker. John had truly come "in the spirit and power of Elijah" (Luke 1:17), for the very history of Elijah was repeating itself in John's life and ministry. Elijah had preached fearlessly against Ahab and Jezebel, whose respective attitudes toward Elijah mirrored Herod's and Herodias' impressions of John. At a much later date John Knox preached in a similar manner against another willful sovereign, Mary Stuart of Scotland. True prophets of God are not respecters of persons. Sin committed in high places must be exposed and denounced as much as any other sin, even if the prophet must shed his blood as a consequence.

And yet it is tempting to label Herod Antipas as another of these "nearly men" of the Bible. Herod was caught on the horns of a painful dilemma, constantly aware of Herodias' spiteful agitations but unwilling to give in to them on account of his genuine appreciation of John's spiritual character. It seems to be the case that Herod heard John with genuine pleasure; it is the same word that described the way in which "the common people" heard Jesus *gladly* (Mark 12:37 KJV). Ungodly men can recognize that which is "righteous and holy" (Mark 6:20) and can be attracted to spiritually minded people without ever being spiritual themselves. How many hours, we may well wonder, did Herod spend in the deep, hot dungeons of Machaerus, by the Dead Sea, hearing the words of John with that strange mixture of fear and fascination?

It was Herodias who was the royal tigress in this intrigue. Just as Jezebel instigated Naboth's death, overriding the king's authority (1 Kings 21:5–15), so Herodias prevailed upon Herod to have John destroyed. She was awaiting an opportunity, and at last one came. It is instructive to notice the circumstances that caused Herod to let down his guard and become vulnerable prey to his wife's sinister machinations. It was his own birthday, and there were many prominent guests present. We are not explicitly told that Herod had been too self-indulgent with his wine, but such a scenario would not be hard to imagine. The dancing of Herodias' daughter, at any rate, had an intoxicating effect upon him. He seemed unable to control himself, and the lavishness of his offer is seen in the public vow that he made, exaggerated far beyond sensible proportions—although the wording may suggest the same kind of courtly hyperbole that we find in Esther 5:3, where King Ahasuerus of Persia employed almost identical language.

The way in which Herodias' daughter went to speak to her mother suggests that she was of tender years, unable to conceive of any reasonable response to Herod's extravagant proposal. Presumably Herodias was not sitting with the men; we read that her daughter "went out" to her and then "came in" afterward. The absence of Herodias from the scene meant that she could concoct her plans at a safe distance. There is no suggestion that the girl herself held strong grudges against John, though it is likely that her mother had already influenced her in that direction.

Thus the grisly request was put before Herod: "I want you to give me at once the head of John the Baptist on a platter" (Mark 6:25). The tetrarch could not possibly back down. He was not prepared to break his oath, just like the Old Testament judge Jephthah, another man who vowed foolishly (Judg. 11:35). The presence of many distinguished guests was also a crucial factor, for how could Herod endure loss of face before their watching eyes? The greatness of his sorrow in contemplating John's execution was overshadowed by the public pressure of the immediate situation. We cannot doubt that he ought to have kept John alive, to have preserved the life of a righteous man even if it meant a loss of reputation. It is surely better to break a foolish vow than to keep it and commit a greater sin, but Herod could not see this.[6] The execution took place without delay, and Herodias had her evil ambition—and ghastly acquisition—granted.

A TORTURED AND TROUBLED MIND

Why is all this recorded for us in the New Testament? For one thing, it shows us that John's end was of a similar kind to that of so many other prophets. To the blood-inscribed list of martyrs from Abel to Zechariah, John's name is now added. What is more, the death of John can be viewed as an illustration of the type of persecution with which Jesus' own disciples will be faced. It is no coincidence that both Matthew and Mark place the account of Herod and John so close to the record of the disciples' first preaching ministry around Israel.

But our main focus must be upon Herod himself. It is in the context of the reports of Jesus' ministry in Galilee that Herod is first mentioned. As tetrarch of Galilee he could not have failed to hear of the amazing works that Jesus had performed. But so tortured and troubled was his mind that "he said to his servants, 'This is John the Baptist. He has been raised from the dead; that is why these miraculous powers are at work in him'" (Matt. 14:2). Do these words imply that Herod believed that John had been physically resurrected? It seems unlikely that such a developed notion had ever crossed Herod's mind. One scholar, Darrell L. Bock, suggests that Herod meant that "Jesus possesses a spirit like John or that John has passed on his authority," in much the same way that Elijah's spirit came to rest upon Elisha.[7]

There is some family history here to reckon with. In one passage Josephus describes how the "ghosts" of Alexander and Aristobulus, the murdered sons of Herod the Great, haunted the royal palace.[8] The same kind of superstition was now at work in the mind of Herod the tetrarch. Although John had never performed any miraculous sign, Herod may have sensed that John's spirit, which had fallen upon Jesus, was intensifying its attack upon his own conscience, compounding his guilt. He felt like Macbeth, tormented by the ghost of the murdered Banquo fixing its gaze upon him across the table. John the Baptist, though dead, would not leave him alone. There was still the vestige of a tender heart in Herod, but how much longer would it remain?

"THAT FOX"

We should look briefly at another gospel reference to Herod before we come to his meeting with Jesus. Herod was famously called "that fox" by Jesus (Luke 13:32). This was undoubtedly a description of his cunning and trickery, with which Jesus was well acquainted. It is certainly a case of "like father, like son." Remember, Herod the Great had tried to "fox" the magi. But foxes are not to be laughed at; they are also destructive animals.

What caused Jesus to designate Herod "a fox"? There were some Pharisees who warned Jesus to move sharply out of the regions of Galilee and Perea because, they said, Herod Antipas wanted to kill him. We cannot be confident that these Pharisees spoke to Jesus with friendly intent. It is possible that they did so, but it is more likely that they wanted to usher Jesus nearer to Jerusalem, to their own power base, in order to seize him. Indeed the most plausible explanation was that Herod and the

Pharisees were in cahoots with one another in their common enmity against Jesus. They were an unlikely alliance because Herod represented Roman power, whereas the Pharisees hated Rome and all that it stood for. But the Pharisees had made common cause with the Herodians—the group who represented Herod's interests—against Jesus before (Mark 3:6).

The Pharisees and Herod had quite different reasons for wanting to get rid of Jesus. The Pharisees were threatened by him, resenting his popularity, his power, and the force of his teaching against them. Herod could not endure Jesus because he reminded him too much of John the Baptist. But both parties knew that their best chance to achieve their desired end would come if Jesus was in Jerusalem. The Lord himself, of course, knew very well that no prophet could ever perish outside Jerusalem, and thus he set his face to go there.

So let us come now to the long-awaited meeting between Herod and Jesus. It is briefly described in just five verses. We can assume it was all over relatively quickly, and yet what we have in these few verses is really one of the most tragic episodes in the whole Bible.

CARNAL CURIOSITY

We are told that Herod was eager to see Jesus. It is usually a good thing to be eager to see Jesus, is it not? There are many instances in the Gospels when people expressed this eagerness for all the right reasons. We can recall large numbers of distressed individuals who came to Jesus in desperation, beseeching him to help them or to help someone dear to them. The friends of the paralytic, Jairus the synagogue ruler, a Roman centurion, a great multitude of the blind, the lame, and the sick—all of these wanted to see Jesus and needed a miracle from him. Herod, too, "needed" a miracle from Jesus. But his motivation was entirely different.

While the chief priests and scribes continued in the same vein as they had with Pilate, vehemently accusing Jesus, all the more desperate to secure his speedy condemnation, Herod sat back in his chair, put his feet up, and waited for the show to begin. His interest in Jesus had descended to nothing more than what we might call carnal curiosity. Herod simply wanted to be amused. He viewed Jesus merely as a performer, someone he could summon to entertain him with a few tricks. Whereas Herod had once heard the preaching of John the Baptist gladly, though most uncomfortably, by now there was no semblance of spiritual interest in his heart.

But not only did Jesus refuse to gratify Herod's desire to see a miraculous sign, he did not speak to him at all. There is a considerable difference in this respect between Herod and Pilate. When Jesus was alone with Pilate, he was prepared to speak to him, even to reason with him. Herod, however, was confronted with deafening silence.

DEAFENING SILENCE

This silence of Jesus Christ in the presence of Herod is dreadfully significant. I use the word *significant* quite carefully, for we can say that Jesus' silence was the only "sign" that he was prepared to give Herod. As we reflect on this, we must surely see that the silence of God is a most terrible indictment, perhaps *the* most terrible indictment, against anyone. It was exactly the same as the judgment that Jesus pronounced against the Pharisees who came to him seeking a sign. It is an evil and adulterous generation that looks for a sign, but none would be given to them—none, at least, that they would see with their own eyes (Matt. 16:4).

One of the most tragic examples of a man who came to know the meaning of God's silence was Saul, king of Israel. Here is someone who began so well, someone who apparently knew the blessing of God. But the second half of 1 Samuel, which is an account of the rise of David, is also a record of the appalling downward spiral of Saul. It was Saul's disobedience of God's clear commands, through Samuel, that began his decline. We see the Spirit of God remaining with David, but at the same time departing from Saul, and a troubling, tormenting spirit coming upon Saul instead (1 Sam. 16:14). These were the days when Saul would habitually sit with his spear, waiting to hurl it at David. King Saul's great atrocity, the murder of the eighty-five priests of God, and the destruction of Nob, the city of the priests, surely sped him further toward a point of no return (1 Sam. 22:18–19). For there came a day when the Philistines were once again attacking Israel, and we read that Saul "was afraid, and his heart trembled greatly. And when Saul inquired of the LORD, the LORD did not answer him, either by dreams, or by Urim, or by prophets" (1 Sam. 28:5–6). It had been much better for Saul when God had been rebuking him through Samuel. It was much better for Saul to hear words of judgment from God than to hear nothing at all. Saul's response to this silence was to consult a medium, which hastened his own death.

In Psalm 28:1 the silence of God is shown to be the most terrifying evidence of his judgment: "To you, O LORD, I call; my rock, be not deaf to me, lest, if you be silent to me, I become like those who go down to the pit." Surely the individual in the most fearful condition is the one who once seemed to hear God's voice, and even to respond to it, but who does so no longer. The great Martin Luther was once asked by a student why it was that God seemed to be "at him" all the time, convicting him of sin, working on his conscience. Luther replied in this way: "Never fear when God is at you; you be afraid when God leaves you utterly alone and lets you go your own way."[9] He spoke from his own experience.

The voice of God through John the Baptist had once troubled Herod. But he had stilled this voice by putting John to death. Now Jesus is telling Herod, by his very silence, that he has chosen to reject God's testimony and therefore he will hear nothing from God any longer.

More evidence of Herod's condition can be seen in the way he responds to Jesus' silence. He does not join in with the accusations of the chief priests and elders; neither, of course, does he jump to Jesus' defense. No, he descends to the level of contempt and mockery. He is like a petulant child who has received a long-anticipated toy, only to find that the batteries do not come with it. So he despises and abuses what he has been given. Human nature and society have reached a particularly galling pitch of depravity when they openly and brazenly mock the things of God. We can be sure that a comedian who seeks to gain cheap laughs at divine, holy things has never begun to understand them. He has never known the fear of God, or what it is to hear the voice of God.

An Unholy Alliance

Finally, notice the concluding observation that Luke makes. "And Herod and Pilate became friends with each other that very day, for before this they had been at enmity with each other" (Luke 23:12). There may be an allusion here to Luke 13:1, where we read of Pilate's massacre of some Galileans who were engaged in worship. This incident may have been one consequence of the enmity that had previously existed between Herod and Pilate. But their encounters with Jesus brought them together.

The early church, in the face of persecution, noticed this unlikely and, we might say, unholy alliance, and saw it as a fulfillment of the second Psalm. We have already commented on the words of Acts 4:26–27:

> "The kings of the earth set themselves,
>> and the rulers were gathered together,
>>> against the Lord and against his Anointed"—

for truly in this city there were gathered together against your holy servant Jesus, whom you anointed, *both Herod and Pontius*

Pilate, along with the Gentiles and the peoples of Israel, to do whatever your hand and your plan had predestined to take place. (Acts 4:26-28)

J. C. Ryle, Bishop of Liverpool, a great and prophetic leader of his day, commented on similar unlikely associations in the later part of the nineteenth century:

> In our own times we sometimes see Romanists and Socinians, infidels and idolaters, worldly pleasure-lovers and bigoted ascetics, the friends of so called liberal views and the most determined opponents of all changes, all ranked together against evangelical religion. One common hatred binds them together. They hate the cross of Christ.[10]

What Ryle wrote well over a hundred years ago might be echoed very loudly today. But I fear that there is something more that we may say. Open hatred of the cross of Christ—at least in Western society—is largely giving way to sheer ignorance and indifference toward it. There is less outward agitation against the gospel of Jesus Christ because fewer people know what that gospel is. Or to put it another way, God is silent toward our present generation. And as we have just seen in the case of Herod Antipas, this is the most perilous condemnation of all.

— 13 —

THE JEWISH CROWD

Pilate said to them, "Then what shall I do with Jesus who is called Christ?" They all said, "Let him be crucified!" And he said, "Why, what evil has he done?" But they shouted all the more, "Let him be crucified!" So when Pilate saw that he was gaining nothing, but rather that a riot was beginning, he took water and washed his hands before the crowd, saying, "I am innocent of this man's blood; see to it yourselves." And all the people answered, "His blood be on us and on our children!" (Matt. 27:22–25)

THE "ARAB SPRING" of 2011 was viewed by millions of people all over the world and was prolonged far beyond the spring of that year. Television pictures—often filmed secretly and broadcast on social networking sites—showed large-scale demonstrations involving the (mostly male) citizens of Tunisia, Egypt, Bahrain, Yemen, Syria, and Libya protesting against their respective governments, with or without ultimate success. The effects of these uprisings have been felt in many other countries, not all so widely reported by the media. Various "days of rage" were witnessed by a worldwide audience.

Then, for several nights in August of the same year, there were violent riots in London, Birmingham, Manchester, and other cities in England. These were sparked by a police shooting in Tottenham in which Mark Duggan, who was believed to be armed, was killed. What began as a peaceful protest against this shooting quickly developed into something much more sinister, and within a few days "copycat" riots had spread to other communities. Watching the coverage of these disturbances made it clear that a considerable number of those involved had no clearly defined idea why they were rioting. Some of them were children as young as eight, though the majority were youths in their late teens. In a crowd the hostile and aggressive element often rises quickly to the top. What might be intended and publicized as a "peaceful protest" can quickly be transformed into a violent, angry mob. When you are part of a spirited and animated crowd it is difficult to avoid being caught up in the surrounding emotion and mass hysteria.

Of course none of this is a fresh phenomenon. We read of a riot that took place in Ephesus when the apostle Paul was there. It had arisen because a silversmith named Demetrius was facing his own serious credit crunch due to Paul's preaching of Jesus. Shrines of the Ephesian goddess Artemis no longer sold as they once did. Discontent rumbled and soon found voluminous expression: "Great is Artemis of the Ephesians!" the crowd declared (Acts 19:28, 34). The people rushed into the massive amphitheater; we read that "some cried out one thing, some another, for the assembly was in confusion, and most of them did not know why they had come together" (Acts 19:32). This is a very telling observation.

How many people caught up in mass protests can accurately articulate the reason for the public discontent? Most of them follow the crowd simply because it is convenient to do so. Nevertheless—and this is the point—they cannot plead innocence because of this. We can go back to the years when Israel was in the wilderness and see that the people of God were strictly warned against acting in such a way: "You shall not fall in with the many to do evil, nor shall you bear witness in a lawsuit, siding with the many, so as to pervert justice" (Ex. 23:2). Justice was to be their guide, not popular opinion, and this can be applied both to an individual and to a group. In this present chapter it will be seen that the crowd that gathered at Jesus' trial before Pilate committed great evil, and that wickedness found particular expression in the words, "His blood be on us and on our children" (Matt. 27:25).

"His Blood Be on Us and on Our Children"

The Pontius Pilate narrative is still not quite finished. He wanted to find a way to release Jesus and to be done with this wearisome, troubling case. Messengers had brought him a report of a strange dream from his wife, which further afflicted his conscience. He sincerely hoped that the crowd, being presented with his customary offer to release one prisoner to them, would do the right thing and ask for Jesus. But to Pilate's intense dismay, they asked for Barabbas to be released and for Jesus to be crucified. And they were insistent. No amount of reasoning could quell the riot that was now simmering. So at this point Pilate took water and washed his hands, demonstrating very publicly and graphically that the condemnation of Jesus was the crowd's responsibility, not his own. What did the crowd make of Pilate's actions? They were only too eager to take this burden upon themselves and thus uttered these deplorable words: "His blood be on us and on our children!" With these words they were effectively acknowledging that the blood that stained Pilate's hands might be transferred to all of them, and indeed to their offspring.

Just how terrible these words were, and what their consequences were, will be seen in due course. But maybe at this stage it is puzzling to account for the extreme opposition toward Jesus that was voiced by the crowd. Good Friday came just five days after what is sometimes called Palm Sunday, the day of Jesus' triumphal entry into Jerusalem, when loud "Hosannas" had rung from the crowd. Poignant expression is given to this in the third verse of the famous hymn "My Song is Love Unknown," written by Samuel Crossman in 1664.

> Sometimes they strew His way,
> And His sweet praises sing;
> Resounding all the day
> Hosannas to their King:
> Then "Crucify!" is all their breath,
> And for His death they thirst and cry.

How can we account for this sudden change of attitude toward Jesus? Our text provides one clear answer. In Matthew 27:20 we are told that "the chief priests and the elders persuaded the crowd to ask for Barabbas and destroy Jesus." Mark, a little more earthy and vivid, records that "the chief priests stirred up the crowd to have him [Pilate] release for them Barabbas instead" (Mark 15:11). A relentless propaganda campaign was being carried out, the chief priests and elders doing all they could to agitate hatred and enmity toward Jesus and stooping at nothing to achieve their desired end.

It is always easier to induce a frenzy than it is to subdue one, just as it is much easier to wreck a precious human relationship than it is to mend one. It need not be imagined that the chief priests employed much artistry in arousing the crowds to hatred. A perusal of the various accusations they brought against Jesus will result in a clear idea of what they would have said to the people. We can be sure that cries of "blasphemy," "false prophet," and "troublemaker" would have been heard and believed.

UNCONVERTED MEN WOULD KILL GOD

But the entire blame ought not to be laid at the feet of the chief priests and elders. It should not be imagined that the crowd were led along in wide-eyed naivety by the sinister machinations of Jesus' enemies. It is blindness and naivety that fails to see that the sinful heart of man can be readily induced to express hatred towards all that is good, fine, and noble. J. C. Ryle knew this well. He wrote

> There are few things so little believed and realized as the corruption of human nature. Men fancy that if they saw a perfect person they would love and admire him; they flatter themselves that it is the inconsistency of professing Christians which they dislike and not their religion: *they forget that when a really perfect man was on earth, in the person of the Son of God, He was hated and put to death.* That single fact goes far to prove the truth of an old saying, that "unconverted men would kill God, if they could get at Him."[1]

The truth of Ryle's observation was strikingly confirmed in one experience of John Marshall, minister of Alexander Road Congregational Chapel in Hemel Hempstead for forty-five years until his death in 2003. As was his regular practice, he was once preaching in the marketplace in Hemel Hempstead when he noticed a young woman listening to him with evident anger on her face. At the end of the sermon she came up to him and began to speak to him, vehemently criticizing everything that he had said. Eventually the preacher, who admitted that she had "got right under his skin," said plainly to her, "You are the kind of person who would have crucified the Lord Jesus Christ." And at that point she seemed to advance to a yet more passionate level of rage, and she exploded, "Yes! That's what I would do to him—I would crucify him!"[2] Surely we see here the most abundant proof of Jesus' statement in John 3:19, with which we began in our first chapter. "The light has come into the world, and people loved the darkness rather than the light because their deeds were evil." It is in this context that we must read the words of the crowd: "His blood be on us and on our children!"

We ought not, of course, read these words in isolation, as if they were expressing a sentiment that was wholly new. We should see them as a summary confirmation of the general position of Israel with regard to Jesus. This imprecation, or curse, that they uttered against themselves is the ultimate expression of their rejection of Jesus. The gospel records are, to a large extent, a detailed description of that rejection.

ISRAEL'S REJECTION OF JESUS

The words in John's prologue, "He came to his own, and his own people did not receive him" (John 1:11), are a concise summary of the public mission of Jesus of Nazareth and the way in which he was received. We surely do not need to multiply texts in order to make this point. Has not a large part of this book already been a comment on the hostility between Israel and the Messiah she did not receive? Nowhere has this been more evident than in chapter 4, where we considered the reaction of the people in the synagogue at Nazareth, his own hometown. When they realized what Jesus was saying, they tried to throw him over the brow of the hill. And early in his ministry Jesus had prophesied both the salvation of the Gentiles and the rejection of Israel.

> I tell you, many will come from east and west and recline at table with Abraham, Isaac, and Jacob in the kingdom of heaven, while the sons of the kingdom will be thrown into the outer darkness. In that place there will be weeping and gnashing of teeth. (Matt. 8:11-12)

But what was it that made Israel's rejection of Jesus so terribly solemn? The answer is that Israel had been blessed with vast and unique spiritual privileges. They had been specially prepared to meet their Messiah. Psalm 147 reaches its crescendo of praise to God with words that underscore the weightiness of these privileges. "He declares his word to Jacob, his statutes and rules to Israel. *He has not dealt thus with any other nation; they do not know his rules.* Praise the LORD!" Truly, as Jesus had declared to the woman of Samaria, "salvation is from the Jews" (John 4:22). Everything that Israel had been taught in their entire history was given to them in order to foreshadow their Messiah. Jesus Christ himself had been represented to the people of Israel through all the revelations God had given in the Law, the Prophets, and the Psalms. Therefore, when these Israelites rejected Jesus, they were sinning against the greatest light that God had ever shone upon men.

"His blood be on us and on our children." It is Matthew alone who records these words. We are told that they were uttered by "all the people." Do we necessarily understand that the whole multitude raised their voices and said this in unison? More likely it is that one of the chief priests or elders made this pronouncement, which was then followed by many cries of assent. But those many voices issued forth from men who had "fallen in with the many to do evil."

A SOLEMN IMPRECATION

We have seen that Pilate's symbolic action of washing his hands was his own public declaration of innocence in the matter of Jesus. He had sought by every means to clear Jesus, but all his designs had failed. Nevertheless, that certainly does not mean that we should accept Pilate's plea and absolve him of all responsibility. He did indeed possess the legal authority to crucify or to release Jesus, and eventually he consented to the first action. The fear of man overrode the fear of God, and we have every reason to suspect that Pilate knew something, however distorted, about the fear of God.

But the point is that the crowd, observing Pilate's actions, readily demonstrated that they were quite content to accept the responsibility for the shedding of Jesus' blood. His condemnation and crucifixion was their own determined course of action. They spoke these terrible words with a grim confidence, indicating how certain they were of the justice of their cause. We can give some idea of the force of their words in this way: "If this man is indeed innocent and we are guilty, then let that blood-guilt attach itself to all of us, and indeed to our children. But we are sufficiently persuaded that Jesus is a false prophet, a blasphemer, so much so that we are prepared to stake our own souls, and the souls of our progeny, upon this claim."

John Calvin, commenting on this verse, wrote the following:

> There can be no doubt that the Jews pronounced this curse on themselves without any concern, as if they had been fully convinced that they had a righteous cause before God; but their inconsiderate zeal carries them headlong, so that, while they commit an irreparable crime, they add to it a solemn impreca-tion, by which they cut themselves off from the hope of pardon.[3]

How weighty and important are our own human words! How carefully we need to deliberate before opening our mouths, and gauge the likely consequences! Speech, our speech, carries with it solemn responsibilities. From time to time we might say to other people that our angry, unwise, or cruel words were spoken "in the heat of the moment." Or we might ask people to forget what we said the day before, because we weren't "think-ing straight." Ecclesiastes 5:2 warns us, "Be not rash with your mouth, nor let your heart be hasty to utter a word before God, for God is in heaven and you are on earth. Therefore let your words be few." The crowd gathered before Pilate and Jesus could not offer any excuse for their words; they amounted, as Calvin noted, to "a solemn imprecation." God heard their words, God knew, and God acted.

THE SINS OF THE FATHERS

At this point it is necessary to pause and ask a question that no doubt will be occurring to the minds of many readers. Would God really curse the children as well as the fathers? Are the children, having been mentioned, to be implicated because of their fathers' reckless outbursts? To many this will seem rather harsh, perhaps even unfair. Clearly we need to deal with this issue in a general sense before turning to the specific incident recorded here.

The postscript to the Second Commandment gives the essential background to this discussion.

> You shall not make for yourself a carved image, or any likeness of anything that is in heaven above, or that is in the earth beneath, or that is in the water under the earth. You shall not bow down to them or serve them, for I the LORD your God am a jealous God, *visiting the iniquity of the fathers on the children to the third and the fourth generation of those who hate me*, but showing steadfast love to thousands of those who love me and keep my commandments. (Ex. 20:4–6)

It is the words in italics that we must especially notice here. Although they are appended to the Second Commandment, they describe God's character and his judgment in a more general sense against all iniquity.

Let us first of all observe that modern Western society reacts strongly against the notion that God has the right to execute his judgment on *any sin at all*. The very concept of God's punishment is regarded as something old-fashioned and outmoded, a relic of a previous era when preachers, teachers, and parents used to "put the fear of God into you." Is not the phrase "divine retribution" heard now only in the context of scorn and mockery, rather like the expression "divine intervention"? How much more unpalatable, then, is the idea that God not only punishes individuals for their own sins, but justly "visits the iniquity of the fathers on the children"? How is this just? Or more precisely, why do people instinctively react against the idea that this *is* just?

The answer surely is that the present Western world has become increasingly individualistic and atomistic, and this attitude has spread into the church. At the base of this is the failure to appreciate the organic, tree-like structure of human society itself. It is true, and accepted without question, that at the most fundamental level children inherit biological characteristics from their parents. But what is of far greater importance—though it is often overlooked or denied—is that attitudes and patterns of behavior are also passed down the family line.

Ultimately this is to be seen in the doctrine of original sin. It is recorded in Genesis 5:1 that "when God created man, he made him in the likeness of God." Adam's created constitution was one of righteousness, true holiness. Then, two verses later, we read that Adam "fathered a son in his own likeness, after his image, and named him Seth." But by now Adam had sinned; he had become a sinner. The consequence was that the offspring of Adam were born in sin, and thus they all died.

Perhaps more relevant to our concern here is that we should see this pattern being reproduced in individual families. Eli, the priest at Shiloh in the latter years of the judges, was visited by a man of God, who spoke to him thus:

> "Why then do you scorn my sacrifices and my offerings that I commanded, and honor your sons above me by fattening yourselves on the choicest parts of every offering of my people Israel?" Therefore the LORD the God of Israel declares: "I prom-ised that your house and the house of your father should go in and out before me forever," but now the LORD declares: "Far be it from me, for those who honor me I will honor, and those who despise me shall be lightly esteemed. Behold, the days are coming when I will cut off your strength and the strength of your father's house, so that there will not be an old man in your house." (1 Sam. 2:29–31)

Here, then, is a very clear instance of the sins of a father being visited upon the children. And what needs to be noted, from the earlier part of this chapter, is that the sons of Eli, Hophni and Phinehas, were acting in such a way that their punishment was entirely deserved. The Judge of all the earth always does right, and no one will ever be able to accuse him of injustice.

JEWISH HISTORY AND PERSECUTION

Therefore the question must now be asked: what were the historical consequences of the words of the crowd that are recorded in Matthew 27:25? We need to exercise special prudence in handling such a subject as this, because it is of course a deeply controversial one. A whole host of related issues might appear to come into the picture: questions on the modern state of Israel and a Palestinian state; the meaning of prophecies that seem to pertain to a great ingathering of Jewish believers at some future date. On these subjects I have no intention of commenting at all. But quite unavoidably, reflections on the fulfillment of these words leads us into deep and emotive considerations. The history of the Jewish people over the last two thousand years has been a story of dispersion, persecution, suffering, and alienation. Most tragically, there have long been professing Christians who have sought to justify ill treatment of the Jews on the grounds that they were "Christ-killers" and who would turn to passages such as this one for support.

It was because of these bleak facts that on October 28, 1965, at the Second Vatican Council, Pope Pius VI issued *Nostra Aetate*, which is translated "Our Times." It was subtitled the "Declaration on the Relation of the (Roman) Church to Non-Christian Religions," in which this subject was addressed. Section 4 dealt specifically with the Jews. "Furthermore, in her rejection of every persecution against any man, the Church, mindful of the patrimony she shares with the Jews and moved not by political reasons but by the Gospel's spiritual love, decries hatred, persecutions, displays of anti-Semitism, directed against Jews at any time and by anyone."[4]

Such a statement was of course extremely timely. John Stott in his celebrated work, *The Cross of Christ*, also addresses this most sensitive of all subjects. "This blaming of the Jewish people for the crucifixion of Jesus is extremely unfashionable today. Indeed, if it is used as a justification for slandering and persecuting the Jews (as it has been in the past), for anti-Semitism, it is absolutely indefensible."[5] Stott's conclusion, of course, must be resolutely upheld. Let us, for the moment, assume that God *has* continued to count the blood of Jesus against all people of Jewish descent throughout the past two millennia. Does this give the smallest excuse for Christians to persecute them on this account? The answer must be an emphatic no. Even if we were to allow that present-day Jews, who reject Jesus as Messiah, continue as enemies of God as regards the gospel (Rom. 11:28), the command to love our enemies would obviously still apply.

But it is necessary to ask a sober question. Is there any biblical warrant to extend the application of Matthew 27:25 to all the generations of Jewish people who lived during the following twenty centuries? The position that is being put forward here can be summarized as follows: the outpouring of God's judgment on Israel's deliberate rejection of Christ evidently came about after some forty years, in the terrible destruction of Jerusalem, which took place in AD 70. It seems prudent not to make any firm pronouncements about what happened after that date and after the close of biblical history.

"ALL THESE THINGS WILL COME UPON THIS GENERATION"

The Gospels contain many clear references to the impending judgment upon Jerusalem. In Matthew 24, in Mark 13, and in Luke 21, this great destruction of the city and of the temple is a central theme in Jesus' discourse, the foreshadowing of the final coming of the Lord himself. Indeed, it is the disciples' remarks concerning the great stones of the temple that bring about Jesus' solemn declaration: "You see all these, do you not? Truly, I say to you, there will not be left here one stone upon another that will not be thrown down" (Matt. 24:2). And there is no more poignant and pointed reference to these terrible events than the words of Jesus that we read in Luke 19:41–44:

> And when he drew near and saw the city, he wept over it, saying, "Would that you, even you, had known on this day the things that make for peace! But now they are hidden from your eyes. For the days will come upon you, when your enemies will set up a barricade around you and surround you and hem you in on every side and tear you down to the ground, you and your children within you. And they will not leave one stone upon another in you, because you did not know the time of your visitation."

Quite evidently, then, Jesus links the destruction of Jerusalem to the unbelief of the Jews, and the unbelief of the Jews reached its highest and shrillest pitch at the very point we are examining in this chapter. But this is the point that needs to be emphasized: we are speaking here of these particular Jews of this specific generation.

At this point we do well to notice again the words of Exodus 20:5, which were quoted a little earlier. God said there that he was "a jealous God, visiting the iniquity of the fathers on the children *to the third and the fourth generation* of those who hate me." These three and four generations are stated in contrast to the "thousands" of those who love him and keep his commandments. It seems indefensible in the light of this declaration to suggest that God's anger against this sin, though it was the greatest sin, would necessarily be visited upon a people for long centuries—let us say for fifty to seventy generations, or even more.

The spotlight must remain firmly fixed upon the Jews of Jesus' own day. Throughout John's gospel, the term "the Jews" invariably refers to the Jewish people *in their rejection of Jesus as Messiah.* Some modern translations—perhaps better termed paraphrases—of the Bible have evidently sensed a degree of unease with the simple and literal rendering of "the Jews" and have preferred to translate these words as "the Jewish leaders" (New Living Translation) or "the Jewish authorities" (Good News Translation). But it is by no means the case that the leaders or authorities are always meant, as in John 6:41, where these translations speak somewhat vaguely of "the people," even though the Greek text states that it was evidently the Jews who were grumbling about Jesus.

We must have the honesty and the courage to acknowledge that the hostility against Jesus sprang from the Jewish people, albeit mainly through the agency of their leaders. We have already seen that Jesus himself admitted as much when he told Pilate that "he who delivered me over to you has the greater sin" (John 19:11). There can be no reasonable suspicion that John was guilty of some form of anti-Semitism—after all, John himself was a Jew. In the book of Acts we see exactly the same pattern as we do in John's gospel. It was "the Jews" in all the cities of the Roman empire who rejected the gospel of Jesus Christ preached by Paul and his companions—with a few noble exceptions like those in Berea (Acts 17:10–12). It was the Jews in Pisidian Antioch who incited the crowds against Paul and Barnabas (13:45, 50). The same was true in Iconium (14:2) and in Thessalonica (17:5). In Corinth the Jews made a concerted attack against Paul (18:12); later, because of the plotting of the Jews, he had to alter his traveling plans (20:3). And it was "the Jews from Asia" who stirred up the crowd in Jerusalem against Paul, leading to his arrest. This opposition of the Jews against Paul and his companions was of a piece with their opposition against Jesus himself, their rejection of the gospel.

A REMNANT WILL BE SAVED

And yet we need to insist that this opposition was general and not total. Paul's clear teaching in Romans 11:5 is that "at the present time there is a remnant, chosen by grace." As it was in the days of Elijah, so it was in the days of Jesus and the apostles. Was Israel utterly sold out to Baal worship when Elijah was prophesying? It may have seemed so to the disconsolate prophet, but he was mightily strengthened to learn of the seven thousand whom the Lord had kept for himself. In the same way there were many Jews, both during Jesus' ministry and afterward, who responded to him in saving faith.

This point is so obvious that it hardly needs to be made. Remember the prophesies of Simeon and Anna, those aged and godly folk who were waiting for the consolation of Israel, to whom was revealed the nature and future work of the child they met in the temple. The apostles were all Jews, as were many others who put their trust in Jesus during the course of his ministry. Does not the conclusion of Peter's sermon at Pentecost underline this even further? "For the promise is for you and for your children and for all who are far off, everyone whom the Lord our God calls to himself" (Acts 2:39). In making this plea, Peter had only Jews in mind, not yet the Gentiles. We then see that in the very earliest days of the church the people of Israel came to their Messiah in great numbers: 3,000, then 5,000. Paul summarizes conclusively in Romans 11:1, "I ask, then, has God rejected his people? By no means! For I myself am an Israelite, a descendant of Abraham, a member of the tribe of Benjamin."

It was indeed a fearful imprecation that this crowd pronounced upon themselves. The physical consequences of it, which came about forty years later in AD 70, were indeed appalling. But there is a further aspect to Israel's general rejection of Christ that we need to understand, and this one does have everlasting consequences.

Israel would no longer, as a nation, continue to be the special objects of God's saving grace. In connection with this, Old Testament scholar O. Palmer Robertson comments, "The solemn consequences of this rejection find expression in the words of

Jesus: 'The kingdom shall be taken away from you and given to a people bearing the fruit of it'" (Matt. 21:43). Israel as a nation would no more be able to claim that they possessed the kingdom of God in a way that was distinct from other nations."[6] From now on, "the Israel of God" (Gal. 6:16) would consist of peoples of all nations who boast only in the cross of Jesus Christ, and in neither circumcision nor uncircumcision. It is faith in God through Jesus Christ that demarcates the people of God.

> There is neither Jew nor Greek, there is neither slave nor free, there is neither male nor female, for you are all one in Christ Jesus. And if you are Christ's, then you are Abraham's offspring, heirs according to promise. (Gal. 3:28–29)

All that was ever uttered to Abraham, to Isaac, to Jacob and to all their seed, by way of promise, now applies to the one worldwide church of Jesus Christ, both Jew and Gentile. The rejection of Israel means the reconciliation of the whole world.

14

THE ROMAN SOLDIERS

And when they came to the place that is called The Skull, there they crucified him, and the criminals, one on his right and one on his left. And Jesus said, "Father, forgive them, for they know not what they do." And they cast lots to divide his garments. (Luke 23:33–34)

WE HAVE JUST WITNESSED the terrible way the Jewish crowd bayed for Jesus' blood and accepted responsibility for it. As we move into the next stage, we can see just how vicious an ordeal they consigned Jesus to. He was now in the custody of the Roman soldiers, who were used to dealing with prisoners in the most barbaric fashion. It was now that the ugliest and basest kind of human behavior came out.

Everything that had happened to Jesus during the previous twelve hours at the hands of the chief priests had been wicked and unjust in the extreme. He had already endured a level of physical torment while he was with the Sanhedrin—though the blindfolding, striking, and spitting were calculated to inflict insult rather than injury. Can any action be more despicable and contemptuous than to spit into someone's face? But it was in this new phase of his sufferings that the shedding of his blood—his own divinely ordained destiny—began.

"WEEP NOT FOR ME"

It is neither necessary nor helpful to describe in detail the nature of Jesus' physical sufferings, especially the scourging, which all four gospel records mention. When the 2004 film *The Passion of the Christ* was released, many churches grasped it as an excellent evangelistic opportunity. Large numbers of seats were reserved and tables containing evangelistic literature were set up in cinemas. Church members were urged to invite their non-Christian friends to watch the film. Undoubtedly those who encouraged such initiatives did so with the utmost zeal and desire to see souls being saved. It should go without saying that we should always applaud these *motives*. But we have to ask whether Scripture itself supports this type of *method*. There is such a thing as zeal not directed by knowledge or wisdom. The underlying idea appears to be that the spectacle of Jesus—or an actor playing the part of Jesus—suffering violently and gruesomely will move the audience and cause them to consider his suffering and death more seriously.[1]

There is no doubt that many people were profoundly moved by this film. It was indeed shocking and horrific. But there is a profound difference between an emotional response to the death of Jesus and a spiritual response to it. We can see this being demonstrated in the case of the women to whom Jesus spoke as he was on the way to Golgotha. Again, it is only Luke who records this incident:

> And there followed him a great multitude of the people and of women who were mourning and lamenting for him. But turning to them Jesus said, "Daughters of Jerusalem, do not weep for me, but weep for yourselves and for your children. For behold, the days are coming when they will say, 'Blessed are the barren and the wombs that never bore and the breasts that never nursed!' Then they will begin to say to the mountains, 'Fall on us,' and

to the hills, 'Cover us.' For if they do these things when the wood is green, what will happen when it is dry?" (Luke 23:27–31)

There is no need to comment on this passage at any length, but it should be observed that Jesus directed the women's sorrow and grief away from his own sufferings and to their future tribulations. It was his own death that would secure everlasting deliverance for all who put their trust in him. It is faith in Jesus that saves people—not pity for him.

In summary, none of the four gospels lingers over the scourging; it is passed over without further comment. It will suffice to say that the Roman scourging was so desperately brutal that it killed some men. In Jesus' case this was followed by the taunting of the soldiers: the purple cloak, the crown of thorns, the mock homage, the striking of Jesus on the head with a reed. So the Jesus who was taken to be crucified had already been subjected to the most merciless treatment. It was a weakened, tortured Jesus who arrived at Calvary, or "the place called The Skull." Thus we come to the cross itself, where we will remain for this chapter and the next two chapters.

SEVEN SAYINGS

When we put the four accounts of Jesus' crucifixion together, we see that there were "Seven Sayings of the Cross." Much attention has been given to these sayings; they have furnished substantial material for many series of sermons leading up to Easter and are often associated with Good Friday. Three of them are unique to Luke's account, three others are unique to John, and the seventh, his cry of dereliction, "My God, my God, why have you forsaken me," is the only one reported by Matthew and Mark.

What are the words of Christ from the cross that Luke records? In verse 34 we hear his prayer at the very moment when he is being crucified: "Father, forgive them, for they know not what they do." In verse 43 we read his words to the criminal who repented and believed: "Today you will be with me in Paradise," and this will occupy more of our concern in chapter 16. Then there are his final words in verse 46 as he breathes his last: "Father, into your hands I commit my spirit!" Amidst the darkness, the violence, the appalling cruelty of that day, Luke gives us these several shafts of pure, brilliant sunlight. For the time being, let us focus on the first of these sayings, his prayer in verse 34. We see in it a precedent for Stephen's dying prayer in Acts 7:60, words which Luke also recorded: "Lord, do not hold this sin against them."

A Gracious Prayer

We should first of all notice that this is a *gracious prayer*, indeed a prayer of unparalleled grace. Of course, all the sayings of Jesus are gracious words. In them we see the most dramatic contrast to everything else that was being said at the time. In the following chapter we will give thought to the words of the chief priests, the scribes, and the elders, "He saved others; he cannot save himself" (Matt. 27:42), by which they sank to their lowest level.

What exactly is this "grace" of which we speak? Grace is love shown to one who is undeserving of that love. But we must surely go considerably further than this as we consider this prayer. The grace God gives to sinners is *the very opposite of what they deserve*. What did these Roman soldiers deserve, putting the Son of God to death as they were? Surely a prayer for strict justice, for punishment and wrath, would have been more appropriate? Why didn't Jesus pray one of the imprecatory Psalms, such as Psalm 109? But grace gives not simply to the undeserving, but to those who deserve the complete opposite.

Our text implies that Jesus was praying this prayer in the immediate aftermath of the action of the soldiers in crucifying him. We must not commit the error of indulging ourselves in expressions of pity for Jesus, as we have seen, but we are bound to look and wonder. How could such a prayer be possible? Jesus was a real man, with real flesh and blood, with real nerves in his hands and feet. He felt the agonizing pain. He had chosen not to drink the wine mixed with gall that would deaden that pain. Jesus knew that he had to enter fully, and with unimpaired consciousness, into the entire horror of the cross. As the nails were being hammered in, his whole body would have been racked with the deepest agony.

But the breathtaking grace of the Lord Jesus meant that now, even now, he prayed for these people, the very people who were inflicting torture on him and putting him to death. We can climb an ascending staircase of grace. First of all, for Jesus *not* to have cursed and insulted these soldiers was itself remarkable. Surely every other victim they had crucified would have done this. Peter draws our attention to this behavior of Jesus: "When he was reviled, he did not revile in return; when he suffered, he did not threaten, but continued entrusting himself to him who judges justly" (1 Peter 2:23). It is a clear demonstration of the sinless character of the Son of God. Second, for Jesus to have positively remembered *anyone* in prayer, anyone perhaps other than himself, is even more astonishing. But we see, third, that in fact Jesus did more—he prayed not for himself, not for his friends, but for the men who were actively engaged in putting him to death.

Here is the unparalleled demonstration of what Jesus had said and taught in his own ministry. "Love your enemies and pray for those who persecute you, so that you may be sons of your Father who is in heaven" (Matt. 5:44–45). What Jesus had preached he also practiced, even—perhaps we should say *especially*—in the most extreme situation. The words of this text from the Sermon on the Mount also reveal to us that Jesus, uniquely, was the Son of his heavenly Father. For in praying that his Father would forgive them, Jesus himself was undoubtedly extending forgiveness to them.

Alfred Edersheim gives powerful and poignant expression to the sublime character of Jesus' prayer.

> In the moment of the deepest abasement of Christ's Human Nature, the Divine bursts forth most brightly. It is, as if the Saviour would discard all that is merely human in His Sufferings, just as before He had discarded the Cup of stupefying wine. These soldiers were but the unconscious instruments: the form was nothing; the contest was between the Kingdom of God and that of darkness, between the Christ and Satan, and these sufferings were but the necessary path of obedience, and to victory and glory.[2]

Then he continues,

> Then also in the utter self-forgetfulness of the God-Man— which is one of the aspects of the Incarnation—does He only remember Divine mercy, and pray for them who crucify Him; and thus also does the Conquered truly conquer His conquerors by asking for them what their deed had forfeited.[3]

A PRIESTLY PRAYER

Second, let us notice that this is a *priestly prayer*. We must begin by asking what exactly is meant by a priest. In these days of ecclesiastical confusion, precise biblical definitions often become distorted in people's minds. A priest is a mediator between God and man, one who pleads and prays to God on man's behalf. A priest is a man who comes before God with offerings to present so that God will receive the people for whom the priest is praying. Throughout the Old Testament there were many priests who lived, prayed for the people, made sacrifices for the people, and then died. The letter to the Hebrews gives memorable expression to the repetitious succession of priests that offered the same sacrifices, which could never take away sins. But it also demonstrates triumphantly that here, in Jesus, is the one great, final high priest (Heb. 10:11–14).

And the point that needs to be understood is that Jesus is acting as that priest from the cross. John 17 is often called the Great High Priestly Prayer. It deserves to be; there is no other point in the Scriptures in which we are permitted to ascend so high and to witness the secret counsel of love and obedience that exists between the Father and the Son. But perhaps what we have here, in Luke 23:34, could be termed the "Short High Priestly Prayer," in itself no less powerful and wonderful. Remember the words of Psalm 110:4, repeated in the letter to the Hebrews; "You are a priest forever, after the order of Melchizedek." A priest forever! The writer to the Hebrews then goes on to say in 7:24–25,

> He holds his priesthood permanently, because he continues forever. Consequently, he is able to save to the uttermost those who draw near to God through him, since he always lives to make intercession for them.

Yes, Jesus was acting as a priest even now. Indeed, Jesus was never so priestly as he was at this point. In the very act of working salvation for his people, in bringing the once-for-all perfect offering for sin, in the very bloodletting that forgives sin, he is interceding for sinners. Here is the view of Jesus that we all need to keep in our minds that will convey to us the deepest spiritual assurance. He is being nailed to the cross, his blood is being shed, and he prays, "Father, forgive them, for they know not what they do."

He is a priest, but see that he is even more. "Yet he bore the sin of many, and makes intercession for the transgressors" (Isa. 53:12). In the same verse Jesus is shown to be both priest and sacrifice. Can we understand that this prayer of Jesus, at the hour of his death, is a summary of all the work he came into the world to do? His whole human existence was geared toward his death. His own death was the only offering, the only transaction, that could bring about the forgiveness of sinners, even those who pursued him to death. Only he, the Redeemer, can "deliver them out of an estate of sin and misery."[4] Every sin that is forgiven, every soul that is cleansed and restored to fellowship with God, is on account of our praying, dying, gracious high priest.

OUR GENTLE HIGH PRIEST

But notice something else even more profound. He prays, "Father, forgive them, *for they know not what they do.*" That is, these Roman soldiers were ignorant. They did not know what a great crime and sin they were committing. Their ignorance is appended to the request and seems to be uttered in mitigation.

Does it follow that it is better to be ignorant than to be wise? Is it really true that "ignorance is bliss," as people say? This is surely dangerous as it stands. If I commit a crime because I did not know anything about the law I had broken, I must still be counted guilty. Ignorance does not excuse guilt. But ignorance certainly *lessens* the intensity of the guilt. In the law that was given through Moses there was a distinction to be made between those who sinned in ignorance, or accidentally, and those who sinned willfully and deliberately. The penalty was much greater for deliberate sin. Thus in Numbers 15:29–31 we read,

> You shall have one law for him who does anything unintentionally, for him who is native among the people of Israel and for the stranger who sojourns among them. But the person who does anything with a high hand, whether he is native or a sojourner, reviles the LORD, and that person shall be cut off from among his people. Because he has despised the word of the LORD and has broken his commandment, that person shall be utterly cut off; his iniquity shall be on him.

An outworking of this principle is subsequently seen in the case of the man who was found gathering sticks on the Sabbath day (Num. 15:32–36); he was sinning with a "high hand."

The Roman soldiers evidently sinned in ignorance; that is the declaration in Jesus' own words. Does that imply, therefore, that the people of Israel, and most importantly the chief priests and elders, had sinned against the clear light of the day "with a high hand" in condemning Jesus? Undoubtedly the Jews were less excusable on this count than the Roman soldiers.

And yet the evidence of the New Testament shows that ignorance was found even among the Jews. When Peter addressed the crowd in the temple in Jerusalem, having healed the lame man, he told them, "And now, brothers, I know that you acted in ignorance, as did also your rulers" (Acts 3:17). Paul echoed this same understanding in 1 Corinthians 2:8: "None of the rulers of this age understood this, for if they had, they would not have crucified the Lord of glory." What had they not understood? The "secret and hidden wisdom of God, which God decreed before the ages for our glory" (1 Cor. 2:7). Those who crucified Jesus were guilty of a great sin against God—but even in their case there was great ignorance. They did not have eyes to see that he was truly "the Lord of glory," though they knew enough to have realized that he was Israel's Messiah.

Let us also consider Paul's testimony in 1 Timothy 1:13–14: "I received mercy because I had acted ignorantly in unbelief, and the grace of our Lord overflowed for me with the faith and love that are in Christ Jesus." Paul knew his Old Testament Scriptures inside and out—but being ignorant of the eternal glory of Jesus Christ, he was shown great mercy and patience. We will devote much more space to this text and to the case of Paul in our final chapter.

This is all part of Jesus' high priestly work. This high priest deals gently with those who are ignorant and going astray (Heb. 5:2). Such is his grace. "They know not what they do." Is there any sinner in the whole world for whom this is not true? How many adult converts to Christ really knew what they were doing in the days when they used to blaspheme Jesus' name? Do they not see, after conversion, the amazing forbearance that God had shown them?

A POWERFUL PRAYER

Then, of course, it was a most *powerful prayer*, a prayer that was to be answered, and not only that, but a prayer that was being answered even during the ensuing hours while Jesus was upon the cross. For whom was Jesus praying, and for whom was this prayer effective? Just who is the "them" of Luke 23:34? The most obvious and immediate reference may seem to be to the very men who were crucifying him, the Roman soldiers. But we can easily demonstrate that the scope of the prayer extends considerably further.

Shortly in this narrative we read about the thief on the cross who repented and believed in Jesus. We will come to consider this in more detail in chapter 16. But for the time being it is well worth noting that it is only Luke who tells us about Jesus' prayer in verse 34, and that it is only Luke who tells us about the repentant thief. How quickly Jesus' prayer was answered! Matthew and Mark tell us simply that both these men reviled and insulted Jesus, just like the passersby and chief priests. "Save yourself and us!" they shouted. But Luke wants us to know more. He wants us to see how powerful and effective this prayer of Jesus was. Luke wants us to see the kind of person for whom this prayer was meant—a robber, a criminal, who had at one time been joining in the bitter chorus of recrimination against Jesus. Now he is told he will be in Paradise that very day. Again, behold amazing grace!

Then take a look at the Roman centurion who was standing by the cross, and hear his great exclamation when Jesus died. He praised God. "Certainly this man was innocent!" (Luke 23:47). Matthew and Mark report that he said more—"Truly this man was the Son of God!" There is no problem with these differing words—he surely made both declarations—and what a confession of faith it was, what an answer to Jesus' prayer! A Roman soldier who had been involved in the whole operation was transformed by the grace and power of the one whose execution he had overseen.

There is a further detail that Luke alone records. Immediately after the centurion had uttered his words, we see the crowds, the Jewish people, returning home and beating their breasts (Luke 23:48). As we read Luke's narrative in particular, we cannot fail to observe the profound change that swept over that whole gathered multitude as that Friday wore on. We must remark how the initial scorn and triumphalism of the crowd was muted as the crucifixion progressed. The deep darkness that fell over the land signaled a great hush. The culmination of this transformation is seen in this guilt-stricken crowd who return home in deep shame and sorrow. The Lutheran New Testament commentator Richard Lenski put it like this: "They came to witness a show, they left with feelings of woe."[5]

THE WIDENESS OF GOD'S MERCY

In the previous chapter we witnessed the way many of these people had not only clamored for Jesus' death, but accepted full responsibility for the shedding of his blood. At one level we might be seeing here the consequences of their fearful words. Blood-guilt in relation to the death of Jesus was already afflicting their consciences. But is it too much to suggest that Jesus' prayer from the cross had been effective for at least some of these people, his own countrymen?

Those who went home beating their breasts must have been convicted of their sin; or at any rate this was a preparatory work for what would follow seven weeks later. For on the day of Pentecost Peter would conclude his majestic sermon—the inaugural address of the Christian era—by telling the assembled crowds, "Let all the house of Israel therefore know for certain that God has made him both Lord and Christ, *this Jesus whom you crucified*"

(Acts 2:36). Three thousand souls that day, cut to the heart by the knowledge of what they had done to Jesus, would repent of their sins and be baptized into his name—the one who was indeed Lord as well as Christ. The number would subsequently reach five thousand (Acts 4:4). Let us also not fail to notice what we are told in Acts 6:7: "And the word of God continued to increase, and the number of the disciples multiplied greatly in Jerusalem, *and a great many of the priests became obedient to the faith.*" What—even some of the priests who had accused him before Pilate and Herod, and who shouted insults at him when he was on the cross? Why should this not be the case—who are we to restrict the extent of Jesus' prayer and the wideness of God's mercy?

"Mercy triumphs over judgment" (James 2:13). The Jewish crowd did indeed call down God's dreadful curse upon themselves and their children. The majority of Jews, during both Jesus' ministry and the apostolic period afterwards, remained stubbornly hardhearted toward Jesus. The destruction of Jerusalem and the end of the temple followed after forty years. But Jesus' gracious, priestly, and powerful intercession from the cross guaranteed the extension of mercy to a great number of Jews as well as Gentiles. Indeed, it encapsulates the very heart and essence of his whole ministry to us.

As Jesus is praying, he surely means this: "Father, completely blot out their sins and transgressions. By your power and grace forgive them fully; give them a new heart and a new mind." J. C. Ryle wrote that "the fruits of this wonderful prayer will never be fully seen until the day when the books are opened, and the secrets of all hearts revealed."[6]

So let me ask the reader a final question. What do *you* make of this prayer? I remember well the first time a Christian told me she was praying for me. At the time I was a curious seeker. It was wholly new to me; I felt touched, though perhaps a little embarrassed at first. Then, when I began to hear other godly believers praying together, I sensed the deepest honor and privilege in hearing their prayers. But here we are permitted to hear this prayer of the Son of God, a majestic intercession that stands for all eternity and is the basis of the salvation of everyone who believes. It is a prayer "to open their eyes, so that they may turn from darkness to light and from the power of Satan to God, that they may receive forgiveness of sins and a place among those who are sanctified by faith in me" (Acts 26:18).

Are you too bad, too wicked, too far gone? Are you beyond the reach of the prayers of Jesus? Stop and look at the people he prayed for here, and see that his prayer was sufficient for them. It is sufficient for you too.

THE CLIMAX OF
JESUS' SUFFERINGS

*And those who passed by derided him, wagging their
heads and saying, "You who would destroy the temple
and rebuild it in three days, save yourself! If you are the
Son of God, come down from the cross." So also the chief
priests, with the scribes and elders, mocked him, saying,
"He saved others; he cannot save himself. He is the King
of Israel; let him come down now from the cross, and we
will believe in him. He trusts in God; let God deliver him
now, if he desires him. For he said, 'I am the Son of God.'"
And the robbers who were crucified with him also reviled
him in the same way. Now from the sixth hour there was
darkness over all the land until the ninth hour. And about
the ninth hour Jesus cried out with a loud voice, saying,
"Eli, Eli, lema sabachthani?" that is, "My God, my God,
why have you forsaken me?" (Matt. 27:39–46)*

TOWARD THE END of George Orwell's dystopian novel
Nineteen Eighty-Four the central character of the story, Winston Smith, is imprisoned by the authorities and then savagely
beaten on the elbow by a guard. In his reeling agony he sees that
"one question at any rate was answered. Never, for any reason
on earth, could you wish for an increase of pain. Of pain you

could only wish one thing: that it should stop. Nothing in the world was so bad as physical pain."[1] Certainly the pain of physical suffering can reach an intensity that surpasses everything else. This reality allows brutal regimes to extract information from people by means of torture.

As we have already observed, we are not called upon to dwell primarily on the physical nature of Jesus' suffering. This has been a danger not only in Roman Catholicism but in certain forms of Protestantism with a mystical tendency. The details of the method by which Jesus was put to death are passed over summarily; the Scriptures do not intend to excite some kind of macabre fascination with the physical horrors of crucifixion. Of course we must affirm that his suffering *was* physical—to deny this would lead us into the realms of heresy—but we learn far more when we seek to understand the deeper, spiritual character of his suffering.

WORDS WILL NEVER HURT ME?

Most readers will be familiar with the old children's rhyme, or something very similar to it:

Sticks and stones may break by bones
But words will never hurt me.

Not only are we familiar with it, we must all know very well—by personal experience as well as by notion—that it is utterly untrue. Indeed, the only time we ever hear it quoted is when its falsity is being demonstrated. Memories of severe physical pain tend to evaporate much more quickly than recollections of cruel and harsh words. The damage done by harmful words often lingers far longer, and penetrates far deeper, than physical suffering. Therefore in many places the Bible emphasizes the great destruction that is wrought by an evil and malicious tongue. The Wisdom Books of the Old Testament, and the letter of James in the New, furnish us with many instances of this observation.[2]

Thus it was at Calvary. The gospel writers provide us with several examples of the extreme callousness of Jesus' enemies as they stood by the cross, taunting and blaspheming him.

We do not read that a small minority of wicked men said a few spiteful words in Jesus' direction. The impression given in our text is that cursing and blasphemy were hurled at him from every direction. In Matthew 27:39 we are told that the passersby vented at Jesus. It is well known that crucifixions generally took place at busy crossroads and thoroughfares; thus in John 19:20 we read that Jesus was crucified "near the city" in order to maximize the impact. It was the intention of the Romans to make a public example and spectacle of those who were being crucified. Most such men were violent criminals, like the other two individuals being executed with Jesus. Their crucifixion in the glare of the public eye was the Romans' way of saying, "Don't let anyone imagine they can get away with crime against Roman author- ity—if they try they'll end up like these men." In a day when there were no newspapers, no television, and no Internet, this was the most powerful medium of communication.

But we should also observe that there is no indication that the many passersby spent any time reviling the other two men on the cross. They all joined in attacking Jesus. Even the two crucified criminals did so for a time, and it is only Luke who records that one of them later repented. Jesus' cross was in the middle, for Jesus was quite literally center stage. See the savage insults he received!

At Calvary, more than anywhere else, it was as though the light of human decency and moral sympathy had been utterly extinguished from people's souls. There seems to have been a complete removal of God's common grace from their hearts and consciences. That is, God's restraining hand, which normally prevents evil from spiraling out of control, seems temporarily to have been withdrawn from many, if not all, of the bystanders. So added to the physical agony and the curse and shame of crucifixion were the taunts and mockery of the people who stood there watching. Jesus was surrounded by a great crowd of enemies. Indeed, on the cross, where he was more terribly alone than he had ever been, almost everyone had become an enemy.

Come Down from the Cross!

Why are these insults and blasphemies recorded for us? They must be seen as the fulfillment of Old Testament prophecy, most strikingly the fulfillment of Psalm 22. Any reader who is not familiar with this psalm should read it at the earliest opportunity; those who know it would benefit from reading it again. Though it was penned by Jesus' ancestor King David a thousand years earlier, it is hard to identify an instance in David's life when he endured such appalling suffering as we read of here. The respected Old Testament scholar Derek Kidner comments. "Whatever the initial stimulus, the language of the Psalm defies a naturalistic explanation; the best account is in the terms used by Peter concerning another psalm of David: 'Being therefore a prophet . . . he foresaw and spoke of . . . the Christ' (Acts 2:30f.)."[3]

Therefore in some respects the Old Testament prophecies of Jesus' suffering and death are an even more graphic and powerful portrayal than the New Testament records, though in this case they are separated by a millennium. Our attention should be especially drawn to verses 7–8 of Psalm 22: "All who see me mock me; they make mouths at me; they wag their heads; 'He trusts in the LORD; let him deliver him; let him rescue him, for he delights in him!'" We can almost see the people wagging or shaking their heads at him, and hear their cries of contempt and ridicule. Just how hollow and ridiculous Jesus' claims seemed to them now! Here was a man who was completely defeated and beyond any help and an easy target for his opponents, who were pillorying him with undisguised glee.

Let us now turn to examine some of the things these people said to Jesus. Both the passersby and the chief priests, with the scribes and elders, sank to a truly diabolical level when they implored him to come down from the cross. I use the word "diabolical" because Satan himself had tempted Jesus to demonstrate his power by a miracle of a similar kind—throwing himself off the pinnacle of the temple. The same request—to come down from the cross—was made by one of the other crucified men, the one who did not go on to repent and believe (Luke 23:39).

Look first at the passersby, who had heard reports of Jesus talking about the destruction and rebuilding of the temple— words which Jesus applied not to Herod's temple, but to his own body (John 2:19–22). In Matthew 27:40 they assailed him. "You who would destroy the temple and rebuild it in three days, save yourself! If you are the Son of God, come down from the cross." Here was the utmost malice: these people, looking upon the crucified Jesus, felt certain that he could never perform this one final miracle. Throughout his ministry he had not made a habit of performing signs when people had demanded it; he had told them that they were "an evil and adulterous generation" (Matt. 12:39; 16:4). Herod the tetrarch had asked for a miracle that very morning and had been denied. These passersby were simply kicking him when he was at his lowest.

Then consider the words of the chief priests in the second part of verse 42: "He is the King of Israel; let him come down now from the cross, and we will believe in him." William Hendriksen observes that between the passersby and the leaders there was this "rather striking difference. The bypassers had addressed Jesus directly, using the second person singular. . . . But not once in the narrative of Christ's crucifixion—whether in Matthew, Mark, or Luke—do the leaders address Jesus directly. Each time they talk *about* him, to each other. They never talk *to* him. So thoroughly do they hate him."[4] When people speak about us in our presence as if we were not there, we feel that they are treating us rudely and contemptuously. This was how these men treated the Son of God.

Further, notice that they used the most hideous sarcasm. Jesus' claim to kingship, as the chief priests interpreted it, was the initial basis of their accusation against Jesus when they brought him to Pilate. Now they began to affirm that kingship in the most hideously ironic manner, just as the Roman soldiers had placed a crown of thorns upon his head and donned him with other mock tokens of royalty. And they had no intention of ever believing in him.

Let us observe in passing that it is sometimes said that "sarcasm is the lowest form of wit but the highest form of intelligence," or words to a similar effect. Whether or not sarcastic speech is indeed a type of sophistication, we should flee from it. It was the form of speech employed by Jesus' enemies on the day of his death. Sarcasm is a form of speech utterly opposed to a peaceable, godly spirit. For the Christian it should be "Let your 'Yes' be 'Yes,' and your 'No,' 'No'; anything beyond this comes from the evil one" (Matt. 5:37 NIV). That was certainly the case here—it further underlines that what was being said by these men was from the devil himself.

And then see their words in verse 43: "He trusts in God; let God deliver him now, if he desires him. For he said, 'I am the Son of God.'" What a bitter, appalling taunt this was! Here these chief priests plumbed the lowest depths of wickedness. They implied that God could never want or desire Jesus. This man could only be suffering the just anger of God for his blasphemous claims. The eternal and intimate bond of fellowship between the Father and the Son, infinitely precious to the Lord Jesus Christ, was being savagely attacked. How wounded his soul would have been by all this!

"HE SAVED OTHERS; HE CANNOT SAVE HIMSELF"

We could spend a great deal of time examining these words that were spoken against the Savior and could denounce them for their barbarity and heinous wickedness. But surely we can do much more; indeed, by examining their words carefully we can even profit from them. Such is the divine depth of meaning that we find in Holy Scripture. For these chief priests and elders really could not understand the full implications of what they were saying, and nowhere is this more evident than in the words we read at the beginning of verse 42. "He saved others; he cannot save himself."

Perhaps we can observe that now, and only now, they are prepared to pay Jesus a tribute. He had saved others; yes, he had saved plenty of others! Pontius Pilate knew that the chief priests had handed Jesus over to him because of envy. Part of that envy was that they could not do the mighty works that Jesus was doing. It was the raising of Lazarus in Bethany a few months earlier that had led to the panicked meeting of the council—they had to do something because Jesus kept performing all these signs and the crowds were following him. Yes, there was no doubting that he saved others. Now that Jesus was safely nailed to the cross it was quite safe to admit that openly. Because now, when it really counted, when they had him in the corner they wanted him in, he could do nothing. What is more, they would have noticed over the course of the last twenty-four hours that Jesus had done nothing to resist his arrest, trial, and sentence. He had not defended himself when he had been charged; he had barely spoken at all. Indeed he could not save himself, but neither had he given the slightest indication that he had tried to do so.

What the chief priests and elders did not understand, in their hour of apparent triumph, was that the very words upon their lips were true words of prophecy whose deeper meaning was completely hidden from them. In this respect they were like their own high priest, Caiaphas, who as we saw in chapter 9 prophesied that Jesus would die for the nation, and not "for the nation only, but also to gather into one the children of God who are scattered abroad" (John 11:51–52). Caiaphas had only evil intentions toward Jesus, but the Holy Spirit intended these words as a prophecy of cosmic dimension.

"He saved others; he cannot save himself." For this was indeed true: on this occasion Jesus could not save himself, or more exactly Jesus *would* not save himself. This was not because of any lack of power on his part. When Jesus was being arrested the previous evening Peter had struck one of the high priest's servants and cut off his ear. Jesus, rebuking Peter, asked him, "Do you think that I cannot appeal to my Father, and he will at once send me more than twelve legions of angels?" (Matt. 26:53). The same power would have been at his disposal on the cross; by the exercise of his divine rights he *could* have come down from the cross. He could have proved his enemies absolutely wrong and silenced them with one final, breathtaking miracle.

But Jesus knew that he had to stay on the cross. The cross was his life's destiny. His non-resistance to the machinations of his enemies was all due to his determination to fulfill the Scriptures and carry out the work that the Father had given him to do. Though in his humanity he shrank from the cross—"My Father, if it be possible, let this cup pass from me"—straightaway he added, "nevertheless, not as I will, but as you will" (Matt. 26:39). He had submitted himself to his Father and bound himself to obedience. In that attitude he went to Golgotha.

So this is the very heart of our text: the only way that Jesus would ever save others—save them spiritually, eternally, utterly; not only their bodies for a time but their bodies and souls forever—was by submitting himself to this sentence. He must not save himself. The greatest imperative of all time compelled Jesus. He "set his face to go to Jerusalem" (Luke 9:51). He said subsequently, "I must go on my way today and tomorrow and the day following, for it cannot be that a prophet should perish away from Jerusalem" (Luke 13:33).

Saved by His Precious Blood

Do you really understand the cross of Jesus Christ; do you know what it means and why Jesus had to go there? Are you able to explain at any length the meaning of the expression "Jesus died for our sins"?

The sufferings of Jesus Christ are sometimes referred to as his "passion" or his "passive obedience." Now although Jesus' suffering was so apparently passive, although his situation seemed so evidently helpless—which is precisely what his foes observed, and the reason they taunted him as they did—we, with the whole Bible in our hands and the eye of faith with which to see, must understand that Jesus was *actively at work* upon the cross. We sometimes speak of the death of Christ as his "work"; the expression "The Work of Christ" is most often linked to his crucifixion. Perhaps this seems rather strange, even macabre. In what possible sense can Jesus' suffering and death ever be described as "work"?

The answer is that the suffering of Christ on the cross was his necessary and unavoidable task if innumerable souls were to be saved. Christ offered himself on the cross in place of sinful men and women, for that was the only way he could deliver them from the power, guilt, and punishment of sin.

We might gain a clearer appreciation of what all this means if we venture to paraphrase the words of the chief priests. "He can't save himself *because*, right now, he is saving others." The wages of sin is death. Jesus came into this world to seek and to save the lost, sinners who are facing eternal death. How can dead, lost sinners ever be saved? Only by Jesus dying in their place, the righteous for the unrighteous. It is precisely because he is engaged in saving others that he cannot and must not save himself. It was wholehearted consent and obedience to the will of his Father that took Jesus to the cross and kept him there. When it was suggested that he might come down from the cross, he would not—not through any lack of divine power, but because of his obedience. "He was held, not by the nails, but by His will to save them."[5]

Here is the supreme demonstration of the love of Christ. "Greater love has no one than this, that someone lays down his life for his friends" (John 15:13). "In this is love, not that we have loved God but that he loved us and sent his Son to be the propitiation for our sins" (1 John 4:10). Furthermore, this love is demonstrated in the Bible to belong to the Godhead—Father, Son, and Holy Spirit. The great plan of salvation is the work of all three persons. To say or imply that the Son loved his people more than the Father did is to create an unbiblical disharmony within the Godhead, and it also flies in the face of the great declaration of John 3:16: "For God so loved the world, that he gave his only Son, that whoever believes in him should not perish but have eternal life."

THE HEART OF HIS DARKNESS

In our previous chapter we considered the Roman soldiers, who by their hands had inflicted physical pain and torture upon Jesus. From there the obvious step seemed to be to move on to the next assailants in the drama, the chief priests and elders who tried to add to Jesus' suffering and pain by mocking and ridiculing him bitterly. These individuals we have now dealt with. We could have left our discussion there, but we still have not descended to the lowest depth of Jesus' darkness. It is necessary to penetrate deeper and to ask the question: what caused Jesus the most intense suffering? Was it nails, was it words, or was it something more overwhelming than either of these?

Recall that the previous evening, when a crowd came to arrest him in the garden of Gethsemane, Jesus had said to them, "This is your hour, and the power of darkness" (Luke 22:53). Our passage describes how from the sixth hour of that day—that is from noon—a great darkness came upon the land. This darkness accompanied the darkness in Jesus' own soul and what has become known as his cry of dereliction: "My God, my God, why have you forsaken me?" (Matt. 27:46) In chapter 2 of this book we saw that the enmity of Satan lay behind all Jesus' conflicts throughout his life. Are we therefore to understand that Jesus was now subjected to the deadliest and most violent assault of Satan and his forces?

We need to exercise caution here because the Scriptures say little about Satan's activity in connection with the events surrounding the cross. It is often implied that Satan was oppressing Jesus to the most intense degree when the Savior was in the garden of Gethsemane. Jesus' appalling agony and the bloody sweat (Luke 22:44) are sometimes regarded as the effects of his adversary's most fearful weapons. Yet we find little biblical warrant to affirm this. In particular, we should see that Jesus' combat with Satan, and indeed his triumph over him, is by no means the only aspect, or even the most significant aspect, of his suffering and death. For Jesus' suffering primarily had what we might call a godward aspect. He was principally enduring the wrath of the Father against his people's sin, not the fury of the Devil against his own obedience. This was true initially in the anticipation that took place in the garden and subsequently in the actual experience on the cross, when the sky darkened and Jesus spoke these words of utter abandonment.

Leon Morris expands on this.

Jesus was in agony as He faced death. Why? Death is never a pleasant prospect, but many have faced it calmly. Significantly, many of Jesus' own followers have faced their death without a qualm, some even with exultation. Jesus was no coward, as many incidents in His life amply testify. It is impossible to hold that He was afraid of leaving this life. It was not death as such that He feared. It was the particular death that He was to die, that death which is "the wages of sin" as Paul puts it (Rom. 6:23), the death in which He was at one with sinners, sharing their lot, bearing their sins, dying their death.[6]

George Smeaton, the nineteenth-century Scottish theologian whose works on the atonement deserve to be read and reread, describes what it was that Jesus endured in great detail:

> The words of Jesus in Gethsemane were uttered under a heaviness and fear which seemed to intimate that body and mind alike were ready to give way, and for ever to be rendered unfit for discharging the task assigned Him with the fortitude and steadfastness, the patience and endurance, that were required. He felt that humanity could bear no higher degree of sorrow. Though His humanity was strengthened secretly by the support of the divine nature, it seemed to Him that His mind and body could not bear more, without dissolution or wholly giving way under the pressure.[7]

Smeaton then goes on to explain the cry of dereliction itself. "What the Lord Jesus thus uttered was His actual experience; and as it was from the faithful witness, it was according to truth. He who was the light of the world was under the hiding of His Father's face."[8]

We hardly dare make any further comment on Jesus' words. Here was uniquely terrible suffering. Here was the righteous Son of God with the sin of the world heaped upon his shoulders; the Lamb of God who was laid out upon the altar of God's wrath, bloodied not only in his body but in his soul.

Jesus Has a Future

And yet we have not quite finished. There is a further observation about the words of Jesus' enemies that we need to make. He would ultimately demonstrate that their words—"He saved others; he cannot save himself"—were completely wrong and he would triumph over them. Jesus would indeed save himself and come down from the cross. Having saved others, he would also save himself.

Jesus' opponents, as we have seen, said what they did with a sense of absolute certainty. They were sure that they could never be proved wrong. Jesus' prophecy about the temple being destroyed could never come true now. They knew that he could never come down from the cross. They knew that now he could never be the King of Israel. And of course he could never save himself.

But they were speaking of matters they had no power to understand. Yes, Jesus is dying, and he will die. He will appear to be beaten. His enemies will seem to be absolutely triumphant. The power of darkness will seem to be established upon the throne of heaven and earth. But very soon all this will be transformed, and the words of scorn and mockery that were spoken against Jesus will rebound on the ones who uttered them. It is most instructive to examine all the words that these enemies spoke in verses 40 to 43, and then to notice that every one of them is satisfactorily addressed in Jesus' dying and in his rising from the dead.

All these statements in these verses meant one thing as far as the chief priests and scribes were concerned. But exactly the same words could reasonably be spoken by a believing Christian with a wholly different meaning. We do well to take hold of these words, understood in this secondary sense, as a basic confession of our faith. Let me explain.

1. Jesus had offered his opponents the opportunity to destroy the temple and said that he would raise it in the space of three days. Now they are doing exactly what he had said, but the temple is his own body, and the rebuilding of the temple will be his imminent resurrection.

2. Jesus will indeed come down from the cross. Not only will his body be taken down when he is dead, but that body will

be raised to life, though still bearing the scars of his death in his hands and his side. The Lamb of God is a lamb who has been slain, and his enemies themselves will one day look on him "whom they have pierced" (Zech. 12:10).

3. Jesus really is the King of Israel. He is demonstrating his kingship now. By dying for his people he is making them his own subjects. Here is true kingly greatness—loving and serving his people to the very end, to the uttermost. He is not king over national Israel, but King over all who willingly bow the knee to him, who love the truth as it is in Jesus.

4. And above all notice that God *is* going to save him! Jesus is the beloved Son of God, the one in whom God delights. As has been already noted, he is in the process of fulfilling Psalm 22. Instinctively, as we turn to that Psalm, our eyes fasten upon the suffering.

> For dogs encompass me;
>   a company of evildoers encircles me;
> they have pierced my hands and feet—
> I can count all my bones—
> they stare and gloat over me;
> they divide my garments among them,
>   and for my clothing they cast lots. (Ps. 22:16–18)

But in the suffering there is the cry of help and the expression of trust in the Father.

> But you, O LORD, do not be far off!
>   O you my help, come quickly to my aid! (22:19)

Psalm 22 ought to be read right to the end, because it tells not only of the suffering of God's Servant, but his glorious triumph. Jesus Christ is the Conqueror who, by the shedding of his own blood, brings many sons to glory.

I will tell of your name to my brothers;
in the midst of the congregation I will praise you. (22:22)

There is a future for Jesus! He *will* come down from the cross. And he will come and make his salvation known among his brothers, in his congregation. The praise of Jesus Christ will be the great and central business of heaven. For all eternity, the Lamb himself, the one who has been slain, will be all the glory of Immanuel's land.

THE CRUCIFIED ROBBER

One of the criminals who were hanged railed at him,
saying, "Are you not the Christ? Save yourself and us!"
But the other rebuked him, saying, "Do you not fear God,
since you are under the same sentence of condemnation?
And we indeed justly, for we are receiving the due reward
of our deeds; but this man has done nothing wrong." And
he said, "Jesus, remember me when you come into your
kingdom." And he said to him, "Truly, I say to you, today
you will be with me in Paradise." (Luke 23:39–43)

GOD, WHO HAS GIVEN us the whole Bible, chose to furnish his people with four accounts of the life and work of his Son. Each of the Gospels has its own distinctive character. Matthew, in stately fashion, demonstrates that Jesus is Israel's Messiah and King, fulfilling the Old Testament Scriptures. Mark gives us a fast-moving eyewitness account of the works of Jesus. John, proceeding from the viewpoint of eternity, writes in order to persuade his readers that Jesus, by his words and works, is indeed the Christ, the Son of God, in whom we have life if we believe. The scholarly and versatile Luke provides his correspondent Theophilus with an orderly account, designed to persuade him of the certainty of all the things that have taken place.

This is a broad-brush sketch, and growing acquaintance with the four gospels uncovers many more detailed features. Luke, for his part, frequently brings out what we might call "personal touches," especially in connection with Jesus' suffering and death. It is Luke alone who records that Jesus warned Simon Peter that Satan wanted to have him so that he might sift him as wheat (22:31), and who informs us that the Lord looked at Peter at the very moment of his denial (22:61). Luke is the only evangelist who tells us about the women who wept for Jesus as he made his way to the cross (23:28–31), and who gives us the words of Jesus' prayer for those who crucified him (23:34).

There is another event we must add to this catalogue, surely the most powerful and memorable of them all, and it is the one we examine in this chapter. Here is the account of the crucified criminal who was brought to repentance and who heard from Jesus these timeless words: "Truly, I say to you, today you will be with me in Paradise" (Luke 23:43).

OUTRAGEOUS MERCY

I have described Luke's distinctive contributions as "personal touches," but it should be understood that they are much more than that. They teach us vital spiritual truths about the saving work of Jesus Christ for his people, truths that magnify the greatness of God's salvation in our eyes. Luke's description of what took place at Calvary, as noted in chapter 14, is characterized by the way he punctuates the thick darkness with many beams of brilliant light; there is more visible light in Luke's account than there is in Mark's, for example. This is not due to his natural temperament, as if Luke were simply a more "upbeat" kind of personality than Mark; it is an indication of his purpose in writing. Luke's record of the events leading up to the crucifixion, and of Calvary itself, anticipates the glorious future that Jesus' suffering and death must bring to fruition.

Leon Morris puts it like this: "Jesus looks past his suffering and past His resurrection and ascension to the culmination that His sufferings would in due course bring about."[1] So it was that on the night before his death, Jesus ate and drank the Last Supper with his disciples and looked ahead with longing to his final destination. "I have earnestly desired," he told the Twelve, "to eat this Passover with you before I suffer. For I tell you I will not eat it until it is fulfilled in the kingdom of God" (Luke 22:15–16).

We must be absolutely certain that Jesus always knew that his mission, obediently executed, would result in eternal blessing for himself and for all the people he had come to save. At the same time he knew that the character of this obedience would involve fearful suffering. The joy that was set before him could be attained only via the path of sorrow. "Out of the anguish of his soul he shall see and be satisfied; by his knowledge shall the righteous one, my servant, make many to be accounted righteous, and he shall bear their iniquities" (Isa. 53:11). If it is possible to speak of this "tension" within the mind of Jesus, then we see it exhibited in statements such as this: "I have a baptism to be baptized with, and how great is my distress until it is accomplished!" (Luke 12:50). And what could the agony of Gethsemane possibly be if it were not the most extreme tension ever experienced by a human being?

This great tension has been in view all along. Thus it was that in the last chapter we dealt with the very darkest hour in the whole experience of Jesus. We saw that this darkness was not ultimately due to the wicked actions or words of his human enemies against him. It was due instead to the Son's voluntary giving of himself as the final and true sacrifice for the sins of his people. He endured the full and terrible weight of his Father's righteous anger against sin. But then we emphasized that the Twenty-second Psalm, that most eloquent prophecy of Christ's sufferings, progresses beyond the physical, the emotional, and even the spiritual horrors of Calvary. It goes on to consider the great end, the eternal reward of these sufferings. Even then, the light shone in the darkness, and the darkness could never wholly overcome that light. Never did gospel light shine so brightly as on this day—as in this very hour when the crucified Jesus showed to his crucified companion the triumph and the glory of his saving work.

We might almost suggest that Jesus showed mercy to this man on an outrageous scale. This outrageous mercy is an aspect of Jesus' work that Luke has already demonstrated. In Luke 7:36–50 we read of a woman who burst into a Pharisee's house while dinner was being served, who began to weep all over Jesus' feet, wiping them with her hair. What is more, she was a notoriously sinful woman. How embarrassing; how this would have made the guests cringe! And then in 19:1–10 Jesus publicly forgives a tax collector, a man viewed by the people as a traitor, called Zacchaeus. Not only does he do this, but he visits his home. What might be called the "shock factor" of these passages is ratcheted up even higher as we come to our present text.

WHO IS THE ENEMY?

One possible objection must be met before dealing with the incident itself. Jesus and his *enemies*? It may well be wondered how this chapter fits into the theme that has been followed so far. If Jesus really has an "enemy" in this short passage, it can only be the criminal who did not repent. The one who *did* repent could surely not be labeled an enemy. This passage abundantly demonstrates that he was Jesus' friend!

And yet he *was* undoubtedly an enemy until a few hours—perhaps less—before the words of this passage were spoken. Apart from the five verses quoted at the head of this chapter, there is nothing at all in the Gospels that differentiates the repentant thief from the unrepentant one.

This is a most important point. Remember that back in chapter 1 it was demonstrated that all Adam's offspring, being born in sin and showing the effects of sin in their lives, are by nature enemies of Jesus Christ. But in that chapter we also saw how Jesus came into this world in order to transform enemies into friends. It is as we focus on the climax of his work, his death and resurrection, that we see this transforming character of his work happening in a number of instances. So whereas all the subjects of the earlier chapters have been enemies who remained enemies, chapters 16 to 18 will focus on one-time enemies of Jesus who were changed, by his love and power, into his friends.

Many have preached and written about this repentant thief. What did J. C. Ryle say of him? "Of all the multitude of saved souls, none ever received so glorious an assurance of his own salvation as this penitent thief. Go over the whole list, from Genesis to Revelation, and you will find none who had such words spoken to him as these: 'Today shalt thou be with Me in paradise.'"[2] C.H. Spurgeon said, "I think the Saviour took him with him as a specimen of what he meant to do. He seemed to say to all the heavenly powers, 'I bring a sinner with me; he is a sample of the rest.'"[3]

What we have in this incident is the very heart and soul of the saving gospel of Jesus Christ, condensed into a brief conversation. The English Puritan Richard Baxter aimed to preach "as a dying man to dying men," and this is quite literally what the Savior did here.

WHY DID JESUS CHOOSE TO SAVE HIM?

Both of these crucified men were literally "evildoers," or as the King James version of the Bible describes them, "malefactors." As such, they were typical of the kind of people one would expect to be subjected to the accursed death of the cross. In the manner of his death, Jesus was truly "numbered with the transgressors" (Isa. 53:12). Matthew and Mark tell us that these men were robbers, which implies that they were violent men. These two evangelists also tell us that both of these criminals were shouting at Jesus and blaspheming him. They record nothing of the spiritual transformation in one of them. It is not for us to wonder why Matthew and Mark omitted this information;

but we should be grateful to God that Luke was moved to report this great act of salvation.

Notice first of all that this man was brought to faith in the Savior at the end of his life; it was in the very act of dying, of being crucified, that his heart was softened and renewed by divine grace. Amidst all the mockery, blasphemy, and savage cruelty of the scene at Calvary, this anonymous individual, who was perishing in his sins, was enabled to understand the true identity of the man who was dying on the cross next to him. He recognized him as the Messiah and the innocent Suffering Servant, and he put his absolute trust in him.

It is necessary to ask a question which must have occurred to many people. What did this man bring with him? Why did Jesus ever choose to save this man? What could he possibly find in a man like this that would ever move him to forgiveness? This man could surely never be commended on the final day, when all the nations of the world would be gathered before God's throne, and the sheep separated from the goats. The Lord could never adjudge him worthy of the commendation, "Well done, good and faithful servant" (Matt. 25:21, 23).

DO YOU BEGRUDGE MY GENEROSITY?

Perhaps the idea that Jesus forgave and saved this man seems repulsive to some people. Is this not sheer injustice? If this man's deeds were weighed in the balance, would not his bad deeds far outweigh his good ones? Our natural fallen instinct is to think in terms of what we deserve, and that is why the mercy of God seems so outrageous to us. This sense of injustice is compounded by the lateness of the hour—this violent robber had only a short time to live.

Jesus, it might be remembered, had told a parable about some laborers in a vineyard. Some worked for the whole day, others for nine hours, others for six, others for three—and then some were hired right at the end of the day, at "the eleventh hour." But the men who had been hired at the end of the day were given the same wages as those who had been hired at the beginning. We see the incredulity of the men who had "borne the burden of the day and the scorching heat" (Matt. 20:12). The punch line comes when the master of the house, the one who summoned the laborers, answered,

> "Am I not allowed to do what I choose with what belongs to me? Or do you begrudge my generosity?" So the last will be first, and the first last. (Matt. 20:15–16)

This is the question: do you begrudge the generosity of God?

It is only when a human soul realizes that he is sinful, guilty, and deserving of God's just punishment that his eyes are opened to the marvel of God's goodness—of his grace. God's grace, as we have seen, is his full and free determination to bless people who deserve the very opposite of blessing. We all deserve God's curse and his punishment. Both the crucified robbers, like the whole of Adam's fallen race, deserved God's wrath, but one received his grace instead.

This account of the repentant thief upon the cross is an "acid test" of our understanding of grace. When the idea of God's grace repels and angers us, then there is a clear demonstration that we are strangers to that grace; we are wedded to a system of works religion that is the natural tendency of the fallen human heart. But if we have truly tasted of God's grace, then it will attract and thrill us. Our wonder and amazement will then be that God does not treat his people—especially *me*—as our sins deserve.

As we look at these two men upon their crosses, we see more starkly than anywhere else the only possible destinies of the whole human race. Both men die, for indeed all people must die. Beyond that there are only two types of people in this world. There are those who are saved by the blood of Christ and those who are not. Nothing differentiates one criminal from the other except the grace of God that led one of them to repentance. When this ultimate reality is rightly understood, then all grounds of self-reliance must be utterly swept aside.

It should never be overlooked that there were two criminals upon the cross and that one of them did not repent and was not saved. How often is *his* end mentioned in sermons? There is surely a cautionary warning here. The idea that the imminent approach of death will usually—if not always—result in conversion is evidently false. Perhaps some of us have relatives who have remained hardened for many years, and we cling onto the expectation that on their deathbed they will turn, repent of their sins, and believe in Christ. We are entitled to pray for such an outcome, but we have no right to regard it as the norm. For some unbelievers, the coming of old age and the prospect of death only hardens their already embittered souls against God.

One great lesson of this text is that nothing, no nothing, can save a human soul apart from the grace of God by the regenerating power of the Spirit. This is the only satisfactory explanation for the phenomenon we see here—one criminal is saved and the other is not. This alone explains why two very similar people— perhaps two brothers or two sisters—can both sit through evangelistic sermons where Christ is preached and salvation is freely offered, year after year, but one comes to repentance and faith, while the other dies in his or her sins.

SPIRITUAL CONVICTION AND ITS CONSEQUENCES

I said earlier on that this passage is "the very heart and soul of the saving gospel of Jesus Christ." The crucified robber, as we have just demonstrated, was forgiven by the sheer grace of Christ alone. It was the power of the Spirit that effected this great change. Now there are further aspects to his spiritual experience that we need to notice.

The previous evening Jesus had given his disciples an extended private discourse, recorded only in John's gospel. This is sometimes referred to as the "Upper Room Discourse," although John 14:31 may indicate that Jesus and his disciples left the room where they had partaken of the Last Supper. In John 16:8–11 Jesus tells his disciples about the future work of the Holy Spirit in the world, that is, among those who are still opponents of the gospel.

> And when he comes, he will convict the world concerning sin and righteousness and judgment: concerning sin, because they do not believe in me; concerning righteousness, because I go to the Father, and you will see me no longer; concerning judgment, because the ruler of this world is judged.

The forthcoming work of the Holy Spirit would be that of *conviction*. That is, he will convince the world of its sin and error; people will see how wrong they have been and will, by God's grace, be directed to the true way of thinking. We have commented earlier on what we might call the "legal overtones" of John's gospel; it is like a great courtroom drama. Therefore Jesus anticipates the time when the Spirit himself will come into the world as the final, perpetual witness. The witness to what, or to whom? To none other than Jesus Christ himself.

It is possible for us to read these verses in John 16 and think about "sin and righteousness and judgment" in a fairly general sense. Moreover, we may find the three respective explanations supplied in the text above somewhat hard to follow. But the key to understanding this passage is to see that these convictions all relate to the person and work of the Savior. What is especially pertinent to this discussion is that these very convictions took place in the heart of the crucified robber. Although Jesus had not yet died, had not yet risen, had not yet been glorified; although the Holy Spirit in his Pentecostal fullness had not yet been given to the church, *the spiritual transformation in this man anticipated the saving work of the Spirit which lay ahead.*

There was *conviction concerning sin.* Perhaps when we think of conviction of sin our minds instinctively turn to private, personal sins. But the great sin of the people of Israel, as we saw in chapter 13, was their refusal to believe in Jesus as the Christ and the Son of God. There is nothing unusual about a man knowing that his life has been wasted, even wicked, but the convicting work of the Spirit is always more—it is Christ-centered. An individual who goes no further than saying, "I'm ashamed of my sins and I'm going to mend my ways," cannot be described as being under this spiritual conviction of sin. Instead they know that their greatest sin has been their refusal to believe in and to worship Christ.

Thus it was the embittered cry of the other criminal, "Are you not the Christ? Save yourself and us!" (Luke 23:39), that provoked a response from the man under conviction of sin. A short time earlier he himself had been joining in with all the insults. He had not believed that Jesus was the Messiah. Now his heart has been changed, and he appeals to the other man,

> Do you not fear God, since you are under the same sentence of condemnation? And we indeed justly, for we are receiving the due reward of our deeds. (23:40–41)

He sees that his own punishment and death are entirely deserved. In saying this he acts as a spokesman for every member of Adam's helpless race. The wages of sin is indeed death, but the greatest sin of all is the refusal to bow down and acknowledge Jesus as the Son of God.

Following this there was *conviction concerning righteousness*. Why in John 16:10 is this connected with Jesus' going to the Father? The answer is that the men who crucified Jesus judged him to be a wrongdoer and a blasphemer. They felt sure that his suffering on the cross was a fitting end for such a wicked man. But the Holy Spirit supplies a wholly different testimony: Jesus Christ is altogether righteous because heaven has received him; heaven would not receive a man who was a sinner. The preaching of the apostles, especially Peter, in the early chapters of Acts, was that the Jews wickedly crucified the Son of God, the Righteous One, asking for a murderer to be released to them. But God vindicated his righteous servant Jesus by raising him from the dead and giving him glory, as all the people now saw.

It is only by the power of the Holy Spirit that the repentant thief is enabled to say that "this man has done nothing wrong" (23:41). He is a lone voice at Calvary amidst all the virulent and blasphemous charges against Jesus—lone, that is, until Jesus dies and the Roman centurion adds his own assent. Jesus has indeed done nothing wrong, as every faithful disciple must confess. "He committed no sin, neither was deceit found in his mouth" (1 Peter 2:22).

Finally there is *conviction concerning judgment*. In reading of judgment we think intuitively of the judgment of God against human sinners. While that is the main sense in which the Bible speaks of judgment, it is not the case here. Rather it is the judgment of the prince of the world, of Satan himself, for it is only by the cross that Christ's greatest adversary is defeated. A little earlier Jesus had proclaimed,

> Now is the judgment of this world; now will the ruler of this world be cast out. And I, when I am lifted up from the earth, will draw all people to myself. (John 12:31–32)

The convicting work of the Spirit causes people to see that Satan's authority over this world has been broken. Christ has crushed the serpent's head and is himself the ruler of his people.

So it is that the dying thief is "a brand plucked out of the burning" (Amos 4:11). He had once dwelt within Satan's domain, a wicked and murderous criminal. Satan had him secure, one of his goods that was locked away in the depths of a dark underground vault. But already the Son of God, infinitely stronger than the devil, was coming to plunder and overturn Satan's kingdom of darkness. It is in his very act of dying that Christ dethrones Satan from his position as "ruler of the world." This repentant thief does not belong to Satan; he belongs to Christ! Men like him, men and women far worse than him, will be transferred from darkness to light, from death to life, by Jesus' victory over Satan. And to guarantee this man's immediate release, and to assure him of the full and imminent blessings of salvation, Jesus tells him, "Truly, I say to you, today you will be with me in Paradise" (Luke 23:43).

"TODAY YOU WILL BE WITH ME IN PARADISE"

The Lord Jesus in this passage provides us with an answer to one of the most frequently asked pastoral questions of all. "I am a believer. What will happen to me immediately after I die?"

This is rather an important question. If the Bible gives us an answer to it then we should find out what it is. Let us suppose someone told you that in a month's time you would be going to live in a country on the opposite side of the world and stay there for the next twenty years. Would that not be a significant fact for you to bear in mind? It would be of the greatest interest to you. How much more then should we be interested in finding out what the Bible teaches us about our existence immediately after we die! Will we be awake or asleep, conscious or unconscious? Will we see the face of Jesus Christ, or will we have to wait?

Notice how the answer that Jesus gave so utterly exceeded the expectations of the criminal. In Ephesians 3:20 Paul reaches a great crescendo of superlatives as he describes the love and power of God in Christ: "Now to him who is able to do far more abundantly than all that we ask or think." This verse is rather like what happened in the experience of the repentant thief on the cross next to Jesus. Jesus gave him a promise that was far better and greater than the dying thief could possibly have imagined.

He had asked that Jesus might remember him; Jesus told him he will actually be present with him. He had asked that this might happen at some future point—whenever Jesus would come into his kingdom; Jesus told him it would be "Today." He had mentioned Jesus' kingdom—Jesus spoke to this man about "paradise."

What was it that led this man to word his question to Jesus in the way that he did: "Jesus, remember me when you come into your kingdom" (Luke 23:42)? The answer must be that he entertained the typical Jewish expectation regarding the coming of the Messiah, that it would be at some far distant future date. The Deliverer would come to the earth in glory at the end of the age, many years from now. The crucified man must have known his Old Testament Scriptures; perhaps he had even heard something of Jesus' own predictions about his sure and certain return. But such is the grace of God that Today, even Today, this sinner would be with Jesus. It was a day on which this man both suffered justly as a criminal and entered into paradise as a redeemed, forgiven man.

But what exactly is meant by "paradise"? Elaborate speculation has taken place about the physical location of the various degrees of heaven and of paradise. Later Jewish rabbis, and some of the early church fathers, believed in seven heavens. But it is safest to understand that "paradise" and "heaven" refer to the same realm. When Paul talks about his amazing experiences in 2 Corinthians 12 he mentions being caught up into "the third heaven" in verse 2 and "paradise" in verse 3. We see that they are one and the same place. After all, why should different words not be used to describe this glorious place where God dwells? William Hendriksen puts it like this.

> Let us say that while you are travelling along the highway, a pretentious house suddenly comes into view. Now is the English language so poor that there is only one word that can properly describe this sumptuous edifice? Is it not probable that this "house" will be referred to as "residence," "mansion," "dwelling," and perhaps even "palace"? If this is true with respect to

earthly objects of splendor or grandeur, why should it not be true with respect to heavenly?[4]

The word *paradise*, as used in the Old Testament, describes a park, an orchard, or a walled garden. In Ecclesiastes 2:5 we read of King Solomon making for himself "gardens and parks," and the Hebrew word for "parks" transliterates, more or less, as "paradise." Revelation 2:7 speaks of "the tree of life, which is in the paradise of God." What *paradise* surely conveys, then, is a picture of a new and better garden of Eden. It is a place where all is holy rest and peace, where nothing can threaten.

THE PRESENCE OF JESUS

But maybe we have a question at this point. Surely the new heavens and the new earth, this new and better garden of Eden, will not begin to exist until Jesus Christ returns to this world? Surely the present creation will continue in its groaning until the day when the sons of God are revealed—when Christ comes back and transforms his people in the twinkling of the eye? It might seem at first that Christ's words are rather premature.

There is only one adequate answer to these questions. It is that *everything which is symbolized by this picture of paradise is bound up in the presence of Jesus Christ himself*. To be in everlasting fellowship with the Savior, freed from the body of sin and delivered from death, is to truly be in paradise. The believer, when he dies, goes to a destination of complete peace and rest, because there he is with his beloved Savior. In view of this, speculations about the precise form of consciousness and existence that Christians have in the intermediate state can be left to one side.[5] If the Lord promises paradise to this man, then surely every dying believer has a right to say, "I am on my way to paradise."

What was it, what is it, that brings ultimate peace and rest to the Christian soul? It is the presence of God in Christ. Because what made the original Paradise, the garden of Eden, a uniquely happy place was that the Lord was there with his people. The Lord was accustomed to being in the garden with Adam and Eve, and they were accustomed to his presence. To be sure, the new heavens and the new earth did not materialize the day that Jesus died, the day that this thief died. Neither have they done so yet. This dying thief was not about to enter a new world full of gardens, parks, and orchards. But the one essential factor that makes for paradise—the conscious presence and enjoyment of the Lord Jesus Christ—was his, and it remains so today. Two thousand years later, the repentant thief continues to be in paradise with his Savior. We need to see this as the highest and best promise of all.

"You will be with me." Remember that Jesus is the promised Immanuel, the God who is with us (Matt. 1:23). When he says he will be with his disciples until the end of the age, he includes the time after they die (Matt. 28:20). Neither death nor life can separate us from the love of God in Christ! He is not a God who is far off, living at a distance like some absentee landlord. The ultimate fulfillment of the covenant promise is that we will have this God dwelling among us, right in our midst. This crucified man, soon to pass through the gates of death, would immediately, that very day, enter the presence of the Savior.

Scripture begins with man in the presence of God. It ends with that reality being eternally recovered and enjoyed. "And I heard a loud voice from the throne saying, 'Behold, the dwelling place of God is with man. He will dwell with them, and they will be his people, and God himself will be with them as their God'" (Rev. 21:3). This is the heart, the center, the essence of what our redemption is all about. Trees, parks, rivers, fountains, the absence of sun and moon in the new heavens and the new earth—all these things are nothing more than the stage upon which our eternal, intimate fellowship with the triune God will unfold and go on unfolding.

— 17 —

SIMON, SON OF JOHN

*When they had finished breakfast, Jesus said to Simon Peter,
"Simon, son of John, do you love me more than these?" He
said to him, "Yes, Lord; you know that I love you." He said
to him, "Feed my lambs." He said to him a second time,
"Simon, son of John, do you love me?" He said to him, "Yes,
Lord; you know that I love you." He said to him, "Tend my
sheep." He said to him the third time, "Simon, son of John,
do you love me?" Peter was grieved because he said to him
the third time, "Do you love me?" and he said to him, "Lord,
you know everything; you know that I love you." Jesus said
to him, "Feed my sheep. Truly, truly, I say to you, when you
were young, you used to dress yourself and walk wherever
you wanted, but when you are old, you will stretch out your
hands, and another will dress you and carry you where you
do not want to go." (This he said to show by what kind of
death he was to glorify God.) And after saying this he said
to him, "Follow me." (John 21:15–19)*

IF THE SUBJECT of the last chapter raised some eyebrows—
the repentant thief on the cross—surely much stronger doubts
will be raised here. How can we possibly explain how Simon Peter
was ever an enemy of Jesus! Here is the bold spokesman of the
apostles, the one whose name is given first in every list of the

disciples that we find in the New Testament. Here is big brave Peter, the rock, who stoutly declared, "You are the Christ, the Son of the living God" (Matt. 16:16). Elsewhere he spoke out in a similar vein: "Lord, to whom shall we go? You have the words of eternal life, and we have believed, and have come to know, that you are the Holy One of God" (John 6:68–69). Here is the great preacher of Pentecost, the one who preached the first, magnificent sermon to the Christian church.

But of course anyone remotely acquainted with the New Testament will be aware that there is another side to Peter. He had his "Simon days" as well as his "Peter days." That great confession at Caesarea Philippi was quickly followed by his attempt to dissuade Jesus from going to the cross, an attempt that brought the withering rebuke from Jesus, "Get behind me, Satan!" (Matt. 16:23). Most tragically of all, he fell into bitter sin and failure when he denied three times that he knew his Lord and Master. On these occasions he acted more like an enemy than a friend. We know that even the mature apostle Peter gave way to a type of peer pressure and had to be sharply rebuked by Paul (Gal. 2:14).

THE SENSE OF DÉJÀ VU

We have left the cross of Calvary behind and we have also left the empty tomb. As we come to the twenty-first and final chapter of John's gospel the risen Jesus has appeared twice to the company of apostles, once with Thomas absent and then a second time, a week later, when Thomas was with them. The Lord has already administered a form of commissioning (John 20:21–23) that anticipates Pentecost, when the Holy Spirit will come upon these disciples in fullness.

Surely these ought to be great and exciting days. And yet the disciples are still unsure as to what they are supposed to do. Seven of them appear in this particular episode, and an air of uncertainty and indecision pervades the atmosphere. Simon Peter's declaration that he is going fishing meets with a kind of nodding assent from his companions. So these apostles are out with their nets on the Sea of Galilee, just as if the clock had turned back several years, to the days before Jesus had called them. Their fishing expedition proves unsuccessful, as it had on an earlier occasion. And even when the stranger on the shore appears to them, as is typical in resurrection appearances, they do not immediately recognize that it is Jesus.

However, the great and miraculous catch of fish that then takes place assures them that this man really is their Lord and Master, and there is no holding them back! Peter hurls himself into the sea, fully clothed, and splashes through the waves to the shore, leaving the other disciples to bring the fish. And there are already fish on the charcoal fire that Jesus has made. The Lord who had multiplied loaves and fishes on two previous occasions, and who had also summoned a great number of fish to the fishermen's nets, is well able to provide a full meal for his friends.

The breakfast that follows, and the subsequent interview between Jesus and Simon Peter, is one of the most poignant episodes recorded in all four gospels. In some ways this chapter of John's gospel resembles a scene shot right at the end of a film, interrupting the credits that are rolling up the screen. The final verse of chapter 20 seems, for all intents and purposes, to mark the end of John's account. "These are written so that you may believe that Jesus is the Christ, the Son of God, and that by believing you may have life in his name" (John 20:31). But we ought not to rush out of the cinema with the crowd and miss this most touching epilogue.

The atmosphere is charged with a hushed emotion even while breakfast is being eaten. No words are exchanged between Jesus and his disciples after he has issued the invitation to come and eat. Solemn joy in the presence of the risen Jesus is the only appropriate response, and yet it is also attended with many memories. Indeed, what should be noted above all is the sense of *déjà vu* that Simon Peter must be experiencing. Had he not been out fishing when Jesus called him? Had he forgotten a previous occasion when his fishing expedition had been fruitless, only for Jesus to order him to put out into the deep and let down his nets for a great catch? Surely he could recall his own words to Jesus at the time, "Depart from me, for I am a sinful man, O Lord," and Jesus' words of exhortation and reassurance, "Do not be afraid; from now on you will be catching men" (Luke 5:8, 10).

A PASTORAL MASTER CLASS

Most gently, most firmly, most deliberately, Jesus now reissues this call to Simon Peter. He, Simon Peter, knows himself to be a desperately sinful man, but he, Simon Peter, is being called to the great task of catching men. Jesus now gives Peter a master class in the work of the pastor, the shepherd of the flock.

Simon Peter, of course, was in the greatest need of exhortation and reassurance. The glaring fact of his threefold denial of Jesus is the unmistakable backdrop to this passage. That does not necessarily mean that Jesus has had no personal dealings with Peter at all since that Thursday evening. Mark—whose gospel account reflects so much of Peter's own influence—records that Peter was singled out by name on the morning of the resurrection. The angel told the frightened women to "go, tell his disciples *and Peter* that he is going before you to Galilee. There you will see him, just as he told you" (Mark 16:7). Jesus in his pastoral love and prayer for Peter was concerned to bring the greatest comfort to him at the earliest opportunity.

The similarities and contrasts between Peter's denial of Jesus and this present conversation between them have been frequently remarked. The three denials of Peter correspond to the three probing questions of Jesus, which Peter answers in the affirmative. There is even a charcoal fire in this scene, as there was when Peter denied Jesus. It had been a dark night of despair when Peter denied Jesus; he was standing in the cold air, surrounded by enemies, warming himself by the fire. Now it is a bright, fresh morning, and Peter with his friends—Jesus and the disciples—are feasting on a breakfast of 153 large fish.

But it is *as the supreme model of pastoral care* that this passage should be examined. Jesus comes to Peter individually, and so it is that believers need individual care from their pastors. It is interesting and instructive that Jesus does not talk "business" with Peter or any of the disciples during the meal. That's not what meals are for! He waits until breakfast is over, and then the serious and important talking begins.

Jesus takes Peter away by himself. This is a private interview between them, out of earshot of the other disciples. Jesus is demanding Peter's complete attention and concentration. The question is addressed to him individually. Peter cannot possibly ignore or sidestep what Jesus is saying to him. He cannot "switch Jesus off" as if he were a television program. This can be a genuine temptation and a tendency today when we listen to sermons. Do we ever hear the preacher as if he were a background broadcast, a sound that is simply going on and on, so that our concentration drifts in and out as we feel inclined? There may be a formality in preaching, but we must not let it lessen the degree of personal urgency.

Like many preachers, I usually stand behind a lectern when delivering a sermon. But on one Sunday morning a few months ago I stepped out and stepped forward, moving among the congregation for a short time. They seemed somewhat startled! Perhaps some of us have forgotten, to our great cost, that preaching is *the Lord himself speaking to us.*

TREATING THE DEEP AND FESTERING WOUND

The connection between Jesus' three questions and Peter's threefold denial would surely not have been lost on Peter. In fact, in this conversation he is not "Peter" but "Simon." Simon was his original name, Simon the son of John. The name "Peter," meaning "rock," had been given to him by Jesus. But now he is being addressed as the old Simon again. He had done so at the Last Supper: "Simon, Simon, behold, Satan demanded to have you, that he might sift you like wheat" (Luke 22:31). As one commentator notes,

> He received his name Cephas, or, in its Greek form, Peter, because of the confession of Christ; but having denied that confession, the name was denied to him. Hence in this tacit refusal to give him his apostolic name, there was an implied rebuke of the severest character, and something that reminded him very vividly of that shameful denial when he forfeited at once his name and his office.[1]

Notice that the Lord does not openly refer to the denials that Peter had made. But Jesus' words must surely have cut Simon Peter to the heart. It is deeply painful for him. On the subject of this healing process A. W. Pink wrote,

> He would not heal Peter's wound slightly, but would work a perfect cure; therefore, does He as it were, open it afresh. The Saviour would not have him lose the lesson of his fall, nor in the forgiveness forget his sin. Consequently He now delicately retraces for him the sad history of his denial, or rather by His awakening question brings it before his conscience.[2]

If there is some physical complaint that we have, then the doctor or surgeon may have to root around deeply in order to remove it. And the deeper they have to probe, the more it will hurt us. No one enjoys having their inner, secret life, their motivations and attitudes, rooted through. It hurts and grieves Peter that Jesus asks him a third time whether he loves him. But Jesus needs to do this in order to restore him. Sometimes it takes three questions to get to the heart of the issue. For a number of years I was a secondary school teacher, and one of the lessons I had to learn was that parents, just like their children, do not always reveal their main grievances straightaway. A wise and experienced deputy head told me that "it's the third complaint parents mention that is the real one." I subsequently found out that exactly the same is true in pastoral work in the church. Very often church members will let the pastor know what is really troubling them only as he turns to leave, or as he stands on the doorstep.

This Pastor knows what needs to be addressed. He is the heavenly Physician—he addresses and treats the deep, festering wound in Peter's life. How does he do so? He asks, "Do you love me? Whom do you love most?" Thus we must see that love to Jesus Christ is the foundation from which all our Christian life and service must spring.

THE GREATEST IS LOVE

The way Jesus asks the first question exposes the great flaw in Simon's character that had given rise to his terrible fall—his utterly misguided impression of the strength of his love and commitment. "Do you love me *more than these*?" It seems most likely that when Jesus asked that question, he meant, "Do you still think, Simon, that your love and commitment to me is greater than the love and commitment of all the other disciples?" Simon Peter had said that he would never deny Jesus; that he was ready to die with him even if the other disciples all abandoned him.

Jesus asks again, and again, "Do you love me?" This question tests and challenges our deepest, inner attitudes. The Christian faith deals with our inner beings, our thoughts, our attitudes, the longings and priorities of our souls. Nothing is more different to true Christianity, more opposed to it, than mere outward actions and the performing of ceremonies. Someone can be a most regular churchgoer and not love Jesus. Someone can know a great deal about the Bible and the Christian faith but not love Jesus. Someone can be a kind, warm-hearted person, apparently active in Christian service, but not love Jesus. Do we think that

Jesus seeks disciples who are very gifted, very active, very knowl-edgeable, even very warm, kind, and "nice"—but who do not love him? This passage teaches us that this is quite impossible.

Love for Jesus Christ is the first and greatest principle of our Christian lives. Everything we would do as a church and as believers, our usefulness in God's kingdom, must flow from the reality of a heart filled with love for Christ.

NO ONE CAN SERVE TWO MASTERS

So having looked back, we now look forward into Peter's future. Peter's lakeside conversation with Jesus should be under-stood in the light of not only his past experiences but also his future life and work. Our passage contains a prophecy of Peter's eventual death; he, like every true follower of Jesus, is called to self-denial for the Savior's sake. The stretching out of Peter's hands is a graphic picture of the way he will be united with his Savior in a death like his. There is a reasonably well-attested tradition that Peter was crucified upside down, believing himself unworthy to die in the same manner as his Master. It is not nec-essary, however, to hold to this tradition in order to appreciate the force of the text here.

Jesus' words have an application that goes far beyond Peter. They constitute a reminder of the command Jesus had given to his disciples before, the command to give themselves to uncom-promising self-denial. "Then Jesus told his disciples, 'If anyone would come after me, let him deny himself and take up his cross and follow me.'" (Matt. 16:24). For whom do we deny ourselves, except for the one we love with an uncompromising, unyielding devotion? We cannot deny ourselves for the sake of more than one person; if we try to do so our loyalties will be in conflict and we will be torn in two. No one can serve two masters.

Jesus is effectively saying this to Peter: "In your old 'Simon' days, you did just whatever you pleased. But now, as Peter, you are the sworn and devoted servant of your Lord and Savior." Peter is no longer his own. Love to Jesus means love to him above all else, above himself. Only love for Christ will enable us to suffer for Christ. This is the whole spirit of Peter's later letters. He is devoted to the care of the flock of God (1 Peter 5:1–4), as Jesus commands and commissions him here. This emphasizes that there is absolutely no biblical warrant for holding that Peter was some kind of senior bishop, even less the first "Pope." The New Testament points to the absolute opposite; he is "a fellow elder" among elders.

WAVES OF PERSECUTION

Peter has left us two letters in the New Testament, and the first of these has a great deal to say about suffering, the suffering that Jesus predicted for him. He tells us that painful trials should not be surprising, as if they were strange. Quite the reverse is true. To see the historical accuracy of his statement we need look no further than the lives and deaths of the apostles themselves. From various sources we can be reasonably sure that several of them were crucified, some beheaded, others killed by other violent methods. John was the only apostle who escaped a violent death, dying in old age.

And that, of course, was only the beginning. We know that both during the times of the apostles and afterward there were waves of persecutions from Roman emperors. Opposition also came from the Jewish opponents of the faith. Seasons of calm prevailed for a while, and then came violent storms of persecution against Christians. It was the general pattern in the early years of the Christian church, and it has remained the pattern ever since. Persecution—of a particularly cruel and physical kind—rages fiercely in many countries of the world today, as all well-informed Christians know. As we consider the general subject "Jesus and his enemies," we need to understand that Jesus' enemies of the present day are also the enemies of his people, of the church. The church on earth is necessarily the suffering church.

A GREAT CONUNDRUM: SUFFERING AND
SPIRITUAL PRIVILEGE

Why must Christians suffer in this way—does it not seem strange? There seems to be a problem here. Doesn't Peter, in his first letter, speak about the amazing and glorious privileges of believers?

> Though you have not seen him, you love him. Though you do not now see him, you believe in him and rejoice with joy that is inexpressible and filled with glory, obtaining the outcome of your faith, the salvation of your souls. (1 Peter 1:8–9)

But what does privilege have to do with suffering? Aren't these two things complete opposites?

Here is one of the great conundrums of the Christian faith. Why does the Bible so often seem to link spiritual privileges with suffering in this world, when these two things seem so utterly different? How can it be a spiritual privilege to be stoned to death or sawn in two? Is it not a disgrace to be a persecuted minority or to suffer? By what kind of perverse reasoning can it be considered a blessing and a privilege?

At the heart of the Old Testament we have the history of Job. Suffering, not knowing why, and not being able to square it with other circumstances is the agonizing issue that confronts Job. Here is an eminently righteous man, one who habitually calls upon God, offers sacrifices to him, and speaks the truth about him. Why does this spiritually minded man suffer so much? It is the question on Job's own lips throughout most of his speeches. We are not even clear, at the end of Job's story, what it was that his suffering accomplished. Job never found out the reasons he suffered, and even if he had more children at the end of his life, he had nevertheless lost his first set of children.

The pattern can be seen elsewhere. Spiritual blessing and earthly suffering are so often linked. The most spiritually rich men have been the most afflicted. It is seen most evidently in the great men of the Old Testament. The patriarchs present to us a picture of mounting suffering. Abraham's life was one of waiting many years and of knowing disappointment, sorrow, and isolation. Jacob knew what it was to be cast out from his family and home, being deceived by his uncle, then experiencing great sorrow because of the wicked deeds of his sons. Joseph's life presents a picture of family strife, unjust accusation, and years of wrongful imprisonment. Later on, Moses, David, and Jeremiah each knew what suffering meant and gave expression to their pain.

Why was this the case? Why must there be this dreadful experience of suffering—in particular, the suffering of persecution—in the lives of these men who, we are told, knew and loved God so well, and indeed were loved by God?

THE REPROACH OF CHRIST

This is where we need the New Testament in order to interpret the Old. The eleventh chapter of Hebrews is rightly celebrated as the great chapter about the faith of the Old Testament saints. But it is also a record of their suffering and persecution. So we read the following in verses 24–26:

> By faith Moses, when he was grown up, refused to be called the son of Pharaoh's daughter, choosing rather to be mistreated with the people of God than to enjoy the fleeting pleasures of sin. He considered the reproach of Christ greater wealth than the treasures of Egypt, for he was looking to the reward.

But how can the author speak of Moses' persecutions as "the reproach of Christ"? Moses lived about 1400 years before Christ was born.

The answer is that Moses, in choosing to identify himself with the suffering people of Israel rather than the privileges of

Egypt, was being united with the sufferings of Christ himself. If the purpose of suffering remained unclear in the experience of Job, if the experience of suffering itself is incomprehensible when we read the Old Testament *in isolation*, it is not so in the New Testament, not so for Peter as he now sees the mystery of suffering explained in the sufferings of Christ. The believer who suffers—when he acts righteously, of course—is a participant in the sufferings of Christ. Peter even says that "the Spirit of glory and of God rests upon you (1 Peter 4:14).

What can this possibly mean? We know that Christ's suffering was glorious because it secured the salvation of all his people from sin. Of course there is glory here, the very greatest glory—glory that will be praised for all eternity. But how can our suffering ever be any kind of participation with Christ's? We must insist absolutely that our own suffering does not redeem our souls. Christ suffered once (1 Peter 3:18); he was laid out upon the altar of God's wrath and endured the righteous anger of the Father once for all. This happened at Calvary, where Jesus himself uttered, on the point of his death, "It is finished" (John 19:30).

However, throughout this book our specific focus has been on the afflictions of Christ that he suffered from his human enemies. The chief priests and elders, as we have seen, opened their mouths to blaspheme him and revile him. It is this particular aspect of Christ's sufferings that continues to be experienced by his people.

The Badge of Honor

Only in this way can we understand Paul's words in Colossians 1:24: "Now I rejoice in my sufferings for your sake, and in my flesh I am filling up what is lacking in Christ's afflictions for the sake of his body, that is, the church." How could Christ's afflictions be lacking in any way? Does this not undermine the redemptive value of Christ's death? Not at all, because Paul is not thinking here about redemption. He is demonstrating instead that the sufferings of Christ—at the hands of his enemies—overflow into the experience of the whole of Christ's body. Moses knew this 1400 years before Jesus, Peter and Paul knew it in the years immediately afterwards, and several million suffering believers across the world could speak of it today.

Jesus had told his disciples the night before his death, "If the world hates you, know that it has hated me before it hated you" (John 15:18). When the world scorns and ridicules us—and worse—it is responding to us in the same way it responded to Christ when he came. But this identification with Christ should cause us joy rather than sorrow. It is proof positive that we really belong to Christ. Edmund Clowney, former professor at Westminster Seminary in Philadelphia, wrote, "The reality of our suffering for Christ becomes a pledge to us of the reality of our belonging to Christ. That in itself brings joy to our hearts. It also strengthens our hope. If, like Christ, we suffer according to God's will, we know that, like Christ, we shall enter the glory of the Father."[3]

It is only by thinking in this fashion that we can be delivered from a sense of despair and melancholy when we suffer for being a Christian. It is only by thinking in this fashion that we can understand that this kind of suffering is not a disgrace. Instead it is a badge of honor—not our own individual honor, but the honor of belonging to Christ.

Peter and the other apostles were taught how to apply and appropriate this Spirit of glory and of God. Insults did not depress them, for by them the whole church was stirred to boldness and to prayer. The Peter of the early chapters of Acts is a stirring, heroic figure, the spokesman of the apostles as before, but now leading the way in Christ-honoring affirmation rather than committing great blunders. Because of Peter's leadership we read accounts such as this:

> When they (the Sanhedrin) had called in the apostles, they beat
> them and charged them not to speak in the name of Jesus, and

let them go. Then they left the presence of the council, rejoicing that they were counted worthy to suffer dishonor for the
name. (Acts 5:40–41)

"UNDERNEATH IT ALL, YOU KNOW EVERYTHING"

There is another aspect of the conversation between Jesus
and Peter that deserves further attention. Are we to understand
that from this day forward Peter would serve Jesus with a heart
and a will that would never waver? When Peter told Jesus that
he loved him, did he mean that his love was perfectly resolute?
Edward Donnelly, addressing a number of Christian pastors
and dealing with this very text, used the following illustration,
a touching one from his own family.

> For over twenty-five years we had on a shelf in our home a
> pretty horrible little lump of hard plaster, a misshapen, ugly
> sort of thing, painted as far as I can remember in bright blue
> and bright red. One of our daughters in P1 went out to school
> one morning and she said "Daddy, I'm going to make a present
> for you and Mummy."⁴ And this was the present; this is what
> she made in school. Now she wasn't Praxiteles, and she wasn't
> Michelangelo. I don't know what it was supposed to be; I think
> it was meant to be an elephant—or something!
>
> And she gave it to us, this present, and you couldn't have
> bought that from me for a thousand pounds. We loved it, that
> ugly little thing. Because we thought of the little, clumsy,
> unskillful fingers that had so patiently tried to shape it and paint
> it "for my Mummy and my Daddy." She was an intelligent child
> and there was a little look in her eyes as she gave it to us that
> said to us "I know it's not very good." And our hearts turned
> over within us and we hugged her, and we said "it's great, it's
> lovely." And it *was* lovely.
>
> And I sometimes feel my work for Christ is like that ugly little
> lump of plaster. I do my best, in my sermons and my pastoral
> work; I try my hardest and I'm not very good.

"You know everything; you know that I love you." Jesus loves Peter. He doesn't say, "Well, you didn't paint that little bit there. Oh—you missed that out!" What sort of parent would that be? "You could have shaped that better!" Oh, no! Instead . . . "you know everything, you know that I love you. Underneath all the garbage, underneath the stupid things that I say and the things that I do, and the failures, and the mess I make, and all the wrong turnings; underneath it all, you know everything, Lord Jesus. And you know that I love you."[5]

There is surely something of this here with Peter. Does Jesus think that Peter's love is perfect? We know that Peter still made mistakes and learned lessons. But Jesus accepts Peter's answer; he does not fault him. He says "Follow me" in verse 19, and he says the same in verse 22. He is once again reminding Peter of that first call.

How far short we all fall of our calling as Christian disciples! At every point in our Christian lives we must be conscious of our sins, our failings, our inadequacy. We might even wonder whether we can honestly say to Jesus, "I love you." Do we not feel like frauds? Are not pastors particularly aware of their shortcomings? Here is the wonder and marvel of it all: Jesus appoints and uses men and women who are so imperfect, so flawed, with a past record of sin and backsliding that would seem to utterly disqualify all of us. He does not wait for us to achieve PhD status. He says to everyone whom he calls, "Follow me." In effect, "Follow me now—don't wait. *If you tarry 'til you're better, you may never come at all.*"

Because in the final analysis, what we see in this passage and in the whole Christian life is the triumph of the love of God in Jesus Christ. We love him because he first loved us. It was the amazing grace of Jesus Christ, in coming now to Peter, that prompted and enabled him to say, "I love you."

If we had asked Peter in his later years about how much he loved Jesus Christ, I think we can be sure that he would have spoken little about his own love for Jesus, but would have dwelled with tears in his eyes on the love of the Son of God for a poor, sinful, stumbling, cowardly Galilean fisherman. And when we rightly understand the gospel of Jesus Christ, our own testimony is exactly the same. Edward Donnelly, who demonstrates a particular insight into the life and mind of Peter, made the following comments:

> But what is the determining factor in our discipleship? Not our faith or devotion, but the fact that God has chosen us to be his. Before the universe was made he set his love upon us. In unfathomable grace, the triune God has decreed to save us, make us perfect, bring us to glory. The Father gave us to the Son, who has enlisted us in his service for ends and reasons of his own, of which we are only dimly and partially aware. The course of our lives has been planned in advance. Everything we do and experience is part of a vast tapestry which he is weaving. We are caught up in something far bigger than we can understand.
>
> God has decided to make us like his beloved Son and the irresistible power of the Holy Spirit is now at work within us with that goal in view. The only reason we will persevere in faith, and we will if we have been born again, is because God will persevere with us.[6]

SAUL OF TARSUS

I thank him who has given me strength, Christ Jesus our Lord, because he judged me faithful, appointing me to his service, though formerly I was a blasphemer, persecutor, and insolent opponent. But I received mercy because I had acted ignorantly in unbelief, and the grace of our Lord overflowed for me with the faith and love that are in Christ Jesus. The saying is trustworthy and deserving of full acceptance, that Christ Jesus came into the world to save sinners, of whom I am the foremost. But I received mercy for this reason, that in me, as the foremost, Jesus Christ might display his perfect patience as an example to those who were to believe in him for eternal life. To the King of ages, immortal, invisible, the only God, be honor and glory forever and ever. Amen. (1 Tim. 1:12–17)

TWO CHAPTERS AGO we looked at the crucified robber whom Jesus saved. It will be remembered that bishop J. C. Ryle referred to him as "Christ's greatest trophy." Here is Christian salvation *in extremis*. Surely, if we scanned the pages of Scripture—and indeed the pages of church history—for the most breathtaking example of God's grace, we could go no further than this.

The trouble is that the Bible itself will not let us rest with this conclusion. Instead we are told that Saul of Tarsus, the apostle Paul, is the most sublime example of God's grace. Our text tells us that according to the apostle himself, he is the "foremost" of all sinners, and that Christ's mercy was shown to Paul as a display of "his perfect patience as an example to those who were to believe in him for eternal life." We will go on to see in this chapter that no man ever sinned against greater light than did Saul of Tarsus. This consideration means that his salvation is the ultimate display of God's amazing grace.

A Trustworthy Saying

The mature apostle Paul is writing to his young charge Timothy, whom he had first met in the town of Lystra during his second missionary journey (Acts 16:1–3). At the time of the writing, Timothy is engaged in gospel ministry in Ephesus, and Paul is instructing him in the work that he has been set aside to fulfill. One of the features of Paul's pastoral letters—two to Timothy and one to Titus—is his use of the expression "the saying is trustworthy." This is found five times in these three letters.[1] Some New Testament scholars, noting—among other observations—that this formula does not appear in the other letters traditionally attributed to Paul, have drawn the unwarranted conclusion that the author of the pastoral letters must be someone other than the author of the other epistles. But there really is no such difficulty. Paul was a versatile enough writer to adopt different styles and phrases when the situation required him to do so. In the specific context in which he wrote to Timothy, and also to Titus, it should be noted that his repeated use of the expression "the saying is trustworthy" was most appropriate.

In the early verses of the first chapter, Paul instructs Timothy to ensure that sound doctrine is preached in Ephesus. There were certain people there who led others in various unhelpful and even dangerous directions. Paul mentions "myths and endless genealogies, which promote speculations rather than the stewardship from God that is by faith" (1:4). He seeks to lead Timothy away from what is doubtful and speculative and toward cast-iron certainty. So when Paul flagged a "trustworthy saying," he surely intended that Timothy should hold such statements, and teach others to hold these statements, as central planks of Christian belief. He is effectively saying to his beloved Timothy, "Give special attention to this! What I am saying here is something you need to constantly hold on to and urge others to do the same. Come back to this again and again in your preaching. 'Christ Jesus came into the world to save sinners—of whom I am the worst.'"

This is one good reason why the church in its happiest and healthiest of times has made good use of creeds, confessions, and catechisms. These keep Christians on the right track and avert the tendency to wander off along unhelpful tangents. We all need to be brought back regularly to the main things.

"PREACH THE MUNROS!"

In Scotland there are some 283 peaks over three thousand feet above sea level.[2] These are known as the Munros. Mountaineers who have scaled all of these peaks are known as "Munroists." Having never reached the summit of any of them—though I have managed three fells in the English Lake District of a comparable elevation!—I think opportunities for me to become a Munroist are running out. But one wise preacher has given this advice to younger ministers: "Preach the Munros!" That is, identify the texts in Scripture that are like these grand mountain summits. The whole of the Bible is inspired by God, breathed out by his Spirit—but there are some texts that stand high above the surrounding plateaus. It would be interesting if a number of Christians decided, independently, to compile a list of 283 "Munro texts"! Surely 1 Timothy 1:15 would be a contender. "Here is a trustworthy saying that deserves full acceptance: Christ Jesus came into the world to save sinners—of whom I am the worst" (NIV).

This is a verse that lies at the heart of the Christian gospel and is designed to bring warm and speedy comfort to anxious souls. What was it that caused Jesus Christ to come into this world? It was the mission given to him by his Father to save sinners. We are on safe ground here. Those who preach a gospel sermon—that Jesus Christ came to save sinners—honor God by doing so. We must beware of those who tell us to find the focus of the Bible, or the focus of Jesus' mission, elsewhere.

During his ministry Jesus made many statements to that effect, many of which we might include as "Munro texts." After the chief tax collector Zacchaeus had been restored, Jesus said that "the Son of Man came to seek and to save the lost" (Luke 19:10). Earlier he said to his opponents, "I have not come to call the righteous but sinners to repentance" (Luke 5:32). And John 3:16, perhaps the "Ben Nevis" of them all, resonates with these other sayings: "For God so loved the world, that he gave his only Son, that whoever believes in him should not perish but have eternal life."

THE CENTRALITY OF GRACE

For this reason the message of the grace of God, in forgiving sinners through Jesus Christ, has been the central burden of the Lord's most faithful servants. John Wesley (1703–91) is a prime example. When he was five, the Wesleys' home in Epworth caught fire during the night. It seemed that all the children in the rectory had been removed to safety, but a count revealed that John was missing. Then a local farmer spotted John looking out of an upstairs window while the flames leaped around him. A number of neighbors quickly formed a human ladder and pulled the child to safety shortly before the whole house exploded into flames. After his evangelical conversion some thirty years later, John Wesley often referred to himself as "a brand plucked from the burning," quoting Zechariah 3:2. This became a great and recurring theme of his life and his preaching, just as it needs to be a recurring theme in the life of every believer and in all the church's preaching.

We rightly refer to 1 Timothy as a "pastoral epistle," and in verse 18 of chapter 1 Paul speaks of his pastoral charge to Timothy. But there are a number of other points that Paul says before he gets down to business. The fact that he had been entrusted with "the glorious gospel of the blessed God" (1 Tim. 1:11) was something the apostle never quite got over; it always astounded him. That is why he feels constrained to pen these beautiful words of personal testimony, of gratitude and wonder to his Savior, that culminate in the grand doxology of verse 17.

Paul begins by writing about the service he was commissioned on the road to Damascus to carry out. He overflows with gratitude to Christ Jesus, who gave him strength, judged him faithful, and appointed him to this particular ministry. But as Paul continues, it is clear that he is dealing not only with his call to be an apostle, but with the whole of his personal salvation. He understands that his own life and character prior to his conversion were all part of God's great purpose: that in him, Paul, "as the foremost [of sinners], Jesus Christ might display his perfect patience as an example to those who were to believe in him for eternal life" (1 Tim. 1:16).

SAUL OF TARSUS AND HIS BACKGROUND

There is a sense in which the life and ministry of Paul is telegraphed prior to his arrival on the New Testament scene. We see instances of this not only in the book of Acts, but in the gospel records. In chapter 6 we saw the prominence of the Pharisees in all the Gospels. This sets the backdrop against which Saul of Tarsus, a Pharisee of Pharisees, was to be converted. Saul of Tarsus had a religious *Curriculum Vitae* that would have been the envy of all his Jewish contemporaries.

If anyone else thinks he has reason for confidence in the flesh, I have more: circumcised on the eighth day, of the people of Israel, of the tribe of Benjamin, a Hebrew of Hebrews; as to the law, a Pharisee; as to zeal, a persecutor of the church; as to righteousness under the law, blameless (Phil. 3:4–6).

"As to the law, a Pharisee"—this was his pride and joy. Everything we have observed in connection with the Pharisees would once have been true of Saul. Why do the Gospels devote so much space to the bitter enmity of the Pharisees against Jesus and to the confrontations in which they were involved? One reason may well be that one of these men, the most pharisaical of them all, is going to become a disciple of Jesus Christ. Not only that, he will become the great apostle to the Gentiles!

Much of Saul's spiritual journey finds an echo in the life of Martin Luther (1483–1546), who said, "If anyone could have gained heaven as a monk, then I would indeed have been among them." One of Luther's biographers records that he "did not simply go through the motions of prayers, fasts, deprivations, and mortifications of the flesh, but pursued them earnestly."[3] While the resemblance between Paul and Martin Luther has been a matter of some controversy, we can see clear parallels. Both men labored with tremendous zeal, and both were determined to achieve "confidence in the flesh." That is, they sought to achieve and maintain righteousness by means of their own human effort—until the day came when their eyes were opened to their need to rest on the grace of God through Jesus Christ alone.[4]

Gamaliel and Stephen

In his defense before the angry crowds in Jerusalem, Paul stated that he was "educated at the feet of Gamaliel according to the strict manner of the law of our fathers, being zealous for God as all of you are this day" (Acts 22:3). This is the same Gamaliel we meet in Acts 5, a Pharisee and teacher held in high esteem by all the people. Strict in his interpretation of the law though he was, he was a man of wisdom. He gave cautionary advice to the Sanhedrin when they wanted to kill the apostles, and addressed them with the following speech:

> So in the present case I tell you, keep away from these men and let them alone, for if this plan or this undertaking is of man, it will fail; but if it is of God, you will not be able to overthrow them. You might even be found opposing God! (Acts 5:38-39)

Although Saul did not follow Gamaliel's advice, he was in time to prove the accuracy of Gamaliel's wisdom. And yet events unfolded in a manner that neither Saul nor Gamaliel could have anticipated. The next important stage in Saul's story is the preaching, the trial, and the martyrdom of Stephen. Indeed the account of Stephen is the catalyst that hastens the arrival of Saul himself.

While Saul is mentioned only twice, and briefly, at the conclusion of the Stephen narrative, a certain prominence is undoubtedly assigned to him. We read that "the witnesses laid down their garments at the feet of a young man named Saul" (Acts 7:58). Although we cannot be entirely sure what this action indicated—were they merely handing their clothes to Saul for safekeeping, or are we to see that Saul acted in some official capacity in Stephen's execution?—it is abundantly clear that Saul was a willing participant in their actions. This is borne out in Acts 8:1: "And Saul approved of his execution."

These verses make it highly plausible that Saul of Tarsus was connected with the same synagogue as Stephen. We can substantiate this with the reference to Cilicia in Acts 6:9. There were people from that Roman province in the synagogue of the Freedmen, whose members rose up against Stephen. And Tarsus, Saul's hometown, was itself a city in Cilicia (Acts 21:39, 22:3). If this connection existed, then we can see that the testimony of Stephen would have had a galvanizing effect on Saul. Elsewhere Paul writes how he was "advancing in Judaism beyond many of my own age among my people, so extremely zealous was I for the traditions of my fathers" (Gal. 1:14). But now Stephen has suddenly become the talk of the town! There he is, "full of grace and power" and "doing great wonders and signs among the people" (Acts 6:8).

Stephen lived and spoke in a way that Saul could not match. The "green-eyed monster" in Saul arose, provoking him to his terrible wrath against Christians. The seventh chapter of Acts contains Stephen's majestic defense—it is really more of a sermon, and it is longer than any other single speech in the book of Acts—which culminates in his stoning. Even as he is dying, he sees his Savior at the right hand of God and he dies in much the same way as Jesus did. "Lord Jesus, receive my spirit"; "Lord, do not hold this sin against them" (Acts 7:59–60). So now it is that Saul, in his pharisaic zeal, is driven into open and furious persecution against Jesus Christ and his followers, "breathing threats and murder" against them (Acts 9:1).

Is Paul Guilty of Exaggeration?

But what are we to make of Paul's words at the end of 1 Timothy 1:15: "Christ Jesus came into the world to save sinners, *of whom I am the foremost*"? Is this simply an example of Jewish exaggeration or hyperbole? Can Saul of Tarsus really have been the "worst" sinner, or "the chief" or "the foremost" of all sinners who ever lived? Does he mean that his sins were the most appalling and atrocious that anyone had ever committed? We do not need to spend long before coming up with many names from history—and perhaps a few contemporary ones too—whose deeds seem to be far more dreadful than those of Saul of Tarsus. Even if we restricted ourselves to the Bible we would quickly discover a number of contenders. We could mention the Pharaoh who cast all the newborn Israelite babies into the Nile, wicked Queen Jezebel who killed the Lord's prophets, and of course Herod the Great, whose deeds of carnage we noted in chapter 3.

But maybe Paul is not really so unique. Have not many Christians, confronted with the pristine purity of God's holiness, felt like uttering words not dissimilar to Paul's? I sit under a penetrating sermon that exposes my guilty soul for what it is, and I say to myself, "nobody, but nobody, has ever sinned as wickedly as I have." While we know only our own hearts—and even our own self-knowledge is fallible, for it was the Lord Jesus alone who "knew what was in a man" (John 2:25)—can we not say that as far as the Christian knows himself, he must confess that when God's righteous character is set alongside his own sinful soul, he believes himself to be the most appalling and wretched sinner who ever walked the earth?

We see such a pattern in many Christians through the centuries. John Bunyan (1628–88) is an example who springs readily to mind. He wrote most eloquently of how great a sinner he was, even in childhood: "I had but few equals, especially considering my years, which were tender, being few, both for cursing, swearing, lying, and blaspheming the holy name of God."[5] From our vantage point it might seem that Bunyan was preoccupied with his sin to the point of mental disorder. Perhaps if he had lived 350 years later he would have been sent to a good psychiatrist or prescribed a dose of antidepressants—but anyone who knows Bunyan's writings can be sure there was nothing unbalanced about him, certainly in his maturity. The fact is that he was experiencing a great conviction of sin prior to the greater blessing of knowing God's grace. It may be that we know little of this type of phenomenon today, but it might be healthier for the church if we saw more of it.

PAUL'S OPPOSITION TO THE GOSPEL

Nevertheless, it is a superficial and inadequate understanding of Scripture that leads us to the conclusion that Paul's pronouncement is nothing other than a subjective personal assessment. On the contrary, "the saying is trustworthy and deserving of full acceptance"!

Yes, Paul means exactly what he says. The language he uses can be taken to mean that of all sinners he stands at the head; he is indeed the "chief." Paul is prepared to place his own sins in the same heinous category as those he has detailed earlier in the chapter, where he has spoken of "the lawless and disobedient," "the ungodly and sinners," "the unholy and profane," "those who strike their fathers and mothers," "murderers, the sexually immoral, men who practice homosexuality, enslavers, liars, perjurers" (1 Tim. 1:9–10). Remember that as a Pharisee Saul would have had a very pronounced sense that people such as these were classed as "sinners." But after his conversion Paul has no difficulty in applying that description to himself as he once was.

This is the point: Paul shows himself to be the foremost example of a sinner *in his opposition to God and to the gospel of Jesus Christ*. He says in verse 13, "formerly I was a blasphemer, persecutor, and insolent opponent." How and in what sense? He expands on this further in 1 Corinthians 15:9: "For I am the least of the apostles, unworthy to be called an apostle, because I persecuted the church of God." We have Paul's own testimony before King Agrippa and the Roman governor Festus.

> I not only locked up many of the saints in prison after receiving authority from the chief priests, but when they were put to death I cast my vote against them. And I punished them often in all the synagogues and tried to make them blaspheme, and in raging fury against them I persecuted them even to foreign cities. (Acts 26:10–11)

So it was that when the risen Lord encountered Saul on the way to Damascus he asked him, "Saul, Saul, why are you persecuting me?" (Acts 26:14). Saul had sinned against God as well as against man—because sin is always, in the first place, an act of rebellion and disobedience against God. "Against you, you only, have I sinned and done what is evil in your sight, so that you may be justified in your words and blameless in your judgment" (Psalm 51:4). Saul's conduct in the early years of the church was that of a man bent on destroying the church of Jesus Christ. His assault upon Christ's body was an assault upon the head, upon Christ himself, for such is the intimacy between the Savior and his people.

The Worst Sin—But Not the Unforgivable Sin

We might even venture to say this: Paul sinned as much as any man could without blaspheming the Holy Spirit himself. In other words, he sinned against God as much as anyone can without putting himself beyond the scope of God's saving power. This may seem a rather bold claim, so let us examine it.

What is blasphemy against the Holy Spirit? It takes place when an individual, having received sufficient revelation to be persuaded that Jesus has indeed come from God, opposes this truth in a stubborn and perverse manner. In chapter 2 we looked at the occasion when Jesus had cast out a demon that had made a man mute; this event is reported in Luke 11:14–23. Mark, in his parallel account, adds the following words of Jesus:

> "Truly, I say to you, all sins will be forgiven the children of man, and whatever blasphemies they utter, but whoever blasphemes against the Holy Spirit never has forgiveness, but is guilty of an eternal sin"—*for they had said, "He has an unclean spirit."* (Mark 3:28–30)

The italicized explanation at the conclusion of this text is all-important; the scribes who observed this miracle sinned against the Holy Spirit because they ascribed to Jesus' works a power that was itself demonic.

In Hebrews 6:4–6, a text that has been much debated, we read,

> For it is impossible to restore again to repentance those who have once been enlightened, who have tasted the heavenly gift, and have shared in the Holy Spirit, and have tasted the goodness

of the word of God and the powers of the age to come, *if they then fall away*, since they are crucifying once again the Son of God to their own harm and holding him up to contempt.

This appears to be something similar to the case with the scribes and the casting out of the demon. In this instance people have been, in some sense, partakers of the Holy Spirit. The Spirit has worked upon their consciences sufficiently to demonstrate to them that Jesus is indeed the Savior and the Son of God. But their falling away consists of their rejection of this truth. This also seems to be the explanation of the "sin that leads to death" in 1 John 5:16. Texts like these are solemn and fearful, but pastoral experience shows individuals who correspond to these descriptions. Having once encountered the gospel, and seemed to embrace it, souls who then reject the Savior are worse off than they were before they ever heard the truth. They become more resolutely worldly, hard-hearted, and intractable.

"Ignorantly in Unbelief"

But this is evidently not the case with the apostle Paul, for he himself says that he "had acted ignorantly in unbelief" (1 Tim. 1:13). The key word here is "ignorantly" rather than "unbelief." Hendriksen comments on this. "During his campaign of aggression the apostle, in his state of 'unbelief' with respect to the truth in Christ, had actually thought that he was offering service to God. . . . He had been thoroughly convinced that he 'ought to do many things contrary to the name of Jesus of Nazareth'" (Acts 26:9)."[6] Men like Saul of Tarsus will truly believe that their violent actions against believers are acts of devoted service to God. In doing so they fulfill the words of the Savior when he said,

Indeed, the hour is coming when whoever kills you will think he is offering service to God. And they will do these things because they have not known the Father, nor me. (John 16:2–3)

Saul of Tarsus was intensely religious, zealous for the God of his fathers, but he was essentially ignorant. His zeal was very great, but it was not according to knowledge (Rom. 10:2). Saul had to understand that the God whom he professed to worship could be known only through the Son he had sent, the Lord Jesus Christ. Without the Son, no one can come to the Father or know him. True conversion comes when a soul perceives that Jesus Christ has come, full of grace and truth, in order to save whomever calls on him. For many years Saul had sought to establish his own righteousness, which came through his observation of the law. But when at last Christ appeared to him, he began to see that Christ himself was the end of the law, and everything he had trusted in prior to this point was simply "dung" (Phil. 3:8, KJV).

We might even see Paul as another of the answers to Christ's prayer from the cross: "Father, forgive them, for they know not what they do." Before Paul had personal knowledge of the convicting power of the gospel, he said, "I too was convinced that I ought to do all that was possible to oppose the name of Jesus of Nazareth" (Acts 26:9). But once the gospel came to him with the authority of heaven, he believed and became the pattern, the example, to all who would follow.

THE SINNER'S PATTERN

For Paul is making a pastoral point here, not only to Timothy, but to every reader of this letter. In 1 Timothy 1:16 he tells us that he is an example, or a "pattern" (KJV) of those who would believe on Jesus and receive eternal life. Paul is walking at the head of a procession that is made up of all souls who will ever be brought to saving faith. There he stands, the man who persecuted Jesus Christ so severely, so determinedly. But he has been forgiven, restored, given fellowship with God and eternal life. Every generation of Christians who has ever followed is able to look at Paul and say, "There, God forgave this man. He was engaged in a full-frontal attack against Christ and his people. He was a blasphemous, violent persecutor. His aim was the extermination of the whole Christian church." Scripture itself declares that he was once the foremost of sinners, but God in his grace is willing to pardon him.

In verse 14 Paul uses the kind of superlative language which is one of his trademarks: "the grace of our Lord *overflowed* for me with the faith and love that are in Christ Jesus." The Christian who feels himself to be the lowest, vilest, most unworthy sinner who ever lived is motivated to look at this example of Paul. If God dealt in such mercy with this foremost of sinners, he will do so with every other sinner. That is why the example of Paul is the most astonishing evidence of the scope of God's grace that flowed from Jesus' cross at Calvary. How great is the grace, patience, and longsuffering of the Savior! Why did he deal with Saul of Tarsus as he did? It was in order to show this grace, patience, and longsuffering to every believer who follows. However great his sin had been, God's grace was so much greater. When Paul said in Romans 5:20 that "where sin increased, grace abounded all the more," he was speaking from personal experience.

The high point in all of Paul's writings comes when he is taken up with the grace of God in Jesus Christ. Christ's great, eternal, universal honor and worship is summarized in the following psalm:

> He raises the poor from the dust
>   and lifts the needy from the ash heap,
> to make them sit with princes,
>   with the princes of his people.
> He gives the barren woman a home,
>   making her the joyous mother of children.
> Praise the LORD! (Psalm 113:7-9)

For we cannot conceive of Christ without his people, any more than we can conceive of the church without Christ, her Head and her Savior. The Bridegroom's honor and glory is in present-ing his beautiful, sanctified Bride to his Father.

Honor and Glory to the King of Ages

That is why blessing, praise, and doxology are the great ends of the Bible, of our salvation, of all the works of God himself. Does that seem repetitive to us? Does the prospect of eternal praise seem rather thin to us? We will never tire of praising God, because we will never become weary of the reasons we have to praise him. It is reflecting upon this great prize, this great sal-vation, eternal life, that causes Paul to break into doxology as he does here. When God's truth is rightly grasped by mind and heart, it must inevitably result in praise and worship. Biblical doctrine humbles and thrills us; it takes our souls and causes them to cry "glory." So it is at the end of Romans 11, and so it is here. Paul's praise takes him and us to the very throne of the Godhead in verse 17: "To the King of ages, immortal, invisible, the only God, be honor and glory forever and ever. Amen."

There is something transcendently glorious about the way Paul describes God here. He sees that his own experiences, his journey from sin and blasphemy to grace and glory, could only have been according to the sovereign decree of the almighty King of heaven. He sees that his life has taken a course that he could never have imagined nor determined before. God, in Jesus Christ, took him while he was yet a sinner, even the chief of sinners, and has led him into his own kingdom. So great has been the love of Christ, the work of Christ, for Paul and for all believers, that we are admitted into the worship of this immortal, invisible God.

We would do well to remember every morning that we stand in God's sight by grace alone. Remembering this will enable us to confess our sins more freely. And to confess our sins regularly—daily, surely—is a necessity in the Christian life. It may seem a strange thing to say, but the more conscious we are of God's grace, the more readily we can confess our sins. Why? Because we know that we stand by grace alone and that all attempts to justify ourselves before God, by our works or our character, fail. We rest upon Jesus Christ—and him crucified—alone.

"He is the true God, and eternal life" (1 John 5:20). See the righteousness, holiness, and sheer attractiveness of the Savior, the good shepherd in distinction to the false shepherds who were the Pharisees and experts in the law. In Jesus Christ we have that key of knowledge that these first-century Jewish leaders, and modern-day equivalents, would seek to deny. Paul, once himself a Pharisee, was graciously delivered out of that system by the Christ he had once persecuted but now preached. Everything he had once counted gain he now counted loss because he had gained Christ.

We can say with Paul, "But far be it from me to boast except in the cross of our Lord Jesus Christ" (Gal. 6:14).

APPENDIX

THE HEROD DYNASTY

THESE DETAILS are included in order to help the reader navigate the complex family structure of Herod the Great and his descendants, who are referred to especially in chapters 3 and 12.

Herod the Great has ten references in the New Testament, most of which are found in the second chapter of Matthew. Herod the Great was the founder of the Herodian dynasty, the king for thirty-three years over the whole land of Israel, and the one who ordered the massacre of the baby boys in and around Bethlehem. From what was said back in chapter 3, it will be clear that Herod had an extremely complex and stormy set of marriages—which is putting it rather mildly—and the intrigue, rivalry, and bloodshed found among his household was prodigious. It might also be remembered that he had caused the death of his wife Mariamne the Hasmonean princess as well as his two sons by her, Aristobulus and Alexander.

Herod Philip was the son of Herod the Great by another Mariamne who was the daughter of Simon Boethus the high priest and was known as Mariamne II. This is the "Philip" referred to in Matthew 14:3 and Mark 6:17; he was the first husband of Herodias, whom Herod Antipas later married. However, Herod Philip never ruled over any territory in Palestine. He dwelt in Rome, very sensibly in view of his father's bloodletting.

Herod Philip is not to be confused with **Philip the tetrarch**, son of Herod the Great by Cleopatra of Jerusalem, who ruled Iturea and Trachonitis.[1]

We then come to **Herod Antipas**. Twenty-four of the New Testament references to a "Herod" apply to him. He was the son of Herod the Great and Malthace of Samaria, becoming tetrarch of Galilee and Perea when his father died in 4 BC. How old he was at this stage we cannot be sure, but he may not have been much more than a youth. Although he is sometimes labeled "King Herod," as in Mark 6:14, he was not a king in anything like the same sense his father had been. The kingdom of Herod the Great was divided after his death, and his sons—Archelaus and Philip the tetrarch in addition to Herod Antipas—ruled over different regions.

Archelaus was the full-brother of Herod Antipas and was the ethnarch of Judea after the death of his father, Herod the Great.[2] It was Archelaus' territory that Joseph, the husband of Mary, was concerned to avoid when he returned from Egypt with Mary and the child Jesus (Matt. 2:22). After nine years he was deposed and Judea was ruled directly by the Romans.

We then come to **Herodias**, who was the daughter of the murdered Aristobulus and therefore the niece—or technically the *half*-niece—of Herod Philip and Herod Antipas, to each of whom she was consecutively married.

The daughter of Herod Philip and Herodias, who danced before Herod Antipas, is known to have been called **Salome**, although this name is not employed in the Bible. To complicate matters a little more, Salome was later married to Philip the tetrarch, her half-uncle.

Next on the list is the third "Herod" of the New Testament, who is referred to only six times, and all these references appear in the twelfth chapter of the book of Acts. He is better known as **Herod Agrippa I**, and he was the son of Aristobulus and therefore the brother of Herodias. He ruled over an area nearly as extensive as the territory as that of his grandfather, Herod the Great. He is the king who killed the apostle James, put Peter in prison, and was later struck down by an angel of God when he accepted blasphemous praise from the people of Tyre and Sidon (Acts 12:23).

Finally, **Herod Agrippa II** was the son of Herod Agrippa I. This is the "King Agrippa" of Acts 25 and 26 who was, famously, almost persuaded to become a Christian by the apostle Paul (Acts 26:28).

NOTES

Chapter One: Why Did Jesus Have Enemies?

1. As in the historical terms *Enlightenment* and *Dark Ages*; although as far as Christian truth is concerned, the Enlightenment (which roughly coincided with the eighteenth century) resulted in increasing skepticism and therefore less light.

2. John Brown, *Discourses and Sayings of Our Lord*, vol. 1 (Edinburgh: Banner of Truth, 1990), 39.

3. Ibid., 42.

4. Leon Morris, *The Gospel According to John*, rev. ed. (Grand Rapids: Eerdmans, 1995), 207.

5. William Hendriksen, *The Gospel of John* (London: Banner of Truth, 1959), 144.

Chapter Two: Invisible Enemies in High Places

1. Wayne Grudem, *Systematic Theology* (Leicester: IVP, 1994), 416. He goes on to refer to Deuteronomy 32:16–17 and Psalm 106:35–37 as specific examples.

2. *Collected Writings of John Murray*, vol. 2, *Systematic Theology* (Edinburgh: Banner of Truth, 1977), 67.

3. Louis Berkhof, *Systematic Theology* (Edinburgh: Banner of Truth, 1988), 149.

4. While it is correct to say that Eve was tempted first, not Adam (Gen. 3:1; 1 Tim. 2:14), it is to Adam that I will mainly refer in this section because he was directly responsible to God as the one who had been commanded to obey (Gen. 2:16–17).

5. John Murray, *Redemption Accomplished and Applied* (Grand Rapids: Eerdmans, 1955), 19.

6. William Hendriksen, *The Gospel of Luke* (Edinburgh: Banner of Truth, 1978), 621.

Chapter Three: Herod the Great

1. See Flavius Josephus, *Antiquities of the Jews*, Books 14 to 16. Available online at http://www.ccel.org/j/josephus/works/ant-14.htm.

2. The appendix describes in detail the members of Herod's dynasty.

3. The Feast of Dedication, mentioned in John 10:22, commemorates these events and is observed by Jews today as *Hanukkah*.

4. Not to be confused with Hyrcanus' brother Aristobulus or indeed Herod and Mariamne's son of the same name. The Herodians contented themselves with a restricted selection of names for several generations.

5. Alfred Edersheim, *The Life and Times of Jesus The Messiah*, vol. 1 (London: Longmans, Green and Co. 1906), 126.

6. Alan Bullock, *Hitler: A Study in Tyranny* (London: Penguin, 1990), 804.

7. John Calvin, *Commentary on a Harmony of the Evangelists*, vol. 1 (Grand Rapids: Baker, 1996), 137.

Chapter Four: The People of Nazareth

1. For those unfamiliar with this term, a "Geordie" is a colloquial expression for a native of Tyneside in northeast England.

2. Philip Schaff, *History of the Christian Church*, vol. 1, *Apostolic Christianity A.D. 1-100* (Peabody, MA: Hendrickson, 1996), 102.

3. David Brown, *The Four Gospels* (Edinburgh: Banner of Truth, 1977), 277.

4. John Calvin, *Commentary on a Harmony of the Evangelists, Matthew, Mark, and Luke*, vol. 3 (Grand Rapids: Baker, 1996), 168.

5. For example Matthew 10:16-25, 24:9-10; John 16:2-3, 33; Acts 14:22; 1 Timothy 3:10-13; 1 John 3:13.

Chapter Five: The Cleansing of the Temple

1. C. S. Lewis, *Mere Christianity* (Glasgow: Fount, 1989), 104.

2. This will be considered in chapter 7.

3. For an excellent treatment of this question, see Leon Morris, *The Gospel According to John*, rev. ed. (Grand Rapids: Eerdmans, 1995), 166-69.

4. Ibid., 171.

5. J. C. Ryle, *Holiness* (Darlington: Evangelical Press, 1997), 34.

6. Abraham Kuyper, inaugural address at the dedication of the Free University of Amsterdam, 1880.

7. Quoted in John Stott, *The Contemporary Christian* (Leicester: IVP, 1995), 282–83.

Chapter Six: The Pharisees

1. These figures are based on a harmonizing of various passages, and on the assumption that the Pharisees *twice* accused Jesus of casting out demons by the prince of demons (Matt. 9:34, 12:24).

2. Flavius Josephus, *Antiquities* XIII.14.2, available online at http://www.ccel.org/ccel/josephus/works/files/ant-13.htm.

3. Raymond E Brown, *An Introduction to the New Testament* (New York: Doubleday, 1997), 79.

4. See, for example, Matthew 6:2, 5, 16; 15:7; 22:18; Luke 12:1; 13:15; 1 Peter 2:1. A most important rule of interpretation is to allow the *usage* of a word, rather than its derivation or etymology, to drive its meaning.

5. See Jeremiah 14:14–15; 23:21, 32; 29:9, 31.

6. I readily acknowledge that the "A to Z" analogy works only in English, not in any biblical language.

Chapter Seven: The Challenge to Jesus' Authority

1. See Matthew 21:12–13; Mark 11:15–16; Luke 19:45–46.

2. *Trend of UK Church Attendance*, from http://www.whychurch.org.uk/images/charts/ch_att_trend.png. It is of course true that the average age of all UK residents has increased over this thirty-year period, but not at the same rate as the average age of those who regularly attend a church.

3. J. C. Ryle, *Expository Thoughts on Luke,* vol. 2 (Edinburgh: Banner of Truth, 1986), 317.

4. D. Martyn Lloyd-Jones, *Preaching & Preachers* (London: Hodder & Stoughton, 1985), 159.

5. These words, adapted from Isaiah 40:3, are found in all four gospels, which underlines how John's ministry was all about preparation for the imminent coming of Jesus.

6. Perhaps the NIV translation of Psalm 18:26 is clearer: "To the crooked you show yourself shrewd."

Chapter Eight: The Sadducees

1. Flavius Josephus, *Antiquities* XVIII.1.4, available online at http://www.ccel.org/ccel/josephus/works/files/ant-18.htm.

2. The belief that the Sadducees accepted the authority of the Pentateuch but not of the rest of the Old Testament is nowhere attested by Josephus or the Talmud.

3. It is true that there is a faint resemblance to the account of Sara the daughter of Raguel, recorded in the apocryphal Book of Tobit (3:7–15). Whether this text inspired the Sadducees' own story is hard to determine, and probably not of great importance.

4. James A. Alexander, *A Commentary on the Gospel of Mark* (London: Banner of Truth, 1960), 328

5. J. C. Ryle, *Expository Thoughts on Mark* (Edinburgh: Banner of Truth, 2000), 258.

6. Carl Trueman, interview with Dr. Mike Ovey, Principal of Oak Hill College, London, April 2010.

7. Origen, "Homily 34," *Homilies on Luke*, trans. Joseph T. Lienhard, S. J. (Washington, D. C.: The Catholic University of America Press, 1996), 138.

8. This is a vast and yet wholly rewarding area of investigation. Readers are directed to Patrick Fairbairn's incomparable *Typology of Scripture* (New York: Kregel Publications, 1989) for a most comprehensive treatment of the subject.

9. Alexander, *A Commentary on the Gospel of Mark*, 331.

10. J. C. Ryle, *Expository thoughts on Luke,* vol. 2 (Edinburgh: Banner of Truth, 1986), 343.

11. James R. Edwards, *The Gospel According to Mark* (Leicester: Apollos, 2002), 365–66.

12. Philip S. Johnston, *Shades of Sheol: Death and Afterlife in the Old Testament* (Leicester: Apollos, 2002), 199.

13. Ibid., 199.

14. We could also mention Elijah's being taken up to heaven, though this event had another important purpose—the expectation that he would return as the Messiah's forerunner (Mal. 4:5; Matt. 17:10–13).

15. Johnston, *Shades of Sheol*, 225.

16. B. B. Warfield, *The Inspiration and Authority of the Bible* (Philadelphia: Presbyterian & Reformed, 1948), 71.

17.Richard Baxter, *The Saints' Everlasting Rest*, available online at http://www.ebooksread.com/authors-eng/richard-baxter/the-saints -everlasting-rest-or-a-treatise-of-the-blessed-state-of-the-saints—txa /page-20.

Chapter Nine: Caiaphas the High Priest

1. William Hendriksen, *The Gospel of John* (London: Banner of Truth, 1959), 146.

2. Flavius Josephus, *Antiquities* XX.10, available online at http:// www.ccel.org/j/josephus/works/ant-20.htm.

3. Ibid.

4. An ossuary is a chest containing human bones.

5. See Matthew 22:21; Mark 12:17; Luke 20:25.

Chapter Ten: Judas Iscariot

1. William Hendriksen, *The Gospel of John* (London: Banner of Truth, 1959), 358.

2. C. H. Spurgeon, *The Treasury of David*, vol. 1, part 2 (Peabody, MA: Hendrickson), 259.

3. Charles Ross, *The Inner Sanctuary* (Edinburgh: Banner of Truth, 1992).

4. Genesis 4:8; 2 Samuel 13:28; 1 Kings 21:13–14. I am aware that there is some speculation about the textual evidence for Cain's words "Let us go out into the field" in the first verse.

5. John Bunyan, *The Pilgrim's Progress* (Oxford: Oxford University Press, 1984), 28.

6. Ibid., 29.

7. This conversation between Jesus and Peter will be considered at greater length in chapter 17.

8. J. A. Alexander, *A Commentary on the Acts of the Apostles* (Edinburgh: Banner of Truth, 2003), 36.

9. Westminster Confession of Faith, 3.7.

Chapter Eleven: Pontius Pilate

1. It needs to be remarked that the Ethiopian Orthodox Church, which is now known as the Tewahedo Church, though of great antiquity, holds to a very divergent canon of Scripture, claiming forty-six

books in the Old Testament and thirty-five in the New. There are also other important departures from true orthodoxy.

2. Edward Gibbon, *The History of the Decline and Fall of the Roman Empire* (Albany: AGES Software, 1997), 25.

3. Philip Schaff, *History of the Christian Church*, vol. 1 (Peabody, MA: Hendrickson, 1996), 80–81.

4. See Luke 3:1. To be somewhat pedantic, Archelaus was not strictly a "tetrarch" but an "ethnarch," meaning a ruler over a particular ethnic group.

5. Alfred Edersheim, *The Life and Times of Jesus The Messiah*, vol. 2 (London: Longmans, Green and Co. 1906), 221.

6. Flavius Josephus, *Antiquities of the Jews* XVIII.3.2, available online at http://www.ccel.org/ccel/josephus/works/files/ant-18.htm.

7. Ibid.

8. Darrell L Bock, *Jesus according to Scripture* (Leicester: Apollos, 2002), 530.

9. William Hendriksen, *The Gospel of John* (London: Banner of Truth, 1959), 408.

10. In connection with this we can think of those who will talk about the "Christianization" of society or culture. But can a state, a business organization, or a school properly be termed "Christian"? The use of the word *Christian* in the New Testament, limited though it is, would suggest that it can be applied only to *people*.

11. In her case, by the Eastern Orthodox Church as well as the Ethiopian.

Chapter Twelve: Herod Antipas

1. William Hendriksen, *The Gospel of Luke* (Edinburgh: Banner of Truth, 1978), 1011.

2. See Joel B. Green, *The Gospel of Luke* (Grand Rapids; Eerdmans, 1997), 804. Green quotes Sherwin-White: "One does not expect a governor of the late Republic and early Principiate, when faced by a malefactor, to bother about the very fine question whether his imperium allowed him to deal with a man who was in but not of his province" (A. N. Sherwin-White, *Roman Society and Roman Law in the New Testament* [Oxford: Oxford University Press, 1963], 28–29).

3. Leviticus 18:16; 20:21.

4. Flavius Josephus, *Antiquities* XVIII.5.1–3, available online at http://www.ccel.org/ccel/josephus/works/files/ant-18.htm.

5. Nabatea was the region immediately east of the Jordan, bordering on Herod's territories.

6. Having said this, we can say that an even greater lesson, as with Jephthah, is that we should not vow foolishly to begin with.

7. Darrell L. Bock, *Jesus according to Scripture* (Leicester: Apollos, 2002), 214.

8. Flavius Josephus, *Jewish War* 1.30.7, available online at www.ccel.org/j/josephus/works/war-1.htm.

9. From a lecture on Luther given by Professor James Atkinson in Newcastle upon Tyne, England, on 7 November 1991. The whole lecture, given under the auspices of *The Christian Institute*, is a mighty and stirring proclamation of the gospel, and is well worth hearing. It can be found online at www.christian.org.uk/resource/martin-luther-2.

10. J. C. Ryle, *Expository Thoughts on Luke,* vol. 2 (Edinburgh: Banner of Truth, 1986), 452.

Chapter Thirteen: The Jewish Crowd

1. J. C. Ryle, *Expository Thoughts on Matthew* (Edinburgh: Banner of Truth, 2009), 387–88, italics mine.

2. From a tape recording of a sermon preached at Alexandra Road on December 31, 1995.

3. John Calvin, *Commentary on a Harmony of the Evangelists, Matthew, Mark, and Luke*, vol. 3 (Grand Rapids: Baker, 1996), 288.

4. Available online at http://www.vatican.va/archive/hist_councils/ii_vatican_council/documents/vat-ii_decl_19651028_nostra-aetate_en.html.

5. John Stott, *The Cross of Christ* (Leicester: Inter-Varsity Press, 1986), 59.

6. O. Palmer Robertson, *The Israel of God* (Phillipsburg: P&R Publishing, 2000), 121.

Chapter Fourteen: The Roman Soldiers

1. We pass over, for the time being, the question of whether the character of Jesus ought to be depicted in *any* visual form, whether illustrated in a book, painted to hang on the wall, or simulated by an actor.

2. Alfred Edersheim, *The Life and Times of Jesus The Messiah*, vol. 2 (London: Longmans, Green and Co., 1906), 593.

3. Ibid., 593–94.

4. *Westminster Shorter Catechism*, Question 20.

5. R. C. H. Lenski, *Interpretation of St. Luke's Gospel*, 1934; quoted in William Hendriksen, *The Gospel of Luke* (Edinburgh: Banner of Truth, 1978), 1037.

6. J. C. Ryle, *Expository Thoughts on Luke*, vol. 2 (Edinburgh: Banner of Truth, 1986), 463.

Chapter Fifteen: The Climax of Jesus' Sufferings

1. George Orwell, *Nineteen Eighty-Four* (London: Penguin, 1990), 251.

2. References in the book of Proverbs abound. See 6:17; 10:31; 11:9; 12:6, 18; 18:21 as an introductory sample. Notice also James 3:1–12.

3. Derek Kidner, *Psalms 1–72* (London: IVP, 1973), 122.

4. William Hendriksen, *The Gospel of Matthew* (Edinburgh: Banner of Truth, 2006), 967.

5. Alfred Plummer, *An Exegetical Commentary on the Gospel according to St. Matthew* (London: E. Stock, 1910), 397.

6. Leon Morris, *The Cross in the New Testament* (Exeter: Paternoster Press, 1965), 47.

7. George Smeaton, *Christ's Doctrine of the Atonement* (Edinburgh: Banner of Truth, 1991), 154.

8. Ibid., 157.

Chapter Sixteen: The Crucified Robber

1. Leon Morris, *The Cross in the New Testament* (Exeter: Paternoster Press, 1965), 99.

2. J. C. Ryle, *Holiness* (Darlington: Evangelical Press, 1997), 178.

3. C. H. Spurgeon, "The Believing Thief" (sermon, Metropolitan Tabernacle, Newington, April 7, 1889), available online at *The Spurgeon Archive*, http://www.spurgeon.org/sermons/2078.htm.

4. William Hendriksen, *The Bible on the Life Hereafter* (Grand Rapids: Baker Book House, 1988), 50.

5. The *intermediate state* is a term that describes the life and existence of the Christian soul between physical death and the second coming of Christ, when believers' bodies will be resurrected as Christ's body was and is.

Chapter Seventeen: Simon, Son of John

1. T. V. Moore, *The Last Days of Jesus* (Edinburgh: Banner of Truth, 1981), 102.

2. A. W. Pink, *Exposition of the Gospel of John*, vol. 3 (Grand Rapids: Zondervan, 1973), 322.

3. Edmund Clowney, *The Message of 1 Peter* (Nottingham: IVP, 1994), 191.

4. *P1* stands for Primary 1, the first year of primary school in Northern Ireland, for children age four and five.

5. Edward Donnelly, "Loving the Lord," (sermon, the Banner of Truth UK Ministers' Conference, Leicester, April 29, 2010.

6. Edward Donnelly, *Eyewitness of His Majesty* (Edinburgh, Banner of Truth, 2005), 42.

Chapter Eighteen: Saul of Tarsus

1. In 1 Timothy 1:15, 3:1 and 4:9; 2 Timothy 2:11; and Titus 3:8.

2. This is the figure I have received; there may be local experts who put the figure slightly higher or lower.

3. James M. Kittleson, *Luther the Reformer* (Leicester: IVP, 1989), 53–55.

4. These plain truths need to be set against various New Perspectives on Paul and on justification, for which N. T. Wright is perhaps the best-known protagonist. This deviant form of teaching, in seeking to reinterpret Paul and First Century Judaism, pulls away at the very foundation of the Christian faith: that we are justified by grace through faith alone, apart from works.

5. John Bunyan, "Grace Abounding to the Chief of Sinners," *The Works of John Bunyan*, vol. 1 (London: Blackie & Sons, 1875), 6.

6. William Hendriksen, *1 & 2 Thessalonians, 1 & 2 Timothy, Titus* (Edinburgh: Banner of Truth, 1983), 74.

Appendix: The Herod Dynasty

1. Cleopatra of Jerusalem is not to be confused with Cleopatra VII, of Antony and Cleopatra fame.

2. An "ethnarch" was a ruler over a specific people group, though the distinction between an ethnarch and a tetrarch did not mean a great deal in practice.